MEXICAN AMERICANS

AMERICAN MEXICANS

MEXICAN AMERICANS

AMERICAN MEXICANS

FROM CONQUISTADORS TO CHICANOS

MATT S. MEIER

AND

FELICIANO RIBERA

AMERICAN CENTURY SERIES

🔖 HILL AND WANG

A division of Farrar, Straus and Giroux

LIBRARY OF CONGRESS CATALOGING-IN-PUBLICATION DATA
Meier, Matt. S.
Mexican Americans, American Mexicans : from Conquistadors to
Chicanos / Matt S. Meier and Feliciano Ribera.—Rev. ed.
p.   cm. — (American century series)
Rev. ed. of: The Chicanos, 1972.
Includes bibliographical references (p.) and index.
1. Mexican Americans—History. I. Ribera, Feliciano. II. Meier,
Matt S. Chicanos. III. Title. IV. Series.
E184.M5M456 1993   973'.046872—dc20   93-3385   CIP

CONTENTS

MAPS

ACKNOWLEDGMENTS

We would like to thank colleagues at San Jose State University and at Santa Clara University as well as library staff members at both universities who gave support to this revised edition of *The Chicanos*. We also owe a debt of gratitude to colleagues elsewhere who made suggestions, over the years, how we might make it a better, more complete history of the Mexican American experience. Special recognition is deserved by professors Alma García, Francisco Jiménez, Ramón Chacón, and Richard García, who read parts of the manuscript; their comments and suggestions have also helped make it a better work. Last but hardly least, we wish to acknowledge the careful and dedicated contributions of our editor and publisher, Arthur W. Wang, who spent uncounted hours going over, clarifying, and improving the various drafts of our manuscript.

MATT S. MEIER
FELICIANO RIBERA

MEXICAN AMERICANS

AMERICAN MEXICANS

INTRODUCTION

The United States is a land of immigrants who have come to the Western Hemisphere over the past 40,000 to 50,000 years. In prehistoric times these immigrants came from northeastern Asia; today a major part of U.S. immigration is formed by Asians and by Latinos descended in part from those ancient Asian migrants. Mexican Americans make up over 60 percent of this latter minority group. Without a sound knowledge of their historical experience, we cannot determine accurately their contributions to American culture.

Today there are over 13 million people of Mexican descent in the United States. A minority traces its origins to early settlers from central Mexico and Spain, some of whom arrived in the Southwest before the *Mayflower* reached New England and all of whom arrived before the 1846 U.S.-Mexican War. Most live in New Mexico and Colorado and, emphasizing their Spanish origins, usually call themselves Hispanic or Spanish Americans.

The second and far larger group consists of somewhat more recent arrivals and their descendants. A substantial migration from Mexico began toward the end of the nineteenth century, was greatly increased by the 1910 Mexican revolution, and continued in cycles throughout the twentieth century. Until the 1920s, Texas served these migrants both as their principal destination and as a way station to the large urban barrios of Los Angeles, San Jose, Denver, Chicago, Detroit, Omaha, and other midwestern cities. Later, particularly after World War II, California became their primary destination. Characteristically many of these Mexicans considered themselves sojourners rather than immigrants—that is, they thought of their move to the United States as expedient and temporary. They believed that they could always return home and eventually would do so.

The history of Mexican Americans is a tale of a frontier people whose land was taken by conquest, whose culture was pushed aside by Anglo conquerors, and who were overwhelmed in this century by Mexican kin who followed in their footsteps. It can be divided into five broad periods.

The first period must consider both their Indian and Spanish backgrounds. It covers the migration of early Asiatic man to the Western Hemisphere, the development of Indian civilizations in Mesoamerica, their defeat by Spanish conquistadors, the blending of Indian and Spanish cultures, the beginnings of physical *mestizaje*, early expansion to the present-day U.S. Southwest, and finally, the achievement of independence from Spain early in the nineteenth century.

The "Grito de Dolores" in 1810 marks the beginning of independent Mexico. Political events soon made clear the gulf that had developed between the Mexican heartland and its distant northern frontier. Local cultures had evolved there based on the mother culture in central Mexico, and continuing isolation led to unrest and mounting political tensions. This period culminated in war with the United States and ended with the 1848 Treaty of Guadalupe Hidalgo, by which Mexico lost half her territory to her expansionist northern neighbor.

The third period, from 1848 to the end of the nineteenth century, is notable for the effects of the change from Mexican to American rule: Anglo migration to the Southwest; investment there of eastern and European capital in railroads, mines, lumbering, cattle, and agriculture; preliminary integration of the Southwest into the larger U.S. economy; and the relegation of *la raza* to a minority position of second-class citizenship in what had once been its own land. Mexican Americans did not just passively accept this change in status. They resisted domination and exploitation through a variety of responses that also served to unite them and to reinforce their cultural distinctiveness.

A rapidly rising rate of migration from Mexico introduces the fourth period. While Mexico's 1910 revolution spewed out its political and social refugees, extreme poverty and future uncertainty impelled Mexican workers to move not only into the U.S. Southwest but increasingly also into the agricultural and industrial centers of the Midwest. Their large numbers modified, reinforced, and revitalized Mexican American culture. This period also witnessed expanded Mexican American social and labor organizing efforts and ended with a reverse migration during the 1930s depression.

World War II marks the beginning of the contemporary period, characterized by renewed heavy migration to the United States; by the *movimiento*, a process of self-identification and heightened awareness of Mexican cultural values; by some improvement in the social and economic conditions of Mexican Americans; by greater acculturation as barriers weakened; and by energetic movements for maximum participation in American life through insistence on better education, full civil rights, and equality of economic opportunity.

Today Mexican Americans constitute the second-largest and most rapidly growing minority in the United States. They are deeply rooted in the Southwest—that is, in the five states of Arizona, California, Colorado, New Mexico, and Texas. Nominally at least, most are Catholic in religion, and a majority are mestizo in racial heritage. They differ markedly from most other immigrant minorities in their close proximity to their cultural homeland and, to a lesser extent, in the recentness of their migration.

Mexicans also differ significantly from most other immigrants to the United States in that they arrive as descendants of a twice-conquered people. Their Indian ancestors were conquered by Spain early in the sixteenth century, and through mestizaje they became inheritors of the enduring Anglo-Saxon Black Legend of unique Spanish cruelty. Their more recent Mexican forebears suffered invasion by the United States in the mid-nineteenth century and endured U.S. conquest and occupation. The continuing consequences of these calamitous events, especially the second, and of their many ethnic implications have engendered over the years a Mexican mind-set that differs notably from the mental attitudes of other immigrants, especially Europeans. Mexicans enter the United States very conscious, even today, that their country was conquered by the Americans. The final result, though complex, is an ethnic minority with a distinct historical experience and a high degree of racial, religious, and linguistic visibility.

Nevertheless, an important characteristic of Mexican Americans is that they do not form a homogeneous group politically, socially, or racially. Since their incorporation into the country in 1848 diversity and complexity have characterized persons of Mexican descent. Some can trace their family residency back 400 years; others migrated north only "yesterday." There are also differences in the varying degrees of Caucasian and Indian ancestry, as well as of acculturation and integration. There are, of course, disparate viewpoints arising out of the varied occupations Mexican Americans pursue. Lastly, there are differences that arise out of their individual historical experience.

Despite this diversity, Mexican Americans have a bedrock of cultural identity. They are united by the Spanish language, a religion which is intimately a part of their daily life and culture, and a concept of individual worth based on respect.

A serious task in writing a history of people of Mexican descent in the United States is determining what to call them. The matter is complicated by several problems: First and foremost, not all persons of Mexican descent agree on a name; second, historically the names they applied to themselves varied by class and region and also changed over time. Additionally, U.S. agencies, especially the Bureau of the Census, have used various identifiers over the years—e.g., country of birth, mother tongue, Spanish surname—making their information not precisely comparable and thereby adding to the difficulties of providing an accurate historical picture of the Mexican American.

The 1992 National Latino Political Survey of nearly 3,000 respondents showed clearly that the large majority, rejecting the broad terms Hispanic and Latino, preferred the nationally specific terms Mexican American, Cuban American, etc. In the nineteenth and early twentieth centuries people of Mexican descent were widely identified simply as Mexicans. Pre-World War II sources commonly use the terms Mexican or mexicano to refer to both Mexican nationals and Mexican Americans. Most Anglos were indifferent or unwilling to distinguish between citizen and foreigner. As Pauline Kibbe of the Texas Good Neighbor Commission observed in the 1940s, "Mexican Americans continue to be considered Mexican though they were born here and know no other country."

The generation of the 1930s and 1940s, nearly all born in the United

States and stressing their Americanism, began thinking of themselves as (Mexican) Americans. After World War II a new generation of youthful activists, insisting on self-definition and seeking cultural roots, preferred the name Chicano, a foreshortening of mexicano. The term dates back to the beginning of this century and originally had pejorative connotations, but was taken in the postwar years by many young Americans of Mexican descent as a prideful identification.

Made popular by militants of the movimiento, Chicano is used after 1940 in this history as a simple alternative to Mexican American. It has the virtue of being short and simple and shunning any implication of divided loyalties. It is particularly useful in writing about Chicanas, avoiding more cumbersome identifications. The reader should be aware that while it is widely used on campuses, it is rejected by some older, more conservative Mexican Americans who find it distasteful because of earlier derogatory implications and more recent connotations of aggressive activism.

Nearly all Americans of Mexican descent agree that they belong to la raza, a Spanish concept connoting ethnic rather than racial solidarity, despite its literal meaning. Although it is an expression widely accepted by Mexican Americans, strictly speaking it belongs to a second, broader category along with Hispanic, hispano, Latin American, latino, Spanish-surnamed, and Spanish-speaking. These seven terms are used to refer to all persons of Spanish cultural background and are used in the text primarily because much information is organized under these categories, especially Hispanic. The term Hispanic is widely used by U.S. government agencies since the 1960s and will appear when statistical information is arranged under that rubric. The reader should note shifts from Mexican American to Hispanic, especially in statistics, and remember that nationwide Mexican Americans make up some 60 percent of the Hispanic population, while in the Southwest the proportion is closer to 80 percent. Latino (and Latin American) appears to be favored over Hispanic as the umbrella term by many. In Texas, Latin American is frequently used simply as a euphemism for Mexican, historically a term of disparagement in that state. For greater detail about specific names the reader is urged to consult the Glossary.

Persons of the southwestern Spanish-Mexican subcultures are referred to in the text as nuevomexicanos, californios, and tejanos in order to distinguish them from Anglos of the three geographical areas. The term Anglo, short for Anglo American, is used to refer to U.S. citizens who neither belong to the above categories nor are Native Americans. Citizens of the United States of America are referred to as Americans, a designation actually applicable to all peoples of the hemisphere.

It is important that the reader have a clear understanding of who is being referred to by the various names. For persons of Mexican descent born in the United States or permanently residing there Mexican American (without hyphen) seems to have the greatest preference and is the basic term used in this work. Where appropriate to the historical period and suitable, other identifiers are also used. The term mexicano is reserved for instances when both Mexican nationals and Mexican Americans are referred to and when sources do not clearly indicate which group is referred to, as was often the case until World War II. After 1940 the terms Chicano and raza are sometimes used simply as appropriate and to avoid overuse of the term Mexican American. No pejorative connotation is implied or intended by the use of any of these ethnic designations.

All of these terms are cultural and ethnic, not racial, and historically have had varying meanings and connotations to members of la raza. Celebrating Mexican Independence Day in San Diego in 1924 with a parade, the Alianza Hispano Americana used on its banner three umbrella terms to refer to mexicanos. The Mexican American *aliancistas* asserted: "La Alianza Hispano Americana [es] La Mejor Sociedad para la Raza Latina."

1

THE MEETING OF
TWO WORLDS

Migration lies at the heart of the American experience. All Americans, north and south, came to the Western Hemisphere; to be sure, some have been here much longer than others. But migration remains the underlying theme of this history. It is the story of a journey both physical and metaphysical, ultimately a journey to the United States and a journey toward full participation in American life. It began with the movement of an early Asiatic people to the Western Hemisphere thousands of years ago. It includes the later arrival of Europeans, both Hispanic and Anglo, as well as blacks from Africa. It describes efforts of Mexican Americans to enter the mainstream of Anglo American life without completely forsaking their cultural roots, and it ends with a brief discussion of efforts to "control" present-day migration from Mexico to the United States.

This history of Mexican Americans begins with the saga of their Indian ancestors' trek from northeastern Asia to the Americas, the chronicle of their Spanish forebears' crossing a fearsome Atlantic Ocean and settling in the land of the Mexica Indians, and the epic of the passage, beginning in the sixteenth century, of mestizo descendants of these two groups from highland Mexico to what is today the Southwest of the United States. Culturally and genetically most Mexican Americans have descended from two great human streams, Amerindian, embracing a wide variety of peoples who lived in what we know today as Mexico, and European, primarily Spaniards, who were also a very heterogeneous people. This mestizo people, whom the great Mexican philosopher José Vasconcelos referred to as *la raza cósmica*, the cosmic race, forms the starting point of our story. We begin therefore with the cultural and social origins of the Mexican American community in the United States—with the story of early humanity in the Western Hemisphere.

Although our knowledge of prehistory in the Americas is limited, recent research indicates that it may go back as much as forty millennia. Various theories about the beginnings of human life in America have been postulated over the years; however, the prevailing belief of anthropologists and archaeologists is that the first humans came to America from northeastern Asia. This does not preclude occasional and accidental later additions of small groups from Europe, Africa, and the South Pacific. However, up to the sixteenth century A.D. most migrants undoubtedly came by way of the Bering Strait, beginning perhaps 50,000 years ago and continuing sporadically over 40,000 years. Sites from Canada to South America have been dated to 10,000 to 50,000 years ago. By 8,000 to 10,000 years ago the basic human population of the New World had been established.

These early people came from Asia in a number of waves, at times perhaps via a land bridge. Slowly they spread southward along the western and eastern edges of the Rocky Mountains, crossed over the Central American isthmus, and followed the spine of the Andes to the tip of South America. Archaeological finds suggest that they reached Tierra del Fuego as early as 7000 B.C. There were, of course, secondary paths of migration eastward from the Rocky Mountains into the St. Lawrence River area, the Mississippi Valley, and the Caribbean islands, and from the Andean region into the Amazon and Río de la Plata basins.

Perhaps forty million or more Indians lived in the Western Hemisphere when Europeans arrived in the fifteenth century. These Amerindian peoples varied greatly in physical appearance and culture; some were nomads who lived from hunting and gathering; others, having developed intensive agriculture, formed villages and reached high levels of civilization. The extensive influence of these latter groups led to a vast arc of societies based on the cultivation of corn. Within this arc extending from the Mississippi Valley in North America southward to

Chile there developed the three most advanced and complex Western Hemisphere civilizations: Maya, Inca, and Aztec.

Major local Indian cultures that evolved in what is now the southwestern United States were part of this arc of maize cultivation and had long-term links with cultures on the Mexican plateau. Many hundreds of years before Christ, Native Americans of the Southwest acquired corn from early civilizations of central Mexico, and later adopted beans, squash, chilies, amaranth, and other important crops from the same source. About 300 B.C. in the valleys of the Gila and Salt rivers of present-day Arizona, a farming people we designate as Hohokam brought irrigation and other innovations from Mexico. The Hohokam center at what is now called Snaketown became the hub from which their culture and influence spread. They were adept at basketry, made pottery, and may even have been acquainted with metallurgy. At their peak they had at least 250 communities centered in the watershed of the Gila River. Over hundreds of years their cultural contributions were extended as far west as the Gulf of California, probably through trade. However, by the time Spanish explorers arrived in the mid-sixteenth century this civilization had either mutated or dispersed, possibly because of ecological factors, perhaps the twenty-four years of drought which climaxed in the 1260s. Some anthropologists think they may have become the historical Pima or Papago Indians.

About 500 A.D. another Indian people of an advanced farming culture began to emerge in the Southwest. Descended from hunting-and-gathering ancestors sometimes referred to as the Basket Makers, these people we call Anasazi, "ancient ones," after the Navajo name for them. Their culture, with its highest development centered in the four-corner area of Arizona, Utah, Colorado, and New Mexico—especially in the Chaco Canyon—depended on agriculture based on the cultivation of corn in irrigated floodplain fields. It was the beneficiary of substantial Mexican influence in cloth making, pottery, architecture, and government. The Anasazi built some 400 miles of roads and extensive apartmentlike dwelling units. They reached their highest levels of development about 1000 A.D. When the area became drier they seem to have migrated southeast to the upper Rio Grande Valley, where they joined people already living there. When the Spaniards first arrived in the Southwest in the mid-1500s thousands of these Indians were still settled there in well-organized, densely populated villages. The Spaniards called them Hopi, Zuñi, and Pueblos.

To the southwest of the Anasazi were the Mogollon people, contemporaries of the Anasazi but less highly developed. Their culture, based on hunting, gathering, and some agriculture, flourished between 500 and 1200 A.D. In the fourteenth century, probably because of severe long-term climatic changes, they seem to have moved southward out of this high plateau area, possibly to the Sierra Madre Occidental of northwestern Mexico.

Far to the east the Mound Builders of the Ohio and Mississippi river basins also reflected Mesoamerican influence in their construction of platform and serpent mounds and small pyramid-based temples as well as in pottery making, agriculture, and other cultural elements. From artifacts found in ancient graves and middens we know that trade between prehistoric peoples of the Americas was extensive. Nearly all archaeologists agree that there was occasional and possibly indirect contact over long periods of time between the area of the southern United States and Mesoamerica. Some see the Mississippian culture as a peripheral or watered-down version of Middle American civilization. In both areas figures of the jaguar, birds of prey, and the earth-water-sky reptile were common cultural elements.

Our knowledge of the ancient history of Mexico is relatively limited. Of thousands of archaeological sites only a few have been investigated and only a handful exposed to intensive study. We do know that 3,000 years ago there began to develop in Mexico a culture of considerable complexity referred to as Olmec or La Venta. In the Yucatán Peninsula and Guatemalan highlands Mayan civilization seems to have evolved from this widespread culture. In the great central plateau farther north there evolved the high cultures of the Teotihuacanos, Toltecs, and later the Aztecs. The last of these peoples, the Aztecs, were also known as Mexicas, and this name came eventually to be applied to the people and country bordering on the United States.

Of all these Middle American peoples the Mayas unquestionably reached the highest levels of development. Sometime between 1500 and 1000 B.C., in a relatively difficult tropical environment, they created the formative stages of Mayan civilization around centers like Uaxactún, Bonampak, Copán, and Tikal. Intensive agricultural practices made considerable population growth possible and led to a highly structured society. From about 200 A.D. to about 1000 there developed what is known as the Classic Period, with its main centers in Guatemala and with some late expansion into the Yucatán Peninsula.

The Mayas reached levels of civilization not attained by any other aboriginal group in the Americas. They developed more than twenty-five large religious centers, each the nucleus of an organized city-state. These ceremonial sites, some linked by a road system, were centers of religion, government, trade, and learning. However, there seems to have been little political interrelationship among Mayan cities of the Classic Period. Governance was based on the clan and tribe; rulers were hereditary and closely allied with the priestly class that headed the Mayas' polytheistic religion. The priesthood dominated a highly stratified social structure that included nobles, feudal lords, warriors, freemen, and slaves.

Mayan culture was shaped by its religious and agricultural base, particularly the cultivation of corn. To a considerable degree life was communal and cooperative, with the seasons determining its rhythm. Crops were raised in a slash-and-burn pattern, although irrigation may have been used as well. Later, terracing, fertilizing, and multiple-cropping seem to have been practiced. The principal crops were beans, peppers, tomatoes, squash, cacao, and, of course, corn. High yields of corn enabled the Mayas to channel part of their energies into building great religious centers and into developing astronomy, mathematics, and other sciences. A thousand years before Europe adopted the Gregorian calendar the Mayas were using a more precise calendrical system; and their invention of the concept of zero also antedated its Old World use by a thousand years. Their amazing civilization is recorded in the ruins of beautiful temples and palaces covered with hieroglyphics, paintings, and sculptured figures.

This highly developed culture reached its peak around 700 A.D. Then gradually, over more than a hundred years, the great Mayan centers declined, decayed, and finally were abandoned. Why, we do not know. Possibly the causes were ecological—such as prolonged drought or perhaps the complete exhaustion of their cornfields. By the beginning of the eleventh century A.D. the Yucatecan cities, which had been on the fringes of the Mayan region, had become its new center. At the same time the Toltecs, a group of more militarized Nahua peoples from the highlands to the northwest, began penetrating deeply into Yucatán. Increasingly the Yucatecan Mayas came under the cultural influence of these vigorous invaders.

The infusion of Nahua culture resulted in a renaissance in the peninsula. This new Mayan era, the Late Classic Period, was characterized by greater militarism and human sacrifice. The Toltec god Quetzalcoatl, the feathered serpent, became accepted as a leading Mayan deity under the name Kukulcán. The first two hundred years of this period were notable for the triple alliance of the leading Yucatecan city-states of Chichén Itzá, Uxmal, and Mayapán. In about 1200 this alliance was broken up by Mayapán, which then dominated Yucatán until the mid-fifteenth century. Around 1450 the Yucatecan cities overthrew the Mayapán hegemony and then fell to warring among themselves. In the process Mayan civilization disintegrated rapidly as roads deteriorated and the great temple complexes succumbed to encroachment by the jungle. By the time the Spaniards began to arrive in 1517 only vestiges of former greatness remained.

In central highland Mexico the most influential early culture to emerge was that of the Teotihuacanos, contemporaries of the Mayas. Northeast of the great valley of Anáhuac they established their center, Teotihuacán, which at its peak had 150,000 to 200,000 inhabitants. Their intellectual developments rivaled those of the Mayas, and the two cultures reciprocally influenced each other as well as many lesser groups. By 850 A.D. Teotihuacán was overrun and burned, and its people disappeared from history.

In about the sixth century A.D. a group of Nahuatl-speaking Indians called Toltecs began to separate themselves from their Chichimec clansmen on the semiarid plateaus of north-central Mexico. As they moved southward they also moved toward higher levels of civilization. Absorbing much of Teotihuacán culture, they built a number of centers, especially Tula, just north of present-day Mexico City. During the ensuing centuries they developed there a civilization noted for its architecture, stone carving, and metalwork. In religion they became widely known for their worship of Quetzalcoatl. At the height of their power in the eleventh and twelfth centuries their hegemony extended to Yucatán and Guatemala. However, a century later Toltec control began to weaken. At the same time it was subjected to encroachment from more aggressive Nahua relatives, including the Aztecs.

Migrating from a northern home called Aztlán in their myths, the Aztecs first settled near Tula and later moved south into the Valley of Mexico or Anáhuac. In the mid-fourteenth century they reached Lake Texcoco and ultimately settled on a barren island which became their future capital, Tenochtitlán (Mexico City today). At first vassals of one of the local tribes, by 1432 they had advanced to an alliance with the powerful neighboring lakeside cities of Texcoco and Tlacopán. By the end of the fifteenth century Tenochtitlán had become the dominant city in central Mexico.

From a tribal organization the Aztecs gradually developed into a strong military state. At its head was the *tlatoani*, "he who speaks," called emperor by the Spaniards. Beneath him in a well-defined caste system were priests, nobles, merchants, free peasants, and slaves. Aztec civilization was based on corn and other crops common to Middle America, including tomatoes, chilies, avocados, maguey, cotton, and tobacco. Between present-day Guatemala and north-central Mexico the Aztecs built great centers. According to the Spaniards who entered Tenochtitlán in 1519, it compared favorably with the great cities of Europe. Its estimated population of 100,000 made it five times larger than contemporary London.

Every town had at least one market, and the markets of Tenochtitlán and neighboring Tlatelolco were so extensive and had such a variety of produce and goods that the Spanish adventurers were amazed. Trade was even more important to the Aztecs than to the Mayas, and traders, called *pochteca*, enjoyed a high position in society. There was an extensive barter in cacao beans, cotton cloth, featherwork, pottery, slaves, and semiprecious stones, especially jade. Aztec culture, influence, and control were spread almost as much by trade as by war.

Aztec civilization is generally considered to have been of a somewhat lower order than that of the Mayas. It was based heavily on the cultures of Toltecs, Teotihuacanos, Mixtecs, Zapotecs, and other predecessors and contemporaries. Although the Aztecs made few original contributions to knowledge, they were highly successful in synthesizing and using cultural elements from the many peoples they conquered. Their special strength lay in the development of the social, political, and military organization needed first to conquer and then to administer their large territory with its population of nine or ten million.

Aztec religion was polytheistic and emphasized human sacrifice. The sun god Huitzilopochtli, who had led them from Aztlán to Tenochtitlán, and other deities required a steady stream of sacrificial victims. On special occasions the number of persons who had their hearts torn out may have reached the thousands. This constant immolation was required to postpone the awful day in Aztec theology when the sun would crash and doomsday would envelop the world. By present-day standards Aztec religion was bloody and violent. Ultimately its demand for sacrificial victims helped lead to Aztec defeat.

By the end of the fifteenth century the Aztecs controlled a confederation that extended from the central Mexican plateau southward to Guatemala and eastward and westward to the Gulf and Pacific coasts. In 1502 Moctezuma II (also transcribed Montezuma) was elected tlatoani. His was the immense task of holding together restless vassals and collecting from them the tribute or taxes levied by Tenochtitlán. He faced his greatest problem when the Spaniards arrived early in the sixteenth century.

The European half of the Mexican American mestizo heritage derives overwhelmingly from the Iberian Peninsula. This area, a crossroads between Europe and Africa, was influenced by various cultural groups from prehistoric times. In the late Paleolithic age Cro-Magnon man decorated the walls of caves in Altamira and elsewhere with magical ceremonial sketches. By the Neolithic period, about the third and second millennia B.C., peninsular inhabitants had learned animal husbandry and some agriculture, as well as the arts of pottery making, basket manufacturing, cloth weaving, and soft metalworking. Trade with the eastern Mediterranean furthered these skills and helped draw the peninsula within the cultural sphere of the Near East. The peninsula became an important source of copper in the Mediterranean trade; however, as the second millennium began, it ceased to be a primary copper source for the East and sank back into relative isolation. Toward the end of the second millennium B.C. Indo-European peoples known as Celts pushed from south-central Europe across the Pyrenees into the Iberian Peninsula and fused with earlier inhabitants to form the Celto-Iberians.

As early as 1100 B.C. Phoenicians from the eastern end of the Mediterranean established trading posts at Gades (Cádiz) and Malaca (Málaga). Late in the seventh century B.C. Greek traders also appeared on the east and northeast coasts of the peninsula until they were displaced by Phoenicians from Carthage in North Africa. Between the sixth and third centuries B.C. these Carthaginians dominated peninsular coastal regions, founding Cartago Nova (Cartagena) as their trading center. At the same time the interior was subjected to another Celtic influx. The three Punic Wars fought between Carthage and Rome for domination in the Mediterranean ended in 146 B.C. With the destruction of Carthage the Romans took over the peninsula.

While there is some debate about the degree of Phoenician influence on Iberian peoples, there is none about the Roman impact. Between the second century B.C. and the end of the fifth century A.D. Rome imposed its government, language, and culture on the peninsula. This Romanizing was gradual and uneven, being more complete in urban areas. By the first century A.D. Hispania, as the Romans called the peninsula, had reached a cultural level that produced such notables as the philosopher Lucius Seneca (4 B.C.–65 A.D.) and the emperor Trajan 52–117 A.D.). Meanwhile, Rome developed networks of roads, bridges, and aqueducts, along with baths, theaters, and forums. A major Roman contribution was a new religion, Christianity, which by the middle of the third century dominated the peninsula.

Roman Spain continued to be subject to further waves of immigrants. Beginning in the second century A.D. Jews of the diaspora added to the earlier ethnic mix of Celts, Phoenicians, Carthaginians, Greeks, and Romans, and in the early years of the fifth century there arrived hordes of vigorous Germanics known variously as Vandals, Alani, Suevi, Goths, and Visigoths. As Roman control faltered and finally collapsed, there emerged in Spain a somewhat Romanized Visigothic kingdom which used vernacular Latin as its language. Despite varying territorial control the Visigothic kingdom survived until the Moorish invasion at the beginning of the eighth century.

The Muslims' conquest of the peninsula between 711 and 719 and their rule in the following centuries over much of Spain, particularly the south, added important new ethnic and cultural elements. Also, during the second century of Islamic control Norsemen began to appear on Spain's western coast and waterways to add one more ingredient to the ethnic potpourri. Between the tenth and thirteenth centuries Arabic Muslims, heirs to the immense cultural patrimony of the eastern Mediterranean, brought to the peninsula this high culture as well as their own contributions to it. In addition to their intellectual baggage in the arts, letters, and sciences they brought new crops like rice and sugar, introduced improved agricultural techniques, and created new industries.

The Spaniards' defeat of the Moors at Covadonga in 718, less than a decade after the Muslim invasion, began the long struggle to retake lost territories. At first it went slowly. However, the *reconquista* was enlivened early in the ninth century when King Alfonso of Asturias announced the discovery of St. James the Apostle's body at Compostela in the northwest. The resultant devotion to Santiago Matamoros (St. James Moor-killer) developed an image of the saint spearheading the fight against Islamic domination and was important in engendering a spirit of Spanish nationalism. By the next century Catalonia and Navarra in the northeast had emerged as independent kingdoms, followed a hundred years later by Aragon in the east and Castilla in the center. Soon the reconquest took on aspects of a religious crusade. By the second half of the thirteenth century Islamic Spain had been reduced to the kingdom of Granada in the south, and the bases for the final step, expulsion, were being laid.

In 1469 Ferdinand of Aragon and Isabel of Castilla married. This was a dynastic, not a political or territorial, union, since neither had yet succeeded to the throne. However, five years later Isabel became queen of Castilla, and in 1479 Ferdinand ascended the throne of Aragon. Their marriage marked a vital step toward the ultimate unification of Spain under their grandson, Charles V. In an anarchic peninsula both monarchs put stress on law and order, suppressing banditry and reducing the powerful and fractious nobles to obedience. They introduced economic, religious, and social reforms and became patrons of learning and the arts. In addition to working for domestic peace, they renewed the war against Islam. In 1492 the conquest of Granada earned Ferdinand and Isabel the title Catholic Monarchs and freed Spain for overseas adventures. A few months later Isabel's persistent petitioner, Christopher Columbus, "discovered" Amerindian America. This event brought to the Western Hemisphere Spanish civilization, a complex cultural and social fabric woven of various African, European, Indo-European, and Middle Eastern strands.

In 1519 the Spanish conquistador Hernán Cortés and about 550 men landed on the Gulf coast of Mexico near present-day Veracruz and in two and a half years seized control of the extensive Aztec domain. Uncertain of the bearded strangers, Moctezuma II initially tried to get rid of them, first offering rich gifts of feathers, jade, gold, and silver, then setting ambushes. From their Veracruz base Cortés and his men advanced toward Tenochtitlán, picking up Indian allies, alternately negotiating and fighting. On a causeway leading to the Aztec island capital they were met by Moctezuma and his imposing entourage.

Cortés and his soldiers were then invited into Tenochtitlán, a magnificent city which reminded some of Venice and impressed them as a place of enchantment and a likely trap. Potentially threatened by thousands of Aztec warriors who surrounded his few hundred men, Cortés boldly seized Moctezuma as a hostage and began ruling the Aztec confederation through him, collecting stores of silver, gold, and precious stones.

In the spring of 1520 the threat posed by a Spanish expedition sent by Governor Diego Velásquez of Cuba to arrest Cortés caused the latter to hurry down to the Gulf coast with some of his men. Without great difficulty he gained control of the new force. Returning to Tenochtitlán, he found that his men had aroused the Aztecs to overt defiance by killing a large number of nobles assembled to celebrate a spring festival. Because of rapidly mounting resistance Cortés soon decided it was imperative to leave the city. On the night of June 30, 1520, subsequently known as "la noche triste," the Spaniards began their withdrawal, which quickly became a disastrous rout. Cortés lost half his men.

This severe setback was only temporary. Cortés withdrew to Tlaxcala, the homeland of his principal ally. There he built a fleet of ships with which to conquer the island capital and enlisted additional men. In May 1521 he landed his small army and his Indian allies at the city. In the process of conquering Tenochtitlán, Cortés deliberately destroyed it building by building, filling in its canals with the rubble. The final conquest was hastened by a virulent smallpox epidemic that broke out among the Aztecs.

The rest of Mexico was conquered only gradually. The Spaniards found the Mayas extremely difficult to subdue and made no serious attempt to defeat the seminomadic Chichimecs. And yet, eventually they took control, however limited, of all Mexico, Central America, and the southwestern part of the United States. Their success was made possible by various advantages possessed by the Spaniards: a large number of Indian allies, mastiffs, horses, firearms, and epidemic disease as well as other factors, military and psychological.

Although the Spaniards imposed a veneer of religion, technology, and government on the conquered, they disturbed only minimally their basic Mesoamerican culture. The Spaniards readily adopted those elements of Mexican society that were compatible with their own. Since relatively few Spanish women came to Mexico, from the very beginning of the conquest there was a physical as well as a cultural blending.

Spaniards of widely diverse peninsular backgrounds combined with Indians of varied Middle American societies to produce a new culture and its protagonist, the mestizo. The modern Mexican is the result of this mestizaje blending process, this combining of Indian and European genes and cultures.

The northward expansion of the Spaniards in the latter two-thirds of the sixteenth century furnishes a concrete example of the continued vitality of the Mexican people. Conquest of the north was carried out with the help of Nahua Indians, particularly the Tlaxcalans. Spaniards used nuclei of Tlaxcalans to colonize much of the northern frontier. Indians and mestizos of the central Mexican plateau accompanied the Spaniards northward as soldiers and settlers, extending Hispanicized Nahua culture to New Mexico and Texas. In their roles as farmers, herdsmen, miners, craftsmen, and servants they were of great importance in settling this region. A few played more exalted roles. For example, Isabel Tolosa Cortés Moctezuma, a great-granddaughter of Moctezuma II, was the wife of Juan de Oñate, founder and first governor of Nuevo México.

A quick and partial survey of expansion northward in the sixteenth century can only suggest the extent of Spanish-Mexican activity in the area. In 1528 Pánfilo de Narváez came from Spain with a small force to explore and conquer the area the Spaniards called La Florida, "discovered" earlier by Ponce de León. The expedition ended in disaster. Alvar Núñez Cabeza de Vaca, one of a handful of survivors, wandered for eight years over much of the southwestern United States and northern Mexico before reaching a Spanish outpost. His reports, which mentioned the fabled Seven Cities of Gold (Cíbola), inspired Spaniards to explore the area further. Fray Marcos de Niza in 1539, Francisco Vásquez de Coronado in 1540, and Hernando de Soto in 1541 undertook broad-ranging surveys of the Southwest, but failed to find either wealthy Cíbola or precious metals. The mid-century discovery of rich silver mines much closer to the Mexican capital diverted Spanish attention from the northern frontier for the next half-century.

After that interval, it was not gold or silver but international rivalry that led to the settlement of the northern frontier. In the late 1570s Francis Drake, the English privateer, sailed across the Atlantic, through the Strait of Magellan, up the west coast of South and North America, across the Pacific, and on around the world. Spaniards believed that Drake had returned eastward via the long-sought Northwest Passage, which Spaniards called the Strait of Anián, believed to be somewhere north of Mexico. To protect Spanish territorial interests in the presumed strait, the crown decided to occupy the region. As a result, Juan de Oñate, son of a wealthy mine owner, led a large expedition to Nuevo México. In north central Nuevo México he founded San Gabriel de los Españoles in 1598, nine years before the English established James-town. In 1610 his successor settled Santa Fe de San Francisco about thirty miles to the south. From this first permanent settlement near the Rio Grande there was a gradual expansion north and south.

Since little mineral wealth was discovered in Nuevo México, Christianization of the sedentary Indians became the primary reason for continuing colonization. After a century twenty-five missions had been established; however, the 60,000 to 90,000 Indians continued to live in the approximately ninety villages they occupied when the Spaniards arrived. In the late seventeenth century Santa Fe, the capital of this northern region, had a population of about 1,000, three-fourths of whom were mixed-bloods. Another 1,500 immigrants lived in scattered settlements along the Rio Grande and its tributaries.

In 1680 colonization efforts suffered a severe setback. After a century of Christianization the Pueblo Indians, resentful of exploitation and upset by the displacing of their leaders, rose up in revolt under Popé and other shamans. In early August a concerted attack on all Spanish settlements killed some 420 men, women, and children. Only Santa Fe was able to withstand the initial assault, but soon the Spaniards were forced to abandon it and all of Nuevo México, retreating down the Rio Grande to the El Paso region.

In the ensuing decade several efforts were made to reconquer the upper Rio Grande area. Finally, in 1693 the newly appointed governor, Diego de Vargas, succeeded in retaking Santa Fe. Popé having died in 1690, the Indian pueblos began reluctantly to resubmit to Spanish authority after Vargas and his soldiers bested them in a number of encounters. When the military campaign ended, the Spaniards acted in a conciliatory fashion, even respecting some Pueblo religious practices. In addition to rebuilding their former settlements, the Spaniards founded Albuquerque in 1706.

Nuevo México was viewed as a buffer between the more valuable mining region to the south and marauding Indians of the northern

COLONIAL NEW SPAIN

0   Scale of Miles   500

frontier. Unremitting hostility from Apaches, Navajos, and Comanches, who surrounded the Pueblo region, continued to make expansion uncertain, and the colony grew slowly as a trickle of settlers continued to move up the valleys of the Rio Grande and its tributaries. In the early 1700s the Apaches came under increasing pressure from the Comanches and for the next 150 years kept the nuevomexicano frontier in a state of terror.

By the middle 1700s a new threat appeared as French traders from Illinois and Louisiana began to penetrate Nuevo México in an effort to initiate trade. The French economic thrust quickly became a matter of great concern to Spanish officials, who responded by expanding the mission system and encouraging settlement. However, efforts to attract more settlers to the region were unsuccessful; at the end of the eighteenth century it had fewer than 8,000 Spanish-Mexican settlers in fourteen towns and villages. It remained an isolated province, with limited and insecure links to the heartland of Mexico. This isolation and intermarriage with local Indians over time led to a strong sense of *patria chica*, little fatherland.

The area that is today the state of Arizona developed even more slowly than the Rio Grande Valley. Colonization was principally the result of Father Eusebio Kino's quarter-century of missionary work in the late 1600s. His efforts were climaxed at the beginning of the 1700s with the founding of missions San Xavier del Bac, near Tucson, and Tumacácori, just south of Tubac. In the second half of the eighteenth century the continued threat of Apache raids, incursions of French traders, and the discovery of some mineral deposits all contributed to the push and pull of settlement. At the end of the 1700s there were fewer than 2,000 settlers living in a handful of pueblos near the present border with Mexico.

———

Settlement of Texas and California had a somewhat different history. In Texas initial interest in settlement resulted from Robert La Salle's expedition down the Mississippi River in 1682, his building a fort at Matagorda Bay two years later, and his subsequent efforts to establish a French colony. Continuing French interest in the area led to increased Spanish military and mission activity. Two missions were established on the Neches River in 1690 and in the following year Texas was given provincial status. During the following decades six additional missions and a presidio were founded. Finally, the founding of San Antonio de Béxar in 1718 firmly established Spanish settlement in the area.

The rivalry between Spaniards and Frenchmen continued until Spain acquired Louisiana from France by treaty in 1763. From that time until 1800, when Spain returned Louisiana to France, Texas developed slowly. Settlement was retarded especially by the aggressive hostility of mounted Comanches. By the end of the 1700s the population of Texas was about 3,500, with approximately half the settlers around San Antonio. Most of the remainder lived at La Bahía, in the southeast near the Gulf coast, and around Nacogdoches, in the northeast near the Louisiana boundary.

It was a very real French menace that encouraged Spanish colonization of Texas, but only a potential threat from Russian and English interests that spurred Spain to settle Alta California. In the 1760s rumors that Russians were advancing southward from Alaska were reported to Madrid. These reports, coupled with activity along the Pacific coast by English explorers, aroused the Spaniards to take immediate steps to counter the perceived possibility of foreign occupation.

In 1765 José de Gálvez was sent to Mexico as a special crown representative with instructions to begin colonizing Alta California. The initial step was taken by an expedition from Baja California headed by the governor, Captain Gaspar de Portolá, and the president of the Franciscan missions, Junípero Serra. Father Serra began his task of establishing missions by founding Mission San Diego de Alcalá in 1769. Governor Portolá built the presidio of Monterey in the following year. Although Alta California was initially colonized as a defense measure, missions came to dominate the province. By 1823 twenty-one missions had been established between San Diego and Sonoma, north of San Francisco. In addition, three presidios and three towns were founded. The total settler population was about 3,500; most of them lived in the coastal valleys.

As we have seen, exploration and colonizing of the Southwest were undertaken by Spain between 1530 and 1800. The two centuries between the beginning of Nuevo México and that of California were years of cultural change and the intermingling of races in both the Southwest and in the Mexican heartland. The people who began the Alta California pueblos of San José in 1777 and Los Angeles in 1781 differed in cultural baggage from those who had established Santa Fe in 1610. In Nuevo México, Spaniards and Mexicans added to their cultural

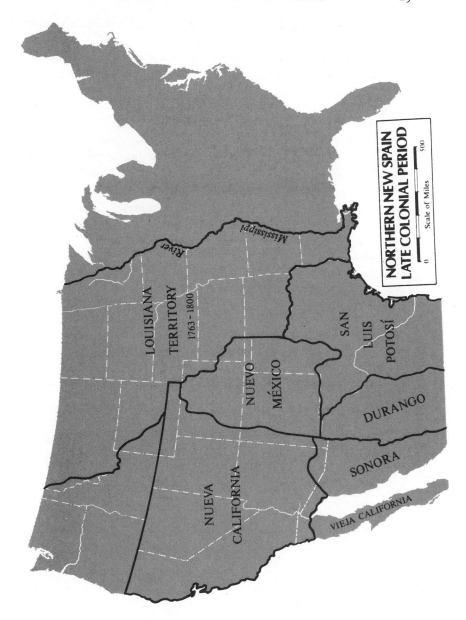

NORTHERN NEW SPAIN
LATE COLONIAL PERIOD

Scale of Miles

0   500

LOUISIANA TERRITORY
1763–1800

Mississippi River

SAN LUIS POTOSÍ

NUEVO MÉXICO

DURANGO

NUEVA CALIFORNIA

SONORA

VIEJA CALIFORNIA

diversity by adapting and incorporating elements from local Indian cultures and by intermarriage.

In addition, varied geographic and economic conditions in the Southwest accentuated differences as time went on. They also determined the manner and direction in which the widely separated areas developed. Although subsistence agriculture was at first the most important activity in all areas, in Arizona and Nuevo México settlements generally evolved around missionary activities and the search for minerals. In Texas and California agriculture and stock raising developed slowly and remained almost the sole economic activity to the end of the colonial period.

The record indicates that most settlers were Mexican Indians, mestizos, mulattoes, and more complex racial mixtures. The government in Mexico City recruited colonists for the northern frontier from among the poorer classes with promises of land, economic aid, and other inducements. As a result, the northern frontier offered opportunities to the more venturesome members of the lower economic strata of Mexican society, as it still does today.

2

REVOLUTION AND DISARRAY

During the last quarter of the eighteenth century and the first quarter of the nineteenth revolutions swept the Western world. The first of these rebellions began in 1775 as a war of independence by some of Great Britain's colonies in North America. That was followed by the French Revolution in 1789, and two decades later Spain's colonies in America revolted. These dramatic events had a profound impact on the history of California, New Mexico, and Texas. Mexicans were directly involved in two of these revolts—the first in England's mainland colonies after 1775 and the second in Mexico beginning in 1810 and ending in 1821.

North American revolutionary leaders seeking foreign support logically turned to England's ancient and traditional rivals, France and Spain. Both responded with aid. Spain became actively involved in the revolt of the thirteen colonies, principally in Florida and the lower Mississippi Valley. She even cut back on her meager defenses of the northern Mexican frontier in order to help the American revolutionaries. Bernardo de Gálvez, governor of Spanish Louisiana, supplied cannons, bombs, muskets, ammunition, uniforms, and tents to the American rebels in their struggle against England and allowed them to cross Spanish territory and to use port facilities at New Orleans. The governor also led a large body of militiamen in a successful campaign against English strong points along the Mississippi River, seizing Natchez, Baton Rouge, and a number of other river ports held by the British. In 1781 he captured the preeminent English New World naval base at Pensacola. By preventing England from gaining control of the Mississippi, the governor greatly aided American revolutionaries. The bulk of Gálvez's funds and supplies came from Mexico and some of his soldiers in the Mississippi campaign were Mexicans. Mexican soldiers were even present at General Charles Cornwallis's surrender at Yorktown. More important in the long run, the success of the American Revolution inspired and encouraged Mexican patriots a quarter-century later. However, the Mexican revolution of 1810 had earlier long-term and fundamental social and economic causes.

From the very beginning of colonization in Mexico resistance to Spanish domination was a recurring pattern in the lives of its Indian people. Over the colonial centuries this opposition had varied manifestations; some appeared to be simple riots, some were rebellions, and some were clearly revolutions aiming at separation from Spain. Most were caused by the dismal conditions of the lowest economic levels of society, namely the Indians. They ranged widely from the ferocious 1541–42 Mixton War, occasioned by Spanish brutality, to the 1692 assault on the government palace in Mexico City that left it a burned-out shell, victim of food rioters. One of the best-organized rebellions took place in 1802 in the west coast provinces of Tepic and Nayarit. This movement, initiated and led by a revolutionary known as "el Indio Mariano," proposed to restore the empire of Moctezuma II. After a prolonged struggle the uprising was suppressed when Indio Mariano was captured and executed by the colonial authorities.

However, as it turned out, the end of Spanish colonialism came not from a racially oriented movement led by Indians but from continuing and escalating conflict between American-born persons largely of European blood, called *criollos*, and peninsular-born Spaniards. In the first decade of the 1800s rising economic and social antagonism between peninsulars, supported by the Spanish crown, and criollos led to the development of small secret revolutionary groups strongly influenced by the French and North American revolutions. The activities of Father Miguel Hidalgo y Costilla, criollo pastor in the small village of Dolores in Guanajuato and a member of one of these groups, led to the outbreak of Mexico's revolution for independence. On September 16, 1810, at his parish church, Hidalgo uttered the now famous "Grito de Dolores," which has come down to us as "Long live our Lady of Guadalupe, down with bad government, death to the Spaniards."

The transition from colonial New Spain to independent Mexico took place during a time of worldwide social and political ferment which had reverberations in Mexico. Motivation for the revolution that ensued was initially social and racial but later became overwhelmingly political and economic. Impoverished Indians formed the bulk of the early revolutionary forces, while much of the leadership was provided by criollos and mestizos who had pretensions to criollo status and sought to achieve higher economic and social positions. In this movement mestizos emerged as a dynamic social force that was to have tremendous impact on the future history of Mexico.

Led by Father Hidalgo, some 50,000 Indians and mestizos united under the quickly and almost instinctively adopted banner of the dark-skinned Virgin of Guadalupe as the symbol of Mexican nationalism. Sweeping southward from Dolores toward Mexico City by way of Celaya, Querétaro, and Guanajuato, Hidalgo's untrained and unorganized horde soon arrived within sight of Mexico City, the heart of Spanish colonial power in North America. Although its capture seemed almost certain, Hidalgo hesitated outside the capital and soon withdrew his forces westward toward Guadalajara. This unexplained action was the turning point in the initial phase of the struggle against Spanish rule. The tide of battle turned in favor of the royalist supporters. The rebel position rapidly deteriorated and Hidalgo was soon abandoned by most of his followers. As he fled northward, possibly to seek aid in the United States, he was trapped by royalist forces and eventually betrayed by one of his own officers. He was quickly stripped of his clerical status, tried for treason, and executed on July 30, 1811.

At this juncture the fallen standard of revolt was picked up by José María Morelos y Pavón, a mestizo priest from the province of Michoacán and earlier one of Hidalgo's students. Morelos possessed a military and political capability notably lacking in Hidalgo. He set about training his revolutionary troops and also assembled a congress which declared Mexican independence in November 1813 and began writing a constitution. Issued a year later at Apatzingán, the constitution officially committed the Mexican revolution to a social and political egalitarianism which Morelos had already initiated informally. Under Morelos the revolution achieved its widest geographical extent, but his strongly egalitarian objectives increasingly antagonized many criollos. With support declining and royalist forces on the increase, Morelos was captured in late 1815 and, like Hidalgo, defrocked, tried, and executed.

Father Morelos's death left the revolutionary leadership crippled and seriously divided. After 1815 activity was reduced to occasional opportunistic guerrilla attacks carried out in Mexico's rugged mountain terrain by small isolated groups of partisans. By the end of the decade the 1810 revolutionary movement had been almost completely suppressed, and the reactionary Spanish government of the restored monarch, Fernando VII, seemed in nearly complete control of the colony.

However, events in Europe soon altered the Mexican situation. In 1820 a revolt by sailors in the Spanish port of Cádiz initiated a revolutionary movement which forced Fernando to accept the liberal constitution that had been drafted by the Spanish *cortes* (parliament) in 1812. In Mexico conservative criollo elements felt that the new constitution and a liberal government in Spain posed a threat both to public order and to their privileged position in society. Their response was a conservative counterrevolution headed by a Mexican royalist officer, Agustín de Iturbide. With the forces under his command Iturbide soon joined the guerrilla remnants of the earlier revolutionary movements and with their leaders declared Mexico independent in 1821. The banner that temporarily united the two groups was known as the Three Guarantees: independence, religion, and equality. One year later Iturbide was inaugurated Emperor of Mexico, Agustín I. His inability to retain support of the numerous political factions that had helped put him in power, especially the liberals, quickly led to his downfall. In March 1823 he was removed from office by a republican revolutionary coup initiated by a youthful criollo officer, Antonio López de Santa Anna.

After deposing Agustín I leaders of the republican movement called a constituent assembly, which proceeded to draw up an extremely federalist constitution. This 1824 document gave virtual autonomy to the states of the new Mexican republic and, despite considerable continuing strife over the issue of federalism versus centralism, remained in effect until 1835. Cumulative reaction to excessive federalism then led to a revolt which overthrew the government and brought López de Santa Anna to the presidency. He quickly called a convention in 1836 to organize a greatly centralized administration. Installation of his new government caused widespread federalist reaction throughout the country, most notably on Mexico's periphery where federalism was strongest. Opposition to the new centralism quickly led to militant action, which broke out in the various provinces, especially in the northern regions that were later to become a part of the United States.

In order to better understand the historical development of this northern region of Mexico between 1810 and 1836, it is necessary to see how political events in central Mexico affected different parts of the area.

For californios, the Spanish-Mexican citizens of the recently settled province of Alta California, the 1810 revolution in central Mexico was the first major political issue. Although they were vaguely aware of the revolt, they remained largely unconcerned and uninvolved with the ideology and events of the independence movement. Indeed, a sense of insecurity resulting from the fact of recent settlement and great isolation made many californios hesitate to break with Spain and thereby risk their future on the unpredictable outcome of the revolt for independence. Moreover, many californios asked themselves whether an independent Mexico would be able to protect remote, isolated California from attacks by foreign powers or Indians. These considerations tended to encourage latent loyalties to the Spanish crown. On the other hand, with the possible exception of government officials, including the clergy, nearly all of whom were Spanish-born, few californios had strong feelings of loyalty to distant Spain. For these reasons they were little involved in the revolution of 1810.

Nevertheless, the fact that supply ships no longer brought luxury items as well as some basic necessities from Mexico made the californios constantly, if indirectly, mindful of the revolt for independence. Inconveniences caused by disruption of trade with the Mexican heartland were minimized by the expansion of mission manufacturing as the missions shifted from subsistence to commercial production. At the missionaries' insistence the Spanish government had sent artisans to teach the Indians a variety of trades. Now mission-manufactured goods supplied most needs of californios. Foreign commerce also expanded as Spanish regulations against trading with foreigners were ignored. After 1810 Boston merchants, English shippers, and the Russians at Fort Ross, north of San Francisco, were able to supply californios with most goods that were not produced locally.

The arrival from Hawaii of the Argentine privateer Hippolyte Bouchard with his two ships, the *Argentina* and the *Santa Rosa*, was the only event that definitely involved californios in the revolution against Spain. In 1818 Bouchard briefly put California under the blue-and-white Argentine revolutionary flag when he landed at Monterey and urged the citizens to rise up and throw off Spanish authority. Since he found little enthusiasm for his incitation to rebellion, he ravaged the town, burning the presidio and the homes of all Spaniards. The two privateering vessels then sailed south to Santa Barbara and San Juan Capistrano, where they engaged in minor skirmishes with local californios, who had been alerted and were prepared for their arrival. Unsuccessful in his effort to solicit revolutionary support, Bouchard finally sailed off to South America.

Californios had already become virtually independent of Mexico City by 1821. Governmental events taking place there had little meaning for and direct impact on them. When they learned of the accession of Agustín I to the Mexican throne early in 1822, Governor Pablo Vicente Solá called a town meeting at Monterey to consider California's relationship to the new government. Discussion indicated only one possible course of action, and thus governor and troops swore allegiance to the new imperial Mexican government on April 11. A few months later a government representative from Mexico City successfully engineered the election of a californio criollo, Luis Argüello, as the first Mexican governor of the province.

Early in 1823, when Iturbide's empire was overthrown and replaced by a republic, Governor Argüello pledged Alta California's support to the new authorities. A year later the federalist Constitution of 1824 reached Monterey and was immediately ratified by the californios. Despite these rapid, but distant, political changes and the acceptance of the new republican constitution, California's social structure and way of life remained relatively undisturbed and unchanged. Because of turbulent conditions and greater instability in central Mexico and sustained economic and political stability in California, during the latter 1820s there was some increase in migration from the Mexican heartland to California.

At the same time various factors were leading to considerable change in Mexican California. These included a rapid rise in anticlericalism after independence, government expectations of revenue from secularization of the missions and transfer of mission lands, the interest of californio landowners in increasing their landholdings by acquiring mission lands, and their expectations of obtaining Indian laborers from the former missions. In the mid-1830s the California missions were secularized by orders from the central government in Mexico City, and a scramble for mission property immediately ensued. Political unrest mounted rapidly when Santa Anna forcibly instituted the Constitution of 1836. This centralist document greatly increased political instability both in central Mexico and on the periphery. On the northern frontier conflict with the United States was already brewing, nurtured by ever-weakening Mexican control and by deepening Anglo American penetration that was beginning to affect local economic and political structures. This trend was particularly noticeable in Nuevo México.

Like California, Nuevo México remained essentially aloof from the kaleidoscopic events in central Mexico during the period 1810 to 1836, generally receiving little help or leadership from the national government. Suppression of Apache depredations had led to renewed migration from below the Rio Grande in the late 1700s and resulted in the expansion of farming and ranching, especially on the northern boundaries of the province. This area had long been an important sheep-raising region and sent large flocks of sheep, as many as 20,000 in one year, south to the mining centers of Sonora. The pioneering use of the Old Spanish Trail from the upper Rio Grande to Los Angeles by Antonio Armijo in 1829 provided an additional market. Early in the nineteenth century mining became especially important because it further expanded trade with Chihuahua to the south, thereby lessening Nuevo México's isolation.

The abating of Indian raids also contributed to revived interest in mining in the more isolated areas of Nuevo México. Some placer gold was discovered in the early 1800s, but copper remained the most important mineral produced in the region. The discovery of copper ore at Santa Rita in the southwestern part of Nuevo México in 1804 led to extensive mining operations there. In some years copper production in the Santa Rita del Cobre mines reached one thousand tons. As a consequence of sizable shipments the trade route between Nuevo México and Chihuahua gained increased importance. At the same time routes from Santa Fe to the United States frontier were being pioneered by Spanish, French, and Anglo fur trappers. However, the Spanish and (later) Mexican governments discouraged contacts with the United States because they wanted to keep all trade within the country and were concerned also about possible American encroachment upon the weakly held northern territories.

The 1810 revolt from Spain and the establishment of an independent government scarcely touched most nuevomexicanos. Primarily, and almost solely, concerned with problems of earning their daily living, they remained passively loyal to Spain and politically inactive. However, their security was diminished by the transfer of frontier troops to central Mexico during the revolution, a move which left the northern provinces more vulnerable to renewed Indian raiding. As Indian depredations increased on the northern fringes of the frontier after 1810, mission activity declined, and settlers living in the more exposed areas either fled southward to towns or were killed. Eventually missions, ranches, farms, and mines were abandoned as missionaries and settlers moved to safer locations, particularly to larger centers such as Santa Fe. Some even fled to Chihuahua and Sonora because problems of labor, transportation, isolation, and security had become too great. The missions were further affected adversely when, in the late 1820s, the Mexican government expelled from its territories all Spaniards, including missionaries, who were unwilling to take an oath of loyalty to the new government.

In 1822 the isolation of northern Nuevo México was reduced when William Becknell opened the 900-mile-long Santa Fe Trail, or Mexican Road, as it was first called. Trade between Missouri and the northern Mexican frontier led to a limited economic revolution and to expansion of the Nuevo México region, particularly along the various alternative routes of the trail. Nuevomexicanos were now able to obtain consumer goods from St. Louis more readily and at lower prices than from the nearest Mexican trading center, Chihuahua. Trade with the United States also provided a welcome and convenient outlet for nuevomexicano products such as mules, horses, woolen blankets, buffalo robes, beaver pelts, and silver, which were exchanged for small manufactured items, hardware, dry goods, and cottons, especially calico cloth.

The Santa Fe trade quickly became an economic mainstay of the area, along with mining and subsistence agriculture, and by the 1830s had become a vital spur to the economy and a source of income to the government. By 1824 the Missouri trade had extended south to Chihuahua and by 1840 50 percent of American trade goods had Chihuahua as its destination. As a result of this extension southward, the Mexican government in 1842 established an annual trade fair at El

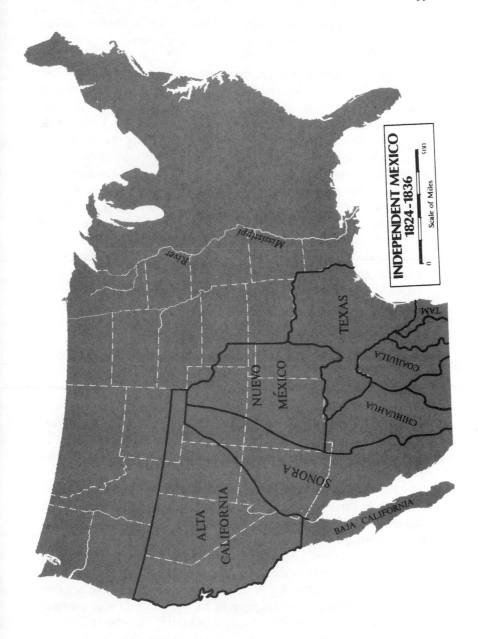

INDEPENDENT MEXICO
1824-1836

Scale of Miles

0

TEXAS

TAM

COAHUILA

CHIHUAHUA

NUEVO
MÉXICO

SONORA

ALTA
CALIFORNIA

BAJA CALIFORNIA

Mississippi

River

Paso on the route to Chihuahua. By this time a number of nuevomexicano elites were deeply involved in the trade, many in partnerships
with Anglos.

A handful of Anglo American frontiersmen and traders who followed
Becknell's lead settled around Santa Fe and some became Mexican
citizens. Some, like Kit Carson, Charles Bent, and James Magoffin,
married into Mexican families, became landowners, and bridged the
gap between Anglo and nuevomexicano society. Others antagonized
nuevomexicanos with their racial arrogance and sneering disparagement
of the Catholic religion, as well as their crude, boorish frontier manners.
Local Mexican officials had well-founded suspicions about the loyalty
of these new citizens and feared that the traders were the vanguard of
a much larger migration. At the same time well-to-do nuevomexicanos
began sending their sons to schools in the United States, particularly
in St. Louis. Thus, as in California and Texas, Nuevo México began
to develop an Anglo faction whose loyalties to Mexico were questionable
and whose religious and social heritage made many at best ambivalent
about Mexican culture.

While these changes were modifying the economic and cultural isolation of nuevomexicanos, the new administrations in Mexico City also
began to affect political and social structures. The 1824 Constitution
organized Nuevo México as a territory with Santa Fe as its capital. The
new territory had a population of some 20,000, most of whom were
mestizos and other mixed-bloods, plus an additional 8,000 sedentary
Indians. The majority lived in small communities in north-central
Nuevo México along the Rio Grande system. In what is today Arizona,
which remained closer to Sonora than to Santa Fe, only Tucson and
Tubac had a few hundred settlers each.

In the years between Mexican independence in 1821 and war with
the United States in 1846 there was considerable migration from the
Mexican heartland into the valley of the Rio Grande, particularly in
the southern area between Socorro and El Paso. At the same time an
important cattle- and sheep-ranching economy continued to develop
in the region north of Socorro. Mining also attracted settlers to Nuevo
México, especially after the discovery of gold in the Sierra del Oro
between Santa Fe and Albuquerque in the late 1820s. One of the most
important mines in this region was the Ortiz mine, the Real de Dolores,
which was producing $20,000 in gold yearly during the middle 1830s.
By the end of the Mexican period yearly production of mines in the

region ranged in value from $40,000 to $50,000. Because of the government's constant and dire need for revenue, discovery of gold in Nuevo México caused Mexico City to take renewed interest in the area.

Of the three provinces in the northern frontier Texas was without doubt most directly affected by political events in central Mexico between 1810 and the 1830s. Before the 1810 revolution, Spanish interest and involvement in Texas had languished because the transfer of adjacent Louisiana from France to Spain in 1763 ended the French expansionist threat. This security, however, was short-lived, as a new challenge to Spanish control of the Texas-Louisiana region loomed, from its next-door neighbor, the United States.

By the last decade of the eighteenth century Anglo American horse traders had begun to be attracted to the eastern Texas plains by the large herds of wild horses and cattle which roamed there. Additionally, after the American purchase of the Louisiana Territory from France in 1803 American frontiersmen became active in general trade with Mexicans and Indians of the area, while others began to acquire land and engage in ranching. A very few had far more ambitious goals. With the backing of some Spanish officials and Americans, Aaron Burr and General James Wilkinson, the U.S. military governor of the Louisiana Territory, developed a scheme, or schemes, for seizing the area and establishing an empire for themselves. The location of Texas far from the centers of power in both Mexico and the United States made it highly vulnerable to infiltration and filibustering by Americans and Mexicans, as well as by knaves and rogues of other nationalities.

Although the 1810 Mexican revolt against Spain initially had little impact on the inhabitants of Texas, the unique location of this Mexican frontier region on the United States border quickly caused it to become a center of intrigue. After the death of Father Hidalgo one of his followers, José Bernardo Gutiérrez de Lara, fled from Mexico and took refuge in the United States. In Natchitoches he met with Zebulon Pike and Augustus Magee, a former United States Army officer under General Wilkinson, and plotted with them to free Texas from Spain. As a result of their intrigues, a Gutiérrez-Magee expedition of about 200 men invaded Texas late in 1812 and captured Nacogdoches, Goliad, and San Antonio. However, Magee was killed and dissension quickly developed among the invaders, enabling Spanish government forces to recapture San Antonio. As a result, Gutiérrez de Lara and his men were forced to flee back across the border into American Louisiana.

Subsequent filibustering in Texas was closely watched and thwarted by the United States government, which did not want to antagonize Spain while it was negotiating a treaty to acquire (Spanish) Florida. Late in 1819 news reached the Louisiana frontier that the United States had obtained Florida through the Adams-Onís Treaty. A clause of this treaty also defined the boundary between American Louisiana and Spanish Texas; thereby the United States gave up claims to parts of eastern Texas. This compromise led to protest meetings among the land-hungry, jingoistic frontiersmen of the early American Southwest.

One of these meetings, at Natchez, Mississippi, led to the organizing of a filibustering expedition into Texas by James Long and Gutiérrez de Lara. Long's ragtag army crossed the Sabine River boundary between Louisiana and Texas, seized Nacogdoches, and declared a republic with Long as president. Moving southwestward, Long and his men captured Goliad in October 1821 and identified their activities as part of the revived Mexican struggle for independence. However, Long's success was short-lived, for his army was defeated. He was captured, taken to Mexico City, and later executed. José Gutiérrez de Lara, on the other hand, somehow managed to avoid a similar fate. In 1824 he became the first governor of the northeastern Mexican state of Tamaulipas, across the Rio Grande from Texas. Although the Long expedition ended in failure, considerable American interest in eastern Texas continued.

After 1821 much of the area between the Nueces River and the Rio Grande was parceled out in land grants by the newly independent government in Mexico City. These grants resulted in an accelerated movement of Mexican settlers into this Nueces triangle. While this northward settlement was progressing there was an even more rapid migration of Anglo Americans into the region north and east of the Nueces. This immigration set the stage for the eventual acquisition of the entire Southwest by the United States.

Mexican independence had limited impact on the northern tier of Mexican provinces. Changes of government in Mexico City had little effect on social, economic, and political structures. Legislatures and other elements of local republican government were established; Indians and mestizos in theory were granted full citizenship. The ideology of republican and egalitarian ideals influenced a few leaders, but many found old authoritarian ways hard to give up. Wealthy landowners, *patrones*, continued to dominate both the economy and local government.

Mexican independence did bring some social improvement to the northern frontier. Increased interest in education, necessary for good republican government, led to the founding of a few schools in major settlements. The introduction of printing presses into California and Nuevo México stimulated interest in the printed word. The chief product of the presses was religious and devotional, rather than educational. Formal book learning was traditionally not a widespread frontier concern or need.

During the Mexican period northern frontier society, particularly in California and Texas, underwent rapid economic change. In California development of the hide and tallow trade led to increased ranching activity, which became conspicuously the economic mainstay during the 1830s. In Texas, stock raising and cotton cultivation grew in importance as the industrial world's demand for cheap protein and textiles increased rapidly. In Nuevo México new trade routes were developed, the most important being the Santa Fe Trail from Missouri and the Old Spanish Trail to Los Angeles. The Santa Fe trade brought about dramatic but limited change as the nuevomexicano economy became increasingly more closely linked to the United States. As a result of expanded trade there were increased contacts with Americans, some of whom settled in all three regions. Many of these new immigrants added to existing unease by their vociferous dissatisfaction with Mexican law and sovereignty. By the mid-1830s the entire Southwest was on the threshold of a new era.

3

MAN AND LAND
ON THE FRONTIER

Political, economic, and religious considerations spurred the initial
movement of Mexicans and Spaniards into the northern frontier region
of New Spain. The peopling of Nuevo México was ordered at the end
of the 1500s by the Spanish crown to forestall presumed English activity
in the region. More than a century later the first effort to settle Texas
was brought about because of the French presence and exploration at
the mouth of the Mississippi River. Three-quarters of a century later,
in 1769, Alta California's settlement began as a result of rumors that
the Russians were moving down from Alaska and reports that the English
also were showing an interest in the Pacific coast.

Over time a typical pattern for settlement of the northern frontier
emerged. First came the initial conquest and occupation, usually impelled by hope of economic gain as well as by other considerations.
This initial stage required the indispensable royal approval and typically
was privately financed. Second came Christianization of local Indians,
undertaken by one of the several missionary orders, in the Southwest
the Jesuits (until 1767) and Franciscans. A third step in this process of
settlement was securing the region, a task carried out by the military,
who established small garrisons, usually near missions or pueblos. Soldiers stationed in these frontier forts were encouraged to remain after

their terms of service with grants of nearby land. In this way population was increased and defense of the province was bolstered. Around the missions and garrisons there grew up settlements which later attracted or developed a small artisan and merchant class.

The societies that emerged along New Spain's northern frontier in these isolated clusters differed not only from the parent society in Mexico but also from one another. There were, of course, many institutions, customs, attitudes, and activities common to all. There also arose regional differences deriving from the colonists' diverse origins, earlier experiences, their adaptation to the local geography and inhabitants, and other factors. Perhaps best known of these cultures is the society which developed in California during the Spanish colonial and Mexican periods.

Alta California was founded as an extension of the mission system which had secured Baja California. Its missions were self-contained socioeconomic units which included substantial numbers of Indians who provided all necessary agricultural and manufacturing labor. Mission Indians were trained in livestock management, farming, and simple building skills. Since missions were acculturating institutions, the Indians were also taught manual arts and Spanish as well as the rudiments of the Catholic religion. Some learned the skills of vintners, weavers, leather workers, blacksmiths, carpenters, and other artisans. While missionaries were not always benevolent, they did provide a degree of protection and economic security for the mission Indians.

Self-sufficiency was based on extensive herds of cattle and horses, flocks of sheep and goats, hogs, wheatfields, orchards, vineyards, garden plots, and workshops. As a result of the zeal and organizing skills of the missionaries and the hard work of the Indians, Alta California became the most prosperous province in northern New Spain. Because of its isolation and self-sufficiency, by the time of independence from Spain in 1821 the province was clearly drifting from the central government's control. Self-sufficiency was an absolute necessity for the californios. They could not depend on supplies or leadership from central Mexico because lines of communication, both by land and by sea, were long and uncertain, and because political confusion reigned in the heartland.

There were two main elements in the economic and social life of California, the mission and the rancho, both highly dependent on the ready availability of land and labor. As elsewhere on the northern

Mexican frontier, missions were granted sufficient land to carry out the tasks of acculturation and Christianization. In addition to mission land grants-in-trust for the Indians, land was also allotted to individual settlers. The first such grant was made in 1775 and by the end of Spanish control in 1821 about thirty private land grants had been awarded in California, principally to former soldiers. These grants remained relatively undeveloped during the Spanish period, since they were used for subsistence agriculture and small-scale ranching. When Mexico became independent nearly all these grants were confirmed by the new government.

Under the Mexican government granting of land in California was rapidly accelerated; between 1822 and 1846 some 780 grants were awarded by officials in both California and Mexico City. Over half these grants were made in the last six years of Mexican rule, between 1841 and 1846. Some went to frontier soldiers whose service was completed, as was the case with Rancho Entre Napa, which was awarded to Nicolás Higuera, a soldier of the San Francisco presidio. Others went to upper-class californios and even to recently naturalized foreigners like William Hartnell, who received title to Rancho Patrocinio Alisal near Monterey, and William Dana, who obtained Rancho Nipomo in San Luis Obispo. By the middle of the 1830s a great expansion of private ranchos got underway.

By the beginning of that decade a few ranchos had begun to compete with the missions for economic preeminence. In this rivalry the rancheros' chief criticism of the missions was that they controlled the main source of labor, the Indians. The Mexican government's secularization of the missions in the mid-1830s helped solve the rancheros' labor problem. Appropriation and sale of mission properties both enlarged rancho holdings and made available the workers necessary for their continued expansion. The rationale for secularization was that it would benefit everyone: the California Indian by making him master of his own destiny, the missionary by freeing him for other work on the cutting edge of the frontier, and the Mexican government by providing a new source of tax revenue.

However, rancheros became the chief beneficiaries. Over 90 percent of mission lands and buildings, as well as other mission property, was leased, sold, or granted to influential rancheros. Although each Indian family was given a small individual plot and had use of the common lands (*ejidos*), ultimately mission lands ended up in private hands. Many

Indians, having sold or lost their allotment of mission land, settled on ranchos and resumed the labors of their former mission life.

California ranchos, like the missions, provided most of the daily needs of their owners and workers, once they had become well established. They raised cattle, horses, sheep, and hogs, and cultivated grapes, fruit, wheat, and other grains. By the beginning of the Mexican period cattle raising had become the largest single industry. The incentive for its expansion came from the rising demand for hides and tallow from New England sea traders. By the end of the Mexican period a quarter-century later, a few larger and more successful ranchos had become virtual self-contained villages similar to large haciendas in north-central Mexico. However, most California rancheros were hardly wealthy elites; they were hardworking frontiersmen with limited leisure and modest two- or three-room adobe homes.

The heart of the rancho was the owner's house, surrounded by various work buildings. Typically, a rancho dwelling consisted of a flat-roofed, one-story adobe building with a hard-packed earthen floor. In these buildings or in adjacent lean-tos, usually referred to as *ramadas*, were performed the routine household tasks—cooking, washing, and the making of candles, soap, cloth, and wine. A nearby garden supplied beans, chilies, squash, onions, and other vegetables. Cattle and sheep, plus an occasional deer from the hunt, furnished meat for the table and leather for harnesses, saddles, boots, and various articles of clothing. Tallow and grease supplied the essential ingredients for candles and soap, and wool was spun and woven into cloth and blankets.

Although greater availability of suitable land and easier access to markets promoted more extensive development of ranch life in California than elsewhere in the Southwest, Spanish urban traditions led to the creation of towns as well. Three pueblos were established by law—San José, Los Angeles, and Villa Branciforte, the last-named near present-day Santa Cruz. Other settlements grew up around forts and missions—Santa Barbara, San Diego, San Francisco, and Monterey, for example. In the southern half of the province Nuestra Señora Reina de Los Angeles de la Porciúncula became the economic, political, and social center because of its location, while in the north Monterey held a similar position.

In these early Alta California pueblos the typical pattern of Spanish-American town layout prevailed. Daily life revolved around the plaza, a parklike square which formed the center of town. On one side of the plaza stood the church. Opposite the church was the town government building, known as the *cabildo*; and on the remaining two sides some of the more prosperous rancheros built their town houses. From the plaza a few muddy or dusty, rutted lanes led out of town, used primarily by horsemen and simple two-wheeled carts.

Like the ranch houses, Spanish-Mexican homes built on the *solares*, or town-house lots, were usually flat-roofed, one-story adobe structures, with thick walls and two or three small rooms. The interior walls were whitewashed, and in the corner there was typically a small shrine to the Virgin and other saints. Most of the furniture, hardware, crockery, and utensils were produced locally, usually on the rancho or at one of the missions. During the Spanish period some household goods were brought from Mexico; later furnishings were supplied by the Boston trade, while luxury items like silverware were imported from England. As rancheros became more affluent their homes were enlarged and better furnished.

On ranchos in California and throughout the Southwest an extended-family pattern was the norm. A household might include parents, children, grandparents, grandchildren, maiden aunts, in-laws, other relatives, occasionally orphans, and Indian servants—all living together. The usually male head of the household filled the role of patriarch and expected unquestioning obedience from all. His authority was recognized and respected by subordinate family members regardless of age. The always difficult conditions of frontier life reinforced this pattern of family cohesiveness and patriarchal dominance.

Another characteristic of colonial California society that arose partly out of its frontier nature was its hospitality, especially to travelers. In the absence of inns ranch owners (and missioners) gladly supplied lodging and food for the occasional traveler because they were happy to have company and news from outside. Indeed, californios were often lavish in their generosity, providing guests not only free lodging and meals but also fresh riding animals to continue their journey and sometimes small amounts of money for their future needs.

Within californio society there was much class-caste stratification, yet social mobility was greater than in other parts of New Spain. The more rigid and almost feudal patterns of patrón and peón relationship never developed in California as they did in Nuevo México, though a caste system did exist. The californios were divided into three classes. At the top were "la gente de razón," mostly members of the landowning class, who constituted roughly 10 percent of the population. Members of this group came from varied backgrounds; most were peninsular Spaniards or criollos, a few were mestizos or mulattoes who had acquired large landholdings and thereby had moved into the upper class. They owned perhaps 90 percent of grant lands awarded before 1840. In addition they held all important social, economic, and political positions and maintained tight control of their privileged status by marrying predominantly within their class. At the end of the Mexican period there were perhaps 10,000 californios, of whom approximately 800 owned ranches of various sizes. Oliver Larkin, the first American consul at Monterey, estimated that about 50 of these were elites who wielded the political and economic power of the province.

The second group constituted a large majority of the population; they were the artisans, small landowners, *vaqueros*, herders, soldiers, some servants, and recent settlers. During the Mexican period *cholo* was the widely used name for members of this class. Composed mostly of mestizos, mulattoes, and other mixed-bloods, they were generally illiterate and poor. Blacks in small numbers also took part in the exploration and settlement of the northern frontier from the beginning. By the end of the colonial period they no longer existed as a distinct group but had become blended into the general population. Some scholars estimate that by 1800 one of five californios was part Negro.

At the bottom of the social ladder was the Indian, who endured a condition of wardship under supervision of missionaries or government officials. Both exploited and protected by the mission system, after secularization the Indian was reduced to a more precarious state— virtual peonage to the californio.

Differences in the quality and composition of dress reinforced class and social distinctions in Alta California. The ranch owner's work clothes were practical and suitable to his daily tasks, but his festive clothing, typically luxurious and of high quality, marked his social class. The clothes of the rancher's wife reflected her social position; she might adorn her rather sedate attire with a colorful *rebozo* of striped silk or fine cashmere or a beautiful lace mantilla from the Far East. Dress among the lower classes reflected their inferior position. Clothing of the humbler members of society tended to be plainer and of lower quality than that of the upper classes—less ornate, more utilitarian, and typically of domestic manufacture. Shirt, trousers, sandals, a wide-brimmed sombrero, and a vest or serape comprised the traditional dress for males. Their women customarily wore homespun skirts and blouses with cotton rebozos draped over their shoulders or wrapped around their youngest offspring.

The californio's entertainment was a natural outgrowth of the isolated communities' daily activities. Much social interaction centered on the church. Weddings, wakes, christenings, and other celebrations were occasions for seeing friends and catching up on local gossip. Social intercourse was also generated by the celebration of individual and town patron saints' days. The roundup or rodeo, an essential part of open-range cattle raising, was another important occasion for socializing. These activities often included processions, music, singing, dancing, horse racing, bull-and-bear fights, cockfights, and bullfights. Picnics and informal evening parties, called *tertulias*, were also common and provided opportunities for card games, music, singing, and recitation of poetry as well as for young unmarried people to become acquainted. Entertainment was provided occasionally by theatrical performances and the rare appearance of a tiny traveling circus. Among men gambling was popular and widespread, a diversion in which all social classes indulged. Hunting, in addition to providing food, was a favorite sport.

Mexican frontier life during this period was a combination of hard work and an occasional fiesta. Literate Anglo Americans traveling or residing in this area during the early nineteenth century failed to recognize and understand or appreciate the positive aspects of its frontier society. All too often they viewed Mexicans as backward and were consequently critical of their lifestyle. Their own cultural heritage was strongly colored by Northern European views, dominated by the Protestant work ethic and a spirit of rugged individualism. Associating their way of life with virtue and godliness, most Anglos regarded anyone who did not accept and adhere to these concepts as not only foreign but inferior as well.

Early Anglo Americans' accounts of the Hispanic-Mexican society often reveal arrogant attitudes of self-righteousness, with disdain and contempt for Mexicans, their (Catholic) religion, and their government. They concluded that the absence of the Puritan ethic reflected laziness, illiteracy implied ignorance, and courtesy or civility was fawning docility. They judged all of Mexico from the little they were exposed to and deplored what they encountered. Mexicans were seen as dirty, lazy, drunken, cruel, violent, treacherous, fanatical, priest-ridden, ignorant, and superstitious. These views were transmitted and perpetuated in accounts which remain an important part of the American literary and cultural heritage. Some are still widely used in our schools. Negative characterizations of Mexicans embedded in this literature still contribute to denigrating stereotypes.

In sharp contrast to this totally negative view, there developed at the end of the nineteenth century a school of writers who embellished and romanticized the Hispanic-Mexican experience, especially in California. Their view was put forward by the writings of authors such as Gertrude Atherton, Helen Hunt Jackson, and Joaquin Miller. They generally ignored or took little account of the Mexican origins of a majority of settlers on the northern frontier and pictured the upper classes as aristocrats and Spaniards of high birth. Life was simple, kind, and gentle; the land was fertile and easily yielded food in abundance; and everyone lived in Arcadian innocence and virtue. This view of early California society, sometimes referred to as the fantasy heritage, is also still with us in literature. The reality of northern Mexican frontier society was far more complex.

Life on the north-central frontier in Nuevo México was different from that of the californios for a variety of reasons. Here, the basis of settlement, after initial concern about the Strait of Anián, was principally economic; and the military played a more important role than in California because of persistent Indian troubles. During the colonial period frequent raiding by seminomadic Apaches, Comanches, Utes, and, up to the eighteenth century, Navajos, all of whom lived largely from pillage, led to close ties to the Pueblo Indians and to a preference, even a necessity, for defensive town living. Towns served as an effective means of protection; each home was virtually a fortress with barred windows, heavy doors, and adobe walls two or three feet thick built around a central patio which usually contained a well. In time of danger the stock could be brought into this patio for protection. Each household included storerooms with provisions for long sieges, which were not uncommon during the 1600s and early 1700s.

Most nuevomexicano farms were located along rivers, particularly the upper Rio Grande and its tributaries. These streams provided water for two agricultural techniques widely used in colonial Nuevo México, floodplain and irrigated farming. The cooperative demands of irrigated farming brought about more communal property holding. Early settlers in the region engaged in subsistence agriculture based on a delicate accommodation to local conditions of soil, climate, and water. Following both medieval Spanish and local Pueblo Indian patterns, nuevo-mexicanos went out each day from the village to the fields to cultivate their crops.

In addition, farmers raised sheep and cattle which they pastured on lands held in common by the villagers. Because there was no accessible outside market for beef, hides, or tallow, cattle raising was of minor importance in Nuevo México throughout the colonial period. Sheep, on the other hand, provided wool to be woven into cloth and could also be driven south to the important market town of Chihuahua when trade routes became less fraught with danger from marauding Indians. In the late 1700s sheepherding began to compete with farming as a way of life and in the early 1800s it became the most important economic activity with some four million sheep providing wool and mutton for the settlers.

In Texas subsistence agriculture was also initially the principal settler activity. Besides the usual staple crops of the northern Mexican frontier, some sugarcane was cultivated. Thousands of wild cattle roamed the Texas plains; and as markets opened up, cattle raising became more important than agriculture. By the eighteenth century the plains of Texas had become a significant source of feral Mexican longhorns, which were rounded up and driven southward across the Rio Grande into the neighboring province of Tamaulipas. Expansion of the Caribbean sugar industry in the 1700s created additional demand for Texas cattle to feed an enlarged plantation labor force, especially in Cuba. After the Louisiana Purchase in 1803, which transferred Louisiana to the United States, the rapidly developing Anglo southwestern frontier created a new and larger market, for which cattle were driven northeastward. Paralleling this increased demand for Texas cattle was an expanding world market for cotton. Thus the economy of Texas during the Mexican period from 1821 to 1836 focused on cattle and cotton; American cotton growers from the Old South were attracted to the area, creating a new stage in Anglo penetration.

Towns in Texas and Nuevo México tended to become self-sufficient entities isolated from one another as well as from central Mexico. Most social and economic activities were closely patterned after models in Old Mexico. In Nuevo México the town marketplace became an economic center where the limited surplus produce of subsistence farmers was bartered or sold. Here dried beef, wild turkey, and venison might be exchanged for leather goods, blankets, and pottery. Mutton, beef, pork, cheese, fruits, herbs, chilies, onions, and other vegetables were sometimes obtainable, as were corn husks for cigarettes. Some nuevo-mexicano towns developed a small but important craftsman and artisan class. Scrap iron was melted down by smiths to manufacture pots and hardware, and Nuevo México became known for its weavers and *santeros* (carvers of wooden statues of saints). Examples of the santero's often anonymous art can still be seen in rural churches of New Mexico and southern Colorado as well as in local museums.

As life became marginally more secure and settlement of the northern frontier expanded, transportation routes opened and trade became increasingly important. In this trade the *arriero*, the muleteer, pushed his string of heavily laden animals from Chihuahua, the terminal point for the early nuevomexicano trade, as far north as Santa Fe and Taos. Some of the bulkier goods like kegs of El Paso brandy and Taos whiskey might be carried in *carretas*, two-wheeled carts. Luxuries such as chocolate, silk shawls, and fine rebozos made up most of the trade goods from central Mexico. In return for this merchandise nuevomexicanos sent furs, hides, woolen blankets, and sheep down the long trail to Chihuahua. By the end of the eighteenth century as many as 400,000 sheep might be driven down the Rio Grande, across the river at El Paso del Norte, and on to Chihuahua 600 miles farther south.

Expansion on the Louisiana frontier in the late 1700s led to a blossoming of trade in Texas after Mexican independence in 1821. The new government cautiously opened the northern frontier to trade with other countries, especially England and the United States. As a result, much contraband trade sprang up both in Nuevo México and in Texas, but especially in the latter. Because of the length of the largely uncolonized Texas coast and the presence there of enterprising privateers and adventurers of various nationalities, including pirates like Jean Lafitte, there was widespread evasion of Mexico's customs regulations.

An especially important aspect of trade expansion during the Mexican period was the annual autumn trade fair at Taos in northern Nuevo México. This fair grew out of mid-1700 trading with Comanche and other western plains Indians at Taos and other northern frontier towns. Chihuahua merchants, who dominated nuevomexicano trade, were a significant part of the fair, but this bustling economic and social event was attended by settlers from all over Nuevo México, as well as by Pueblo and plains Indians. After 1800 American and French Canadian mountain men also began to take part in this lively affair at which there was brisk trading of livestock, horses, mules, furs, hides, calicoes, hardware, silver, and liquor. Indians and trappers exchanged their year's catch of beaver pelts and other furs for the necessities of life, bright cloth for their wives, alcohol, and gewgaws. After days of intensive trading, gambling, prodigal living, heavy drinking, and general debauchery this yearly commercial and social event wound down to an unrueful end, and the various participants dispersed to their daily routines for another year.

After 1821 Santa Fe became the dominant trading center in northern Nuevo México because of its proximity to the U.S. frontier, its importance as a local distribution center, and the size of its population. Also, after 1829 it was linked to Alta California by the Old Spanish Trail to Los Angeles, the first interprovincial trade route. Its expanding trade attracted a vanguard of American interests and led to closer economic ties with the United States than with Mexico City. Some nuevomexicanos became consignees for American goods, extended credit, and even acted as fiscal agents for Anglo traders. As a consequence, American traders and a small group of nuevomexicano associates soon dominated the local economy, and the provincial government became heavily dependent on income generated by customs duties. It was a time of turbulence from the Mexican government's viewpoint, but the evolving nuevomexicano middle class saw it as a time of rising prosperity. Even officials like Governor Manuel Armijo, despite some misgivings about the foreigners, joined them in trading partnerships. By 1830 the small nuevomexicano middle class enjoyed a relatively high standard of living as a result of the trade. The relationship of prosperity to the Santa Fe trade and to the economic alliance of nuevomexicanos with American traders smoothed the way for later Anglo American conquest.

Long before trade began to expand and change Santa Fe, a relatively isolated village culture had become firmly entrenched due to regular, almost continuous, though limited, settlement in Nuevo México from the end of the sixteenth century. Because of its deep roots nuevomexicano society had a greater degree of stability as well as a more rigid social stratification than California or Texas. From the beginning of Hispanic-Mexican occupation and colonization, cohabitation and intermarriage between settlers and local Indians took place, and mestizos continued to form the largest racial element in Nuevo México.

Mestizos and Indians, who made up the lower classes of Nuevo

México and Texas, lived in circumstances ranging from the very humble to the impoverished. Mestizos, most of whom were peones or share-croppers, called *medieros*, existed just above the subsistence level of the Indians. Of course, any mestizo who was able to raise himself out of the lower classes, usually by owning land, became a criollo almost automatically. Indians were the poorest of the poor, exploited by the upper classes, including government officials who were supposed to protect them. Some Indians were ill-used to the point of enslavement, especially in Nuevo México, where slavery of blacks was virtually un-known. In Texas the expanding cotton economy led to greater use of Negro slaves, especially after the beginnings of Anglo American settle-ment in the 1820s.

In Nuevo México a distinct, semifeudal social pattern evolved. In this patriarchal structure a wealthy few known as patrones or ricos ruled over the peones in a despotism that typically was relatively benevolent. This influential oligarchy of about twenty closely interrelated families generally considered itself to be of Spanish origin, its members descen-dants of early pioneers. By the time of the Mexican period the church had become a powerful social and religious force that played a prom-inent role in daily life, as it also did in Texas and California. Along with the patrón, the missionary and the parish priest held top positions of leadership and were not afraid to contend with the governor himself.

The society of the nuevomexicano and the tejano, like that of the californio, was derived from Spanish and Mexican cultural traditions. In Nuevo México, however, Pueblo Indian culture was also important in molding both the economy and society. Because of Pueblo cultural sophistication some of their religious rituals were adapted to Christian practice. *Compadrazco* between the two groups became fairly common during the 1700s in a move to heal the rift between Pueblos and Span-iards in the aftermath of the Popé revolt. Some Indian agricultural techniques, especially in irrigation, were fundamental to their subsis-tence economy and were adopted by the settlers. In times of poor crops, as in 1753, nuevomexicanos even hired themselves out to work for Pueblos.

Education was never a major concern on the northern Mexican frontier from Texas to California—an attitude common to all frontiers. Literacy and formal education were seen as luxuries that might be indulged in only after the rigorous daily demands of life were met. However, missionaries and priests ordinarily provided a basic education for the children of the more prominent colonist and Indian families. Throughout the colonial era Jesuits and Franciscans practiced a rudimentary form of bilingual education. Late in the Spanish colonial period and in the Mexican era a few public schools were organized in the larger towns of Texas, Nuevo México, and California, but they usually had an ephemeral existence because of poor pay and an extreme shortage of teachers.

At the beginning of the nineteenth century Spanish governor Juan Bautista de Elguézabal of Texas issued a compulsory school attendance law for children up to age twelve, but it could not be enforced for want of buildings and teachers. Nuevo México, older, more stable, and with a much larger population, experienced limited intellectual development. Some leading nuevomexicano families sent sons to schools in central Mexico and even to Europe, especially to study for the priesthood. During the Mexican period they began sending them to the United States, mainly to St. Louis.

After the first decade of Mexican rule intellectual aspects of society were negatively affected by the exiling of Spanish missionaries along with all other Spaniards. On the other hand, reading material became marginally more available to nuevomexicanos toward the end of the Mexican period when a printing press was shipped to Santa Fe. In the summer of 1834 the first nuevomexicano newspaper, *El Crepúsculo de la Libertad*, was published with this press by Antonio Barreiro. Later the press was sold and moved to Taos. There it was used to print school manuals and religious works by the Taos pastor Antonio José Martínez, a member of one of the most prominent nuevomexicano families and an important leader in the Mexican period.

The most important single factor affecting the evolution of institutions and attitudes in all the regions of Mexico's northern frontier was unquestionably the cluster pattern of settlements and their isolation both from each other and from central Mexico. Isolation and long neglect by the bureaucracy in Mexico City engendered on the frontier a spirit of self-reliance and independence which affected the whole range of human activities in society and government. The brief decades of independent Mexican rule, 1821 to 1846, characterized by the political instability of transitory governments in the Mexican capital, helped bring about the greatest and most dramatic change in the history of Mexico's northern frontier—its loss to the United States.

4

MANIFEST DESTINY

As Mexican federalists and centralists struggled for political power and domination of the country, rapid change, uncertainty, and chaos spread. In the eleven years between 1824 and 1835 there were sixteen changes in the presidency of Mexico. The First Republic of 1824, strongly federalist in philosophy and organization, was headed by the old revolutionary leader and now first president, Guadalupe Victoria. However, federalism, and the liberalism which was a part of it, ran counter to Mexico's colonial political experience and at best meant local autonomy, at worst virtual anarchy. Plagued by lack of unity and inexperienced leadership, the federalists proved incapable of controlling and effectively governing the country. By the mid-1830s passage of (for the times) very liberal legislation such as secularization of the California missions, suppression of the clerically controlled University of Mexico, government domination of appointments to the church hierarchy, and reduction in the powers of church and army courts led to mounting political unrest, especially among wealthy criollos and the clergy. Spreading tensions eventually culminated in a successful centrist revolt in 1834.

The change in government brought to power Antonio López de Santa Anna, a rising young political and military leader whose actions were to affect Mexican politics profoundly for the next quarter-century. Once in office, this sometimes morose, sometimes charming caudillo proceeded to put into effect his limited views of centralist government. When he initiated steps to draft a unitary constitution, there was an immediate strong federalist reaction.

On the entire periphery of Mexico—in Yucatán, Sonora, Nuevo México, California, and Texas—opposition to centralism led to militant action as local leaders refused to accept control by Mexico City. Yucatán declared its independence and submitted to central authority only after a long struggle ending in 1843. In Texas reaction to the new government was more violent and more successful largely because of the overwhelming number of recent Anglo immigrants. Although California and Nuevo México continued to be largely unconcerned about Mexican national politics, they did exhibit considerable adverse reaction to this change which directly affected them. Centralism played an important role in the subsequent loss of the entire northern frontier to the United States.

California was first affected by the centralist movement in Mexico City when Mariano Chico, an unimportant Mexican congressman, was appointed the new governor in a political payoff. Because of his arbitrary actions as governor, Chico soon became intensely disliked by the californios and was forced to return to Mexico City early in 1836. At this point, Juan B. Alvarado, a leading young californio, led a successful revolt against the provisional governor and took his place. The Alvarado government declared California independent until Mexico City would agree to return to the federalist constitution of 1824. This autonomous government lasted until 1840, when californios accepted Manuel Micheltorena, the new governor appointed by President Anastasio Bustamante. Micheltorena's unsuccessful attempt to put centralism into effect was the government's last effort to control California and clearly demonstrated Mexico's tenuous hold on the province.

At first Nuevo México experienced only mild unrest when the centralists imposed their rule and reforms. However, in 1835 Colonel Albino Pérez, the civil and military governor sent from Mexico City, was overthrown and killed in an apparently spontaneous uprising. This Santa Cruz rebellion of lower-class elements against new, direct taxation and other centrist actions took over the provincial capital, Santa Fe. A few weeks later a counterrevolt led by former governor and wealthy merchant Manuel Armijo suppressed the rebellion. Armijo then maneuvered himself into the provisional governorship and subsequently was confirmed by Mexico City. He then dominated nuevomexicano politics until the outbreak of hostilities between the United States and Mexico a decade later.

The northeastern border province of Texas was also the scene of a revolt against Mexican centralism. Here, however, the local political circumstances were quite different and so was the outcome. The Texas uprising was not only a reaction to the termination of local political control; it was also the outcome to the preceding half-century of Texas history, a history of neglect by Spain and Mexico and of poor judgment by both in permitting Anglo settlement. In addition, it was a result of Anglo convictions about self-government and Manifest Destiny.

Manifest Destiny was a peculiarly Anglo American version of the concept of a chosen people. By the beginning of the nineteenth century North Americans began to believe that their country was destined by divine providence to settle and control the area from the Atlantic seaboard to the Pacific Ocean. Subsequently more extreme exponents of this concept were convinced that the Arctic Circle to the north and the Strait of Magellan in the south were the only logical limits to inevitable Yankee expansion. The country to suffer most in the nineteenth century as a result of Manifest Destiny was Mexico, since approximately half its territory, about one million square miles, lay between the American southwestern frontier and the Pacific Ocean.

After Spain acquired the Louisiana Territory in 1763 the security of adjacent Texas ceased to be of major concern to her. Troops were withdrawn from the Texas region, which in turn led to an increase in Indian harassment. As a result of this more aggressive hostility, many missions and small settlements were abandoned, leading to a decline in tejano population. By the end of the eighteenth century only six of twenty-seven Texas missions were still functioning, and the civilian population had declined to about 3,500.

When the United States purchased the Louisiana Territory from France in 1803 there was limited emigration of Spanish speakers from that area into Texas. Despite government encouragement of settlement in Texas, its population continued to decline. This trend became even more pronounced after the 1810 revolution for independence broke out. By the end of the revolutionary decade the population had dropped to about 2,000 and the governor was pressing for settlers from central Mexico to populate his vast province. His request was made in vain.

Unable to persuade Mexicans to move into this buffer area, the Mexican government encouraged foreign colonization. Unfortunately for Mexico, this attempted solution to the serious problem of underpopulation ultimately helped bring about the loss of Texas.

Meanwhile horse and cattle traders on the southwestern U.S. frontier and southern cotton farmers were becoming keenly interested in eastern Texas. As early as 1815 a few aggressive Americans, ignoring the boundary, had crossed the Sabine River and established themselves on farms around Nacogdoches near the Louisiana border. In 1821 the Spanish government gave to Moses Austin of Potosi, Missouri, an *empresario* land grant, under which he was to receive free land for bringing a specified number of settlers into Texas. Austin, a Catholic and former Spanish subject (Missouri was a part of Spanish Louisiana until 1800) who still held a Spanish passport, died before he could carry out his project to bring in 300 families from formerly Spanish Louisiana.

Two years later his son Stephen received a similar grant from the newly independent Mexican government and began to implement it. Thus an approved influx of Anglo American settlers began. Eventually some fifteen empresario grants were awarded to United States citizens and other foreigners, mostly by the state of Coahuila-Texas. Stephen Austin chose his immigrants with considerable care and was generally scrupulous in carrying out the terms of his agreement with the Mexican government. These terms required that all settlers be of good moral character, that they either be, or be willing to become, Catholics, and that they swear an oath of loyalty to Mexico. Most empresarios, however, failed either to respect or to complete the terms of their grants, while their settlers generally ignored Mexican regulations and institutions. In 1826 the Mexican government tried to compel one of the Americans, Haden Edwards, to abide by provisions of his empresario grant, particularly to recognize earlier titles within its limits. This caused a minor uprising known as the Fredonia Revolt, which broke out at Nacogdoches and was supported by many recently arrived Americans. However, Austin and his colonists refused to side with the Anglos in the uprising and helped Mexican authorities suppress it.

By the end of the 1820s there were in Texas about 25,000 North American immigrants, including black slaves, and about 4,000 Spanish-speaking Mexicans. Many of the Americans were illegal aliens who had migrated from the slaveholding South and had set themselves up as cotton growers. Increasingly they saw themselves as on the way to becoming subjects of a country that they were convinced was politically and morally inferior to their own. Contemptuous of Mexican culture, government officials, and laws, most resisted integration into Mexican society. Because of this attitude the Mexican government became concerned in the late 1820s about the rapidly increasing number of aliens in Texas and tried to stem the tide of migration from the United States.

Alarmed by efforts of the American minister to Mexico, Joel R. Poinsett, to purchase Texas, and encouraged by the British chargé d'affaires, Henry George Ward, President Guadalupe Victoria sent General Manuel Mier y Terán to study the Texas situation in detail. Mier y Terán was critical of both Mexican and Anglo settlers and eventually recommended that the government take vigorous measures in Texas before serious problems arose. In 1829 Mexico's second president, former revolutionary leader Vicente Guerrero, implemented Mier y Terán's recommendations and abolished slavery in Mexico by executive decree in order to make Texas less attractive to cotton planters from the American South. Threatened economically by this law, Texas landowners protested vigorously, and the decree was suspended in Texas, the only Mexican state in which slavery was still important. However, in the next year the Mexican Congress, also following Mier y Terán's advice, enacted legislation completely prohibiting importation of slaves and severely curtailing legal North American immigration into Texas. At the same time, to offset the already sizable Anglo population, the government began to strongly encourage European immigrants. Another law established customhouses and presidios along the Texas–United States frontier, and soldiers were dispatched to enforce Mexican laws, especially customs regulations, since the seven-year tax exemption on imports granted to American settlers was beginning to expire. In eastern Texas, where most of the U.S. immigrants had settled, the conflict of cultures began warming up.

Collection of customs duties quickly became the most abrasive issue between Anglo colonists and the government, leading to organized anti-customs actions. At San Antonio de Béxar, Stephen Austin led a movement to seek legal redress and was successful in obtaining some concessions. Other colonists took a more radical approach. Some activists launched guerrilla attacks on customhouses and presidios, and in 1832 fighting broke out in Texas between Mexican troops who supported centralism and those who favored federalism. That same year Texas held a convention to discuss relations with the central government. Seeking repeal of the 1830 legislation and separation of Texas from Coahuila, a second convention voted to send Austin to Mexico City to petition for these changes. Austin found little sympathy for the Texas viewpoint and was jailed after he sent a letter to the Texas colonists urging them to form an autonomous Mexican state government. Finally, after a year, he was released and returned to Texas. Further changes introduced by the centralist government added fuel to the fire. On November 7, 1835, the Texans declared conditional independence, adding their voices to those of other Mexican federalists demanding a return to the 1824 constitution as the price of resubmission to Mexico City.

In response to these events early in 1835, President Antonio López de Santa Anna sent to Texas 4,000 federal troops under his brother-in-law, General Martín Cos. After establishing his headquarters in San Antonio at a former Franciscan mission popularly called the Alamo, Cos was soundly defeated by a group of federalist rebels in late 1835 and forced to withdraw. President Santa Anna, who had suppressed a similar federalist revolt in Zacatecas the year before, assumed personal command of an army to force the Texans to submit to his authority. Recruiting, training, and organizing a conscript army as he marched north to Texas in 1836, he was determined to avenge Cos's defeat. Santa Anna's subsequent actions must be viewed in proper historical perspective. Directed by the Mexican Congress to suppress the seditious revolt in Texas, he rightfully considered Texas rebels to be traitors and set out to smother the flames of rebellion.

Meanwhile, a Texas convention of Anglos and tejano federalists declared by a two-to-one vote that it wanted reinstatement of the federalist constitution of 1824. It also appointed Sam Houston commander of all Texas forces. Political differences within the provisional Texas government led to a second convention at Washington-on-the-Brazos, during which fifty-nine delegates unanimously declared complete independence on March 2, 1836. A few days later they elected David Burnett provisional president and Lorenzo de Zavala, a prominent Yucatecan federalist and Texas land empresario, vice president. They reappointed Houston to head the army.

The first major encounter between the soldiers of the fledgling republic and the forces of Santa Anna took place in San Antonio at the Alamo. Here the Texans let themselves be caught by surprise even though they had been warned of the Mexican army's imminent approach by tejano scouts. After a ten-day siege 187 defenders led by

William Travis and including tejanos under the leadership of Captain Juan Seguín, all fighting under a 1824 Mexican federalist flag, were wiped out. Seguín himself escaped the massacre because he was sent to seek help before the final Mexican assault began. A month later the Mexican army reinforced this Alamo victory by slaughtering 450 Texas rebels at Goliad. However, Santa Anna's victories were costly and short-lived. Hundreds of Mexican soldiers lost their lives in massive frontal attacks, and the army's ruthlessness generated fierce resistance on the part of the Texas rebels.

On April 21 an overconfident Santa Anna and his army were routed at San Jacinto by a Texas attack in which tejanos under Seguín played a key role. Santa Anna himself was taken prisoner and a counterslaughter took place. This Texan victory led to the so-called Treaty of Velasco, by which Santa Anna agreed to Texas independence in exchange for his freedom. Needless to say, the government in Mexico City repudiated Santa Anna's personal arrangement, but it was unable to force the Texans to resubmit to Mexican authority. By 1840 the Texans had succeeded in obtaining recognition of their independent republic from the United States, France, and Great Britain.

Having achieved de facto independence from Mexico, Texas pressed for annexation to the United States. However, annexation posed a problem for antislavery congressmen and the country, which was trying to maintain a balance between the admission of slave and free states. As the slavery issue grew more intense in the United States and the abolitionist movement gained support, Texans devoted less and less effort to annexation. Instead, attainment of economic and political stability by other means became their prime concern. To achieve national viability some Texans suggested expanding the republic to the Pacific, while others preferred merely to annex the Nuevo México area with its valuable Santa Fe trade.

In an effort to persuade nuevomexicanos to secede from Mexico and become part of the Texas Republic an expedition to Santa Fe was organized by Texas president Mirabeau Buonaparte Lamar. If the nuevomexicanos refused, the Texans were willing to settle for a share in the lucrative Santa Fe trade, as documents carried by the leaders of the expedition indicated. With twenty-one wagons loaded with $200,000 worth of trade goods some 300 Anglo and Spanish-speaking Texans, organized into five military companies under General Hugh McLeod, left Austin for Santa Fe in June 1841. On the way they

**TEXAS CLAIMS AND
MEXICAN WAR RESULTS**

0   Scale of Miles   500

encountered blistering heat, raging prairie fires, and hostile Indians; and they also lost their way, thereby adding to their 600-mile journey. The poorly managed and ill-fated expedition split into two groups, believing that this would speed up the journey. When the members finally reached Nuevo México they were suffering intensely from hunger, thirst, and exhaustion. Here the naive participants allowed themselves to be disarmed by a ruse and were taken prisoners by Governor Manuel Armijo without a shot being fired. At Santa Fe some of the Texans were executed and the remainder were sent on a grueling death march to prison in Mexico City. The survivors were eventually released only after strong American and British protests.

The failure to annex Nuevo México and to participate in the Santa Fe trade on the one hand and reports of the brutal treatment of prisoners on the other incensed public opinion and contributed to further antagonism between republican Texans and nuevomexicanos. The threat of further expeditions caused the Mexican government to tighten its control of the Santa Fe trade until war with the United States ended Mexico's authority.

Meanwhile, the United States and Mexico were moving rapidly toward a war which neither country wanted. In Texas conflicts between Anglos, especially recent arrivals, and tejanos coupled with border raids by both Mexicans and Texans intensified mutual antagonisms. Between 1836 and 1846 various serious but unsuccessful attempts by plundering Mexican armies to reconquer Texas kept the border in a constant state of tension. Because of perennial financial difficulties Mexico was unable to pay its acknowledged claims debts to the United States, and the latter's repeated efforts to buy part or all of the Southwest were viewed in Mexico with great alarm. In the early 1840s new American claims against Mexico arising from border difficulties and outrages against American citizens kept animosities at fever pitch and helped provide excuses for U.S. intervention.

The climax came in March 1845 when the United States, by a joint resolution of Congress, annexed Texas, an action which Mexico had previously warned might lead to war since it had not recognized Texas secession and independence. The Mexican government immediately broke off diplomatic ties with the United States, and relations between the two countries became critical. In August, President James Polk sent John Slidell to Mexico with instructions to purchase Alta California and Nuevo México for as much as $25 million and to discuss settlement of the disputed Texas-Mexican boundary. However, Mexican officials were reluctant to discuss these matters with Slidell because of intense anti-American feeling. Finally, Slidell was forced to leave Mexico by a new, strongly anti-American administration, installed by a coup.

Failing in his attempt to acquire the territory by negotiation and purchase, Polk sent General Zachary Taylor to the Nueces River area in southeastern Texas in hopes that a military clash with Mexico might lead to war and bring about acquisition of the entire Southwest. Polk made this provocative move in response to a widespread arrogant American conviction that the country was manifestly destined to rule over all North America. Armed hostilities soon broke out between the two countries.

As a result of a clash between American and Mexican troops in the disputed triangle of land between the Nueces and the Rio Grande, the United States declared war on Mexico in May 1846. Both sides saw the conflict as not just a fight for territory but as a struggle between two "races," cultures, and religions. Ordered to carry the war into the heart of Mexico, General Taylor crossed the Rio Grande and occupied Matamoros. In September he moved west from there to capture Monterrey. Meanwhile, Santa Anna, who had been returned to the presidency, organized another army to turn back the American invasion. The following February at Buena Vista near Saltillo, Coahuila, a hard-fought, indecisive battle took place between Taylor's troops and soldiers under Santa Anna. The ill-equipped and fatigued Mexican recruits fought valiantly against the Americans. Santa Anna, unaware of Taylor's plan to withdraw to Monterrey because of overextended supply lines, disengaged his forces during the night and headed back to Mexico City as his army disintegrated. Both generals claimed victory.

Meanwhile, Nuevo México was initially taken by the United States without a fight. Anglo traders in Santa Fe and the profits of trade with the United States had convinced many nuevomexicano businessmen that the province would be better off as part of the United States than under the ineffectual and unstable government in Mexico City. After organizing a large body of militia, Governor Manuel Armijo decided not to oppose the invading army of 1,500 Americans under Colonel Stephen Kearny. Instead, he suddenly disbanded his larger force and departed southward for Chihuahua. Armijo's change in plan was perhaps influenced by Kearny's assurances to nuevomexicanos that he came as protector rather than conqueror.

When Kearny entered Santa Fe in mid-August, acting governor Juan B. Vigil and some twenty leading nuevomexicanos greeted him and the American troops warmly and promised that all citizens would be loyal to the United States. In response to this friendly reception Colonel Kearny assured them that the United States government would respect the property and religious rights of all who showed peaceful intent. Then, while the townsmen and Kearny toasted each other with wine and brandy, the American flag was raised over the governor's palace. Two days later a group of Pueblo Indian leaders came to Santa Fe and declared their allegiance to the United States, stating that their traditions foretold that one day they would be redeemed from Spanish injustice and oppression by men from the east. The apparently easy transition to U.S. control was in some ways anticlimactic, but disquieting portents of resistance and rebellion were heard from time to time.

After completing the formalities of imposing military control in Nuevo México, Kearny ordered the drafting of a framework for the establishment of a new American government in the Southwest. Known as the Kearny Code, this instrument was based on American and Mexican law and included provisions for the appointment of government officials. Despite President Polk's orders to retain the existing nuevomexicano political power structure, Kearny, after discussions with officials, generally ignored leading Santa Fe and Taos families in organizing the new government. He appointed Charles Bent, a leader of the Santa Fe traders and the pro-American faction in Nuevo México, as acting governor. Equally at home in the two cultures, Bent was a well-educated landowner and merchant of Taos, married into a wealthy nuevomexicano family since 1835. He had held minor political offices. From the existing Spanish-speaking political structure, Kearny appointed Donaciano Vigil secretary of the territory and named Antonio J. Otero one of three territorial court judges. Other high officials were merchants and recent arrivals from Missouri. Most minor Mexican officeholders, after taking an oath of allegiance to the United States, were continued in office.

With Nuevo México presumably secure, the ambitious Kearny set out for California late in September 1846 to help complete the conquest of that province. Shortly after leaving Santa Fe he encountered the Taos-based scout Kit Carson, who informed him that California was already under Anglo control. Upon arriving in southern California, however, Kearny found californios in full revolt and his dragoons opposed by a small force under the local commander, Andrés Pico. In the battle of San Pascual east of San Diego, Kearny's troops were severely defeated by Pico's lancers and he himself was wounded. Kearny was forced to seek help from Commodore Robert Stockton, who had arrived earlier on the California coast as commander of the Pacific Squadron. With support from Stockton's forces Kearny finally reached the security of San Diego on December 12, 1846.

To understand more clearly the californio experience during the war between Mexico and the United States, it is necessary to review some of the history that led to hostilities in California. Prior to 1846 California underwent economic and sociopolitical experiences similar to those of Texas and Nuevo México. As in those areas, the process of economic detachment from the central government began with trade. Starting in the 1820s, sailing ships from England and the United States began to bring manufactured goods to California in exchange for hides, tallow, and furs. This trade also initiated a small influx of Anglo American immigrants. Those who came in the 1820s and 1830s, nearly all by sea, tended to become an integral part of California society. Many married into californio families, accepted Catholicism at least nominally, became Mexican citizens, and acquired land grants; a few even held public office. However, Anglos who began to arrive in the early 1840s by way of the Oregon Trail were of a different type. Many came with their families, had no intention of becoming Mexican citizens, and deliberately settled in areas remote from Mexican control, especially in the Sacramento Valley. Supported by a firm belief in Manifest Destiny, they came as a vanguard of North American expansionism.

Accelerated American immigration, coupled with californio dissatisfaction with Mexican centralist government, led to a rebellion which broke out in northern California just before the war between Mexico and the United States began. This uprising, centered in the Sacramento region and known as the Bear Flag Revolt because its banner depicted a bear, quickly became a part of the Mexican War. Initially spearheaded by a group of Anglo adventurers, the revolt established a basis for Anglo conquest of California. John Charles Frémont, a United States Army captain who was illegally in the province on a reconnaissance expedition for the government, quickly took command of the revolutionaries. When word came that Mexico and the United States were at war, the Bear Flag was replaced by the Stars and Stripes. The arrival of the Pacific Squadron, at first under the command of Commodore John

Sloat and later under Robert Stockton, readily secured American control of the entire area without bloodshed. However, inept leadership of the occupation forces in Los Angeles brought tensions to a climax that led to a californio revolt in September 1846 and to the only serious fighting in California.

Commodore Stockton had quickly antagonized californios, both by initiating a large number of restrictive and tactless controls and by placing Captain Archibald Gillespie in command of southern California. Gillespie, insensitive to local feelings and cultural practices, issued further unnecessary and irksome regulations, which caused the southern californios to launch a successful attack against his forces. Eventually, however, through the combined efforts of Gillespie, Stockton, Kearny, and Frémont the southern California revolt was subdued. American control was reestablished through negotiation of the so-called Treaty of Cahuenga with the californios in January 1847. This agreement, independent of the government in Mexico City, terminated hostilities in California. Nevertheless, in the heated atmosphere rumors persisted that californios were plotting further resistance.

Meanwhile, far to the south in central Mexico, Santa Anna and another hastily organized army battled American general Winfield Scott, who had landed near Veracruz with 10,000 men. The war went badly for Mexico. She was severely divided by internal bickering, her leaders were deeply mistrustful of each other, and the majority of Mexicans were demoralized and unclear as to the objectives of the struggle with the United States. Some Mexican states even refused to provide troops to defend the country against the invaders. The majority of the troops were poorly motivated, ill-trained Indian conscripts.

Within six months Scott's forces advanced from Veracruz to Mexico City, reaching the Valley of Mexico by mid-August 1847. In the last days of the fighting, at Chapultepec Hill just outside the capital, one hundred young Mexican military cadets showed how well Mexican troops could fight when trained effectively and motivated by patriotism. However, the bravery of these "Niños Héroes" was in vain. They were unable to turn back the United States invasion, and on September 14 the North American army successfully occupied the Mexican capital. With the conquest of Mexico essentially completed, the only item remaining on James K. Polk's agenda was to write a treaty of peace.

Earlier in 1847 Polk had sent a personal representative, Nicholas Trist, to Mexico to negotiate a treaty which would secure his expansionist goals. However, because of personal antagonism between Trist and General Scott, the president ordered Trist's recall. Trist ignored the order and continued negotiations with the provisional Mexican government. Finally, on February 2, 1848, agreement was reached and a treaty was signed in the village of Guadalupe Hidalgo outside Mexico City.

Although Polk was irritated by Trist's insubordination, the treaty basically achieved the president's original territorial objectives, and he therefore submitted it to the Senate. Widespread support of Manifest Destiny had led to a strong demand that the United States take all of Mexico, with Democratic representatives leading the cry in hopes of regaining fading political popularity. The U.S. Senate quickly studied the proposed treaty and made some changes. Article IX, dealing with the political rights and eventual citizenship of the inhabitants of the territory to be transferred, was replaced with a similar but shorter article taken from the Louisiana Purchase treaty of 1803, and Article X, which the Senate felt would have raised problems of landownership in Texas, was completely excised. However, when the amended treaty was discussed with the Mexican representatives in May, assurances were given that titles to all kinds of personal and real properties existing in the ceded territories would be recognized and protected. Moreover, all civil, political, and religious guarantees specified in the original Article IX would be retained. These promises were put into writing after the amended treaty had already been ratified by the Mexican Congress at Querétaro on May 21, 1848, and are known as the Protocol of Querétaro. Four days later, with the exchange of ratifications, the treaty went into effect. The protocol itself was never ratified by either government and therefore technically had no validity in international law.

By the provisions of the Treaty of Guadalupe Hidalgo the United States acquired the territory that now forms the states of Arizona, California, Nevada, New Mexico, and Utah and half of Colorado, and received clear title to Texas with the Rio Grande boundary that the Texas government had previously claimed. Mexico lost about one million square miles and was paid $15 million in partial compensation. Although Mexico lost approximately 50 percent of her national territory, she lost less than 1 percent of her population. Nearly all 80,000 Mexican citizens living in the ceded territory ultimately became U.S. nationals. Relatively few kept their Mexican citizenship. In Nuevo México about 1,500 to 2,000 moved southwest across the new political border and another 2,000 remained but retained their citizenship. In Texas about 1,000 crossed the border, and several hundred californios went south to Baja California and Sonora. Although the Mexican government encouraged settlement in Mexico both at the end of the war and in the following decades and sent agents to arrange details for those who wished to leave the United States, few accepted the proffered help.

The chief provisions of the Treaty of Guadalupe Hidalgo that relate to Mexican Americans are those concerning citizenship and property. Mexicans living in the ceded area had a year in which to decide whether they wanted to retain Mexican citizenship or to become nationals of the United States. Those still living in the area at the end of the prescribed time who had not specifically declared their intentions to remain Mexican citizens were presumed to desire U.S. nationality. Article IX of the treaty guaranteed that these former Mexican citizens would ultimately become U.S. citizens and meanwhile would receive the protection of the United States government in the exercise of their civil and political rights. It also specifically provided that they would have the right to worship freely and that their property rights would be protected. It is interesting to note that no mention was made in the treaty concerning the political and civil rights of local Indians, the more acculturated of whom had been given citizenship under Mexican law but had continued to be treated as second-class citizens.

A second important provision dealt with real and personal property of the inhabitants, whether or not they continued to reside within the bounds of the area. It stipulated that full title to all property would be retained with rights of disposal and inheritance, and it guaranteed complete protection of these rights by the United States government. Item Two of the protocol which "supplemented" the treaty specified that valid Spanish and Mexican land grants would be recognized by the United States and that the United States would accept as legitimate all property titles recognized under Mexican law.

By the terms of this treaty the United States gained not only an immense new territory but also a sizable group of new nationals who would become citizens when Congress so determined. Although they were left in their same geographic and cultural setting, these new United States nationals were now exposed to unfamiliar legal, political, and social institutions. Guaranteed freedom of religion, they remained Catholic, but they were inundated by a flood of Anglo-Saxon Protestants, many of whom held Catholicism in contempt. Guaranteed full protection of property rights, they soon became enmeshed in a web of confusing Anglo-Saxon law which based ownership on criteria unfamiliar to them and often difficult to provide. Most were unaware of the great changes that were in store for them.

Some conflict was unavoidable as Anglo American and Mexican societies met. The Treaty of Guadalupe Hidalgo as supreme law of the United States proposed to solve the problems of change in nationality, but many obstacles inevitably arose from differing cultural viewpoints and historical experience. Anglo Americans stressed heavily the role of the individual, who was expected to use his rugged individualism and drive for personal benefit. On the other hand, the Spanish-Mexican view tended to subordinate individual advantage to community welfare. Although the treaty included guarantees of individual rights to former Mexican citizens, it failed completely to take into consideration their community rights as a distinct and dissimilar cultural entity.

The U.S.-Mexican War was merely one conspicuous event in a corrosive and acrimonious conflict of cultures that had begun years before and simmered long after the ratification of the Treaty of Guadalupe Hidalgo. Racism existed long before the 1800s. Racial hatred and violence during the 1830s and 1840s created a climate of conflict that has endured for generations. In the long history of this confrontation antagonisms between Anglos and Mexican Americans have continued to fester. Although discrimination has diminished in recent years, it still exists at both a conscious and a subconscious level.

Neither Anglo nor Mexican was prepared by historical experience to consider and respect the other's heritage and culture. Years of misunderstanding and conflict between the two groups led to a situation in which Mexican Americans found their lands gone, their religion denigrated and challenged, and themselves nationals of a country whose language, laws, and social customs they did not fully understand. A prejudiced Anglo majority isolated and dominated them within American society and did not permit significant acculturation to the majority. Thus, despite treaty guarantees of property rights and equal protection under the law, bitterness and estrangement between Anglos and Mexican Americans grew during the years following the Treaty of Guadalupe Hidalgo. The depth of this animosity is especially apparent in relations between the two communities during the latter half of the nineteenth century.

5

ROOTS OF THE POISON

With the stroke of a pen the Treaty of Guadalupe Hidalgo extended the borders of the United States to include 80,000 people with a culture that was different not only from that of the United States but also from that of the traditional European immigrant. Without moving, these people became foreigners in their native land. This unique experience inevitably led to misunderstanding, problems, and conflict. Notably absent from the treaty, and not a part of nineteenth-century thinking, were provisions to protect their social institutions. The treaty pledged to these new nationals the protection of U.S. laws for their religion, property, and political liberty and promised them eventual citizenship. Facilitated by the American system of public education, the acculturation of immigrants was presumed to be virtually automatic and held little concern for the American West.

Following the war, the Far Southwest remained culturally much as it had been under Mexican rule. Popular reaction to the new conditions was mixed; some accepted, some resisted, and most were simply unconcerned or indifferent. There was little immediate change in language; Spanish continued to predominate. Traditional Mexican living patterns persisted except in eastern Texas and in northern California, where an immediate and massive influx of Anglos brought far-reaching change. Even in these two areas many Anglos adopted other Mexican ways in addition to techniques in mining, ranching, and agriculture. By the time of statehood in 1850 the Spanish-speaking population of California had declined to 15 percent of the total. The advent of a large Anglo majority quickly reduced californios to economic subordination and political powerlessness at the state level, but Mexican influence persisted in the southern half of the state until the 1880s. Then large-scale Anglo immigration once again brought considerable change.

The discovery of gold in 1848 had a sudden and sweeping impact on California's economy and society. The gold rush of 1849 and the following years brought prosperity—even wealth—to some californios, but it also brought rapid and overwhelming Anglo penetration and domination. Along with Anglos, californios, more than a thousand of them, hurried from town and rancho to the goldfields. In the Sierra foothills they were joined by other adventurous miners, including several thousand Mexicans from Sonora, who introduced such successful mining techniques as panning and dry-wash separation of gold. Resentment engendered by the success of these Sonorans was one of the important factors in the antagonism that mushroomed between Anglos and Spanish-speaking. Initial hostility between the two groups was fostered by attitudes formed more than a decade earlier during the Texas independence movement and in the recent U.S.-Mexican War. Acute competition for the better mine sites rekindled and intensified existing animosities and eventually led to open conflict.

In this inflammable situation californios and Mexicans became the focus of discrimination. In the mining areas posters soon appeared warning that foreigners had no right to be there and threatening violence if they remained. Californios found that they were unable to convince some 80,000 suspicious or hostile Anglos that they too were Americans. The presence of some 8,000 Mexicans, 5,000 Chileans and Peruvians, and numerous French, Germans, and Irish further complicated the situation. Anglos, uninterested in distinguishing between californios and Spanish-speaking foreigners, lumped them all together under the denigrating term "greasers." Anglo behavior, based on a combination of economic, racist, and jingoistic attitudes, quickly moved from suspicion to threats, to violence, to restrictive legislation, to litigation, and back to violence. In the spring and summer of 1849 vigilante groups, insisting that mineral wealth was peculiarly reserved for Americans, forced many Spanish-speaking miners from the northern mining region (above the Mokelumne River).

Meeting at San Jose before statehood had been achieved, the first California Assembly, by a vote of 22 to 2, supported this view by asking the United States Congress to bar all foreigners and californios from the mines. A foreign miners' tax law, aimed primarily at californios and Sonorans, was passed by the state legislature in the following May, but it was neither uniformly enforced nor uniformly accepted. Partly because of loose and selective enforcement Mexicans and other Hispanic miners were terrorized by vigilante groups and their property often was taken or destroyed. Sonora, a California foothill town established by miners from that Mexican state, was put to the torch by 2,000 rioting Anglo miners. Shooting at every Mexican in sight, they continued to harass the townspeople for days. Scores were murdered or lynched, causing most of the terrified inhabitants to flee farther south. Hispanos were blamed for subsequent highway robberies and violent deaths, which, of course, led to further vigilante action. Rampant xenophobia and nativism encouraged widespread claim jumping, extortion, shootings, and lynching. Although this persecution of Mexicans and other Latino miners had widespread popular support among Anglos, the injustice repelled some, who dared to speak out against it. Early in 1851 the miners' tax was repealed. During the few months it was in effect, however, it had served to eliminate most Spanish-speaking miners.

The influx of 100,000 people into California in 1849 created other difficulties, most notably an immediate and critical need for adequate civil government. Seeking a solution to this problem, the military governor, General Bennett Riley, called a constitutional convention to meet at Monterey in June 1849. Of the forty delegates elected to this convention, eight were californios of the landowning elite. They took active roles in committees and in writing the constitution; one of them, Mariano Vallejo, was elected the following year to the first California Senate.

Concerned especially for their lands and civil rights, this handful of Spanish-speaking delegates at the constitutional convention were modestly successful in securing a degree of protection for themselves and their fellow californios. By participating actively in committee work and by addressing the delegates on issues of significance to them, they helped mold the constitution. Among their transitory victories was securing a unanimous vote in favor of a proposal that the legislature print all laws in Spanish as well as in English. However, after 1855 the legislature ceased to provide funds to do so; it also ended public school instruction in Spanish. The eight californios obtained the right to local election of tax assessors as a protection against potential future discriminatory taxation of their lands. In the matter of suffrage they were less successful. They argued that the Treaty of Guadalupe Hidalgo guaranteed the political rights of all former Mexican citizens and would be violated by limiting the vote to white males. Nevertheless, the convention did so, with the face-saving proviso that the state legislature might, by an (unlikely) two-thirds vote, extend suffrage to Indians and mestizos.

This 1849 constitution is the only major state document which californios helped shape and in which their legal heritage was represented. When the constitution was completed, they were reasonably well pleased with the results and joined in the widespread celebration of the work. Three decades later, when the Spanish-speaking numbered only about 4 percent of the state's population, this document was replaced by the 1879 constitution, which marked an end to even minimal support of biculturalism as well as bilingualism in California public schools, courts, and public administration. In subsequent years Hispanic-Mexican legal traditions formed the basis for California's communal property and water rights laws and for mineral rights and mining legislation.

While the 1849 constitution was being written, changes were taking place in the northern half of the state; these were to have far-reaching economic and political effects for many californios. As placer gold deposits became exhausted, many miners turned to other pursuits, including farming; squatting on the lands of the californios became increasingly common. On the heels of early miners came Anglo farmers, who with their ideas of preemption and occupancy rights, sought out apparently vacant lands to establish homesteads. In complete disregard of grantees' rights they settled on the most desirable agricultural lands. Some loudly argued that victory in the war with Mexico gave them the right to oust californio grantees. Later these squatters filed numerous complicated land title suits which choked the California courts for decades.

The history of land in California after the gold rush is in many instances a story of greed, acquisitiveness, and outright robbery. Land-ownership formed the basis of California's economic and social system under both Spain and Mexico. Millions of acres of prime land were held by californios under titles from the Mexican and Spanish governments and Articles VIII and IX of the Treaty of Guadalupe Hidalgo. However, pressure from increasing numbers of U.S. immigrants motivated some Anglo politicians to seek a solution to the squatter problem by questioning the validity of all land titles and then seeking legal means to vacate as many as possible. Violent Sacramento squatter riots in 1850 lent a sense of urgency to the issue. Congress was persuaded by California congressmen to pass the Land Act of 1851 to clarify land titles. The act created a Board of Land Commissioners and required all grant holders to appear before it to prove their titles, despite the guarantees of the Treaty of Guadalupe Hidalgo.

The Land Act gave the ever-increasing number of squatters support for their illegal actions and hope that they might keep "their" lands. Each new wave of squatters added to the conviction of the righteousness of their position and to their fierce determination to retain the land they occupied. Even renters who had earlier accepted californio ownership now withheld further payment until their landlord's title was confirmed. At the same time efforts were made to pass legislation making grant lands available to settlers. In 1856, after the board had completed its task, a law was passed converting all unconfirmed grant acreage into public domain, thereby making it accessible to settlers. However, in the following year the law was declared unconstitutional by the state supreme court.

Californios made many serious and justifiable complaints against the attitude and actions of the board and its implementation of the 1851 law. Much of their criticism grew out of ambiguities directly resulting from the land law itself. Additional californio resentment against the board arose from the unfamiliarity of commissioners with Mexican and Spanish legal traditions in land usage. Under the Spanish legal system landownership was ratified largely by length of occupancy and use, and exact boundaries were much less important and often were not precisely delineated. At best a sketch map, called a *diseño*, was included with the grant papers. Subsequent transfers of land could be made by verbal contract and were not always officially recorded. Accustomed to Anglo-Saxon legal standards, accurate surveys, and complete documentation, Americans were appalled at Mexican norms of indeterminate boundaries, widespread absence of surveys, and failure to register grants officially. In addition to difficulties created by these anomalies, the board insisted on complete and exact fulfillment of grant conditions and tended to decide cases on technicalities rather than on broader issues of justice and fairness.

The board met from January 1852 to March 1856, when it finally adjourned. Californio grantees appeared before it with their Anglo lawyers, their grant papers, maps, proof of long possession, and other evidence of ownership. Californios put forward 467 of the 813 claims submitted; Anglos, who had received or purchased grants, filed 346 claims. Initially the board rejected 273 claims and confirmed 521; 19 were discontinued. Grantees and government attorneys appealed 549 rulings of the board. Some cases were appealed as many as six times and 99 were appealed all the way to the U.S. Supreme Court. Government attorneys clearly showed excessive zeal in trying to vacate a maximum number of California land grants. The general attitude was that grantees were to be considered guilty of fraud until they proved their innocence. Ultimately 614 of the 813 claims, about nine million acres out of thirteen million, were validated.

The process of confirming land grants was long, arduous, costly, and in the long run a disaster for californios. The slowness of validation was unfair to both Mexican Americans and Anglos and served to increase hostility between them and to delay Anglo settlement in California. To establish clear title took an average of about seventeen years, during which time the owner's control of his land was limited. Although about three-fourths of the grants were eventually confirmed, the process proved extremely expensive for most grantees. In order to meet the heavy costs of proving title many had to borrow at high interest rates, using their land as collateral. Even when they eventually won clear title, they lost. Most were eventually forced to sell part of their landholdings or cattle to pay court costs, lawyers' fees, and other expenses.

Moreover, confirmation did not necessarily assure security of title; some rancheros continued to be harassed and persecuted by persistent and determined Anglo squatters. For example, one notable family in the San Francisco Bay area, the Berryesas, were harried by acts of terror and violence that brought some of its members to insanity or death. As a result of litigation, forced sales, intimidation, unscrupulous lawyers, and out-and-out robbery, landownership in California underwent drastic change by 1856. Loss of lands was an important factor in the erosion of californio political power in the second half of the nineteenth century.

Town and mission land grants posed additional problems. Not until the 1860s were these worked out. San Jose, Los Angeles, and San Francisco all had their titles to the customary four square leagues confirmed. The Catholic Church received patents only to mission church sites; the lands held in trust for the Indians had long since been sold or granted by the Mexican government to important citizens, including some Anglos. California's economic development was held back by the uncertainties in landownership. Without clear title few settlers would risk buying and improving land. It might have been better for California and the nation if the government had purchased title, as it did to 75 million acres in Texas in 1850, and then made land available to settlers. By placing the heavy costs of proof on the grantees the United States clearly failed to live up to the spirit of the Treaty of Guadalupe Hidalgo.

Arrogant squatter conduct was only one form of lawlessness that harassed californios as a result of the gold rush. In addition, the presence of large numbers of adventurers, outcasts, and societal misfits from many lands and the absence of a police force led to considerable violence. Thievery, robberies, and murders were common throughout the gold-mining period. Because of the widely held stereotype of Mexicans, they often provided convenient scapegoats for these crimes. There were, of course, thieves and bandits among the Spanish-speaking just as there were among Anglos. However, Mexican "bandit activity" was often a response to Anglo persecution and violence. The response of some individual Mexicans led to great notoriety. Joaquín Murieta is perhaps the best-known, if largely legendary, californio bandit-hero. He was credited with terrorizing much of Calaveras County in 1852–53. His alleged activities and those of other highwaymen, such as Juan Flores and Three-Fingered Jack García, led to retaliation against all mexicanos. Indeed, many innocent Mexican Americans suffered as the result of legal and extralegal efforts to reduce crime and banditry in California. To accuse a mexicano of stealing gold or a horse was tantamount to finding him guilty and often led to his sudden demise.

A number of Joaquíns were so accused, but Anglo Californians tended to blend them all into one and credited Joaquín Murieta with numerous violent crimes committed in the state. According to the folklore that sprang up, Murieta was a peaceful Mexican miner whose claim was jumped by gold-greedy Anglos, who whipped him, hanged his brother, and raped his wife in his presence. Enraged by these vicious acts, Murieta dedicated his life from then on to avenging family honor by bringing death and destruction to all "gringos." As more and more travelers reported that they had been robbed by him, his reputation grew to legendary proportions and he became the Robin Hood of the mexicanos.

The California legislature early in 1853 created a special ranger force under Captain Harry Love to hunt down the "five" Joaquíns, listing them as Murieta, Carrillo, Valenzuela, Ocomorenia, and Botilleras or Botellier. A $1,000 reward was also posted. Californio legislators protested in vain that this was an open invitation to hunt mexicanos. After chasing alleged Joaquíns through the entire southern mining region for several months, in July, just as their commission was about to expire, Love's rangers killed two mexicanos, one of whom was identified by them as Joaquín Murieta. In order to collect the reward, they brought back with them a head they claimed to be Murieta's, preserved in whiskey. However, from the very beginning there was some question about this identification as well as the events of Murieta's life. The historical reality of Murieta's origins, life, and death continues to be disputed.

Anti-Mexican feeling in California was not limited to the mining region. Anglo prejudice against Mexican Americans, especially those of marked Indian appearance, existed statewide. In Los Angeles the Spanish-language newspaper *El Clamor Público* championed the rights of the Spanish-speaking, describing their persecution and criticizing unequal application of American law. However, no relief was forthcoming. Some californios even considered emigration and a few tried it, but most preferred to remain in California, hoping that the situation would improve.

During the 1850s a number of factors in the Los Angeles area eased the adjustment of Mexican Americans to American rule. Because of the absence of gold and the scarcity of water a limited number of Anglo settlers were attracted to this area. In addition, a moderate but fairly steady influx of Mexicans from Sonora into southern California maintained a Spanish-speaking majority there until the 1870s. This majority position helped ease the political transition. Throughout this period californios continued to fill important positions in local government; Juan Sepúlveda was named a Los Angeles alcalde, and Antonio Coronel became Los Angeles's first superintendent of schools and later held other high offices. Many others occupied positions of lesser importance at various levels. Nevertheless, the Spanish-speaking were soon dominated by Anglos in both government and business in the south, as well as in the north.

Another factor easing the position of californio elites in the southern counties was the economic prosperity of the 1850s. During the decade these pastoral counties supplied large numbers of cattle at rapidly rising prices to easily accessible markets created by thousands of gold miners. For a while large incomes from cattle sales enabled many southern California rancheros to enjoy a hitherto undreamed-of standard of living. However, Texas and Sonora cattle drives in the late 1850s combined with a long California drought of the early 1860s to put an end to this immensely profitable cattle boom. Cattle which had sold for $5.00 a head before 1849 and for as much as $100 during the height of the gold rush were selling for less than $1.00 each in the spring of 1864. Many rancheros, heavily in debt as the result of extravagant living and the cost of proving landownership, lost their lands to creditors or the tax collector. Over the long term the end of this cattle boom had a diversifying effect on land use, leading to expansion in sheep raising and wider cultivation of grapes, citrus, wheat, corn, and other crops for market. Southern California's sheep industry spread, especially as the Union Army's demand for wool soared during the Civil War.

Mexican Americans, like other Americans, were divided in their sympathies during the War Between the States. Because there were many Confederate supporters in California, especially in the south, President Abraham Lincoln had special cause to be interested in the loyalty of the recently acquired nationals. Although not well informed about the issues of the war, a large majority were at least passively loyal to the North, and Mexican Americans served in the Union forces. Two Spanish-speaking soldiers were awarded the nation's highest citation for valor—the Medal of Honor. The most notable Hispanic group in the struggle was a battalion of 450 californio cavalrymen, led by Captain Salvador Vallejo. Patrolling the Mexican border and fighting Apaches, these troops also helped frustrate Confederate plans to seize control of New Mexico.

The Civil War also had a direct political impact on Mexican Americans. Because most Confederates were Democrats, Republicans labeled the Democratic Party as the party of treason—a tactic which brought great electoral success for the Republican Party, to which most Mexican Americans belonged at this time. As a result, a larger number of californios and nuevomexicanos were elected to political office in the years during and immediately after the war, as political passions ran especially strong.

———

During the second half of the nineteenth century cultural and historic ties to Mexico and a continuing movement of Mexicans into California turned californios' eyes toward Mexico. Both the civil strife there during the late 1850s known as the War of the Reform and subsequent French intervention in the 1860s served to direct their interest to what was taking place in Mexico. Using the Mexican government's suspension of payment on its foreign debts in 1861 as justification, France invaded Mexico early in the following year. Initially thwarted at the city of Puebla on May 5, 1862 (Cinco de Mayo), the reinforced French forces pushed on to capture Mexico City a year later. A combination of the ambitions of Napoleon III and Mexican conservatives' desire to reestablish monarchy brought the Archduke Maximilian of Austria to Mexico as its French-supported emperor in 1864.

In this critical situation Benito Juárez, a Zapotec Indian from Oaxaca, assumed leadership of the resistance to French intervention. The great Mexican liberal leader fought desperately against the combined forces of Mexican monarchism and French imperialism. Finally the Juárez government was forced to withdraw to the northern frontier of Mexico. Driven to desperate measures by French military success, President Juárez sent General Placidio Vega to California to seek both financial aid and volunteers. The latter's activities brought some results. Mexican patriotic and benevolent societies mushroomed in the south, $200,000 was raised to continue the fight against the French, and some californio and Anglo volunteers enlisted in Juárez's army. However, few actually ever reached Mexico.

After Juárez's army successfully overthrew Maximilian and drove out the French invaders in 1867, the activities of Mexican patriotic societies in the American Southwest continued. Californios felt a greater sense of identification with Mexico than they had before. The annual celebration after the 1860s of two national holidays, Cinco de Mayo and the Grito de Dolores (September 16), reflects this new attitude. Another factor in this change was the continuing immigration of Sonorans who typically showed a stronger sense of affection for their country than did most californios. The Sonoran immigrants, with their greater patriotic zeal, reinvigorated and reinforced the earlier cultural patterns of mexicano society. As they became a major group in the Spanish-speaking community of southern California, there was some blurring and a breaking down of distinctions between Mexicans and californios.

The Mexican Americans of southern California faced a new era in the late 1870s with the arrival of the transcontinental railroads. In 1876 the Southern Pacific Railroad reached Los Angeles, and a decade later the Santa Fe gave southern California a second connection with the Midwest and the East. The two railroad lines brought into the southern half of the state large numbers of Anglo Americans, who overwhelmed the Mexican culture there. These new settlers bought small farms and sections of ranchos for raising oranges and grapes or they leased or rented rancho lands to run sheep. They also established their own churches, schools, and other cultural institutions. By 1880 Anglo immigration had reduced Mexican Americans to about 25 percent of the southern California population, and ten years later they comprised only 10 percent.

The impact of heavy Anglo migration was negative for californios. They soon found themselves in new social and economic roles. Loss of lands had eaten away at their economic base, and many now found themselves pushed out of middle-class ranks into work as ranch hands or unskilled labor. Some wives and daughters were forced into the labor market as laundresses, seamstresses, and cannery workers. Those with lighter skin color, status, or a claim to Spanish identity were the only Mexican Americans likely to be accepted by Anglos, and only partially at that.

A tiny Mexican American middle class existed in the south, made up largely of small service businessmen in the mexicano community. It included doctors, teachers, stonemasons, jewelers, leatherworkers, hat makers, tailors, and other shop owners. This middle class lived widely dispersed throughout Los Angeles and enjoyed considerably better conditions than the rest of the mexicano population. Because of economic and social changes, by 1900 a separate californio culture, developing for over a century, became almost extinct. As immigration from Mexico increased toward the end of the century, poorer californios became increasingly identified with the newcomers and began to face residential segregation.

By the end of the century there were as many immigrant Mexicans as californios in the state. A majority of the immigrants lived in a *colonia* known as Sonoratown, south and east of Los Angeles plaza, and worked

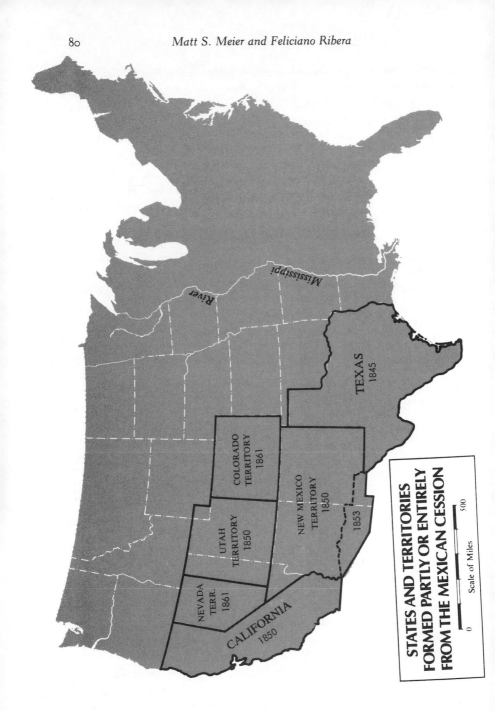

STATES AND TERRITORIES
FORMED PARTLY OR ENTIRELY
FROM THE MEXICAN CESSION

TEXAS
1845

COLORADO
TERRITORY
1861

NEW MEXICO
TERRITORY
1850

UTAH
TERRITORY
1850

NEVADA
TERR.
1861

CALIFORNIA
1850

1853

Mississippi

River

Scale of Miles

0   500

in low-paying jobs as farm workers, day laborers, slaughterhouse workers, and domestics. Californio culture was swallowed up by the flood of Anglos and by waves of immigrants from Mexico fleeing economic injustice, social turmoil, and political repression. A new period was about to begin for the Mexican American in California.

The Mexican American experience in Texas during the second half of the nineteenth century differed in many respects from that of the californio. After Texas gained independence in 1836 a strong and continuing flow of Anglo migration into the area quickly reduced tejanos to a small percentage of the population, and they lost the few prominent political positions that pro-American elites like José Antonio Navarro, Lorenzo de Zavala, and Juan Seguín had held. By 1840 they constituted only 10 percent of the total population. When Texas became a state in 1845 José Antonio Navarro was the only Spanish-surnamed delegate elected to the constitutional convention. After the mid-1840s tejanos lost to the rising tide of Anglos even the political control they had wielded in largely mexicano San Antonio. However, some continued to be elected to local positions in the border region, where the population remained overwhelmingly mexicano. During this period the new international boundary set by the Treaty of Guadalupe Hidalgo was disregarded by all, allowing a constant flow of sojourners and immigrants to southern Texas.

Early social interaction between the upper economic strata of tejanos and Anglos, especially Catholics, was based on mutual interests and resulted in considerable intermarriage, leading to a degree of acculturation during the quarter-century following Texas independence. After the 1870s, intermarriage, while not impossible, was nearly unthinkable, especially to old Anglo Texan families. Upper-class, lighter-skinned tejanos, many of whom were Canary Islanders or their descendants, tended to be accepted and have their civil rights respected. They formed a small, tightly knit elite whose members considered themselves culturally superior to both Anglos and Mexicans. Ignoring public affairs, they left the political field to Anglo newcomers.

The rise in the United States of the ultranationalistic, antiforeign, and anti-Catholic Know-Nothing Party during the 1850s added to the difficulties of tejanos and intensified the relation of ethnicity to social class. Discrimination was widespread, especially against the poorer class of darker-skinned mexicanos, who were widely accused of helping run-away slaves escape across the border into Mexico. Mere accusation was sometimes enough to cause them to be driven from their homes and out of the region. Living in segregated barrios, they provided labor and services and were "kept in their place." Border banditry involving Anglos, tejanos, and Mexicans, especially in the heavily Mexican area of the Nueces triangle, aggravated the troubled relations among these three groups. Tejanos who successfully competed with Anglos became particular targets for violence.

The Cart War of 1857 was one example of their difficulties. From colonial times Mexicans had been extremely able teamsters and had organized successful businesses carrying goods between the Texas coast and the interior, particularly San Antonio. Because they charged lower rates than Anglo competitors, they became the focus of their wrath. Bitterness finally led some Anglo teamsters and others in Goliad and Karnes counties to attack Mexican freight trains, stealing goods, burning carts, and even murdering drivers. Despite fairly widespread Anglo and tejano condemnation of the crimes and demands that the United States provide troops to protect cart trains, the depredations went on for six months. Finally, after Mexican government complaints, federal troops were sent into southern Texas. Their presence and Anglo vigilante action against some of the guilty teamsters brought the Cart War to an end. It exemplifies the tribulations suffered by border mexicanos, as did the Cortina conflict, which followed it.

At the close of the 1850s Juan Nepomuceno Cortina excited popular imagination along the border much as had the legendary Joaquín Murieta in California. After an uneventful early life as a member of a prosperous border ranching family, Cortina first came to public notice in 1859, when he shot a Texas marshal while rescuing a peón whom the lawman was brutally mistreating. Then, early on the morning of September 28, 1859, Cortina and a band of about 100 followers burst into Brownsville, shouting, "Viva Cortina! Mueran los gringos!" ("Long live Cortina! Death to the gringos!"). They quickly took over the town, killed three Americans accused of mistreating Mexicans, attempted to raise the Mexican flag, and finally left. From his hideout Cortina issued statements saying that he would continue fighting to emancipate his fellow mexicanos.

The Anglos of Brownsville, alleging that Cortina was trying to exterminate the Anglo border population, appealed for American troop protection. Failing to receive it, they sought help from the Mexican Army, which chased Cortina across the Rio Grande into Mexico. Evidently genuinely interested in redressing wrongs committed against mexicanos, Cortina attracted strong support. Subsequent clashes between Cortina and American forces resulted in victory for Cortina, who became a hero to Latinos on both sides of the river. His temporary success was brought to an end three months later in December by the arrival of additional American troops, who chased him deep into Mexico, where he continued to enjoy some fame. In subsequent roles as a supporter of Benito Juárez, as governor of Tamaulipas, and as a brigadier general in the Mexican Army, he continued to support forays into the Nueces triangle until the 1890s. His career illustrates the ambiguity of nationality along the border.

Continued enmity between Anglo and mexicano was in evidence during the Civil War. After Lincoln was inaugurated in March 1861, a Texas convention voted 109 to 2 to join the Confederate States of America. There is little to indicate whether most tejanos concurred in this overwhelming support. They fought on both sides. Many became Union supporters, harassing Anglo Confederates by "liberating" their cotton, cattle, horses, and other property. On the other hand, as inhabitants of a Confederate state a majority of the 3,500 tejanos who fought in the Civil War fought for the South.

After the war swarms of unpaid and destitute Confederate veterans ranged the Texas countryside. Robbery and violence became widespread and indiscriminate; often mexicanos were the targets. In western Texas a running border war developed out of a series of events that started during the Civil War. At the beginning of the 1860s mexicanos at San Elisario, near El Paso, were taking salt from the Guadalupe salt lakes. These lakes, located east of El Paso, had always been considered open to communal use. In 1866 Samuel Maverick of San Antonio, using government land scrip, preempted a section of the best area in the salt licks and attempted to charge for taking salt. The salt lakes quickly became a political issue, as well as a point of conflict between Maverick and El Paso mexicanos. For the next ten years the dispute took numerous complex turns; however, mexicanos continued to take salt from areas not held by Maverick.

In 1877 a Democratic politician, Judge Charles Howard, laid claim to the salt lake area not already claimed by Maverick and posted notices that henceforth he would charge a fee for taking salt. Trouble began when Howard had two mexicanos arrested for allegedly trying to take salt from his claim. Mexicano frustration and anger led to a citizen's arrest of Howard, who was forced to sign papers renouncing his claim. Humiliated and angered, Howard shot his political opponent, Luis Cardis, who had supported the mexicanos in their fight for the right to take salt. In retaliation a mob of mexicanos executed Howard, killed other Anglos, and inflicted considerable property damage in El Paso. Racial feelings and violence ran high as adventurers rushed into the area to join in the fight. The violence continued. Officials on both sides of the Rio Grande seemed little interested in suppressing the looting, robbery, rape, and murder. Finally relative peace was restored by the arrival of a United States investigating commission and the subsequent stationing of troops at Fort Bliss, newly established in 1878 near El Paso. In the end everyone had to pay to take salt from the Guadalupe lakes.

During the post-Civil War era the entire southwestern frontier became a refuge for social outcasts and misfits, defeated Confederate soldiers, and the dregs of western mining booms. Violence between Anglo and mexicano continued, often provoked by bandits from both sides of the border. Along the Rio Grande there were many callous killings by American and Mexican gangs, who found the border region a safe haven, adequately controlled by neither the United States nor Mexico. Mexicanos unfairly received most of the blame for these brutal crimes, and indiscriminate retaliation by Anglo posses against mexicano suspects was common. By the mid-1870s violence had become so widespread that many mexicanos and Anglos moved from their ranches and farms into town for safety. Mexicanos even moved across the Rio Grande into Mexico. There was some demand that the United States annex the border areas of Mexico in order to restore a semblance of order. However, by the end of the decade border conflict had subsided considerably, largely as a result of Porfirio Díaz's rise to political power in Mexico. During the 1880s the Díaz administration was able to extend its control to the northern border region, and collaboration between Mexican and American forces brought the beginnings of law and order to the sparsely populated area.

Texas experienced fewer problems with issues of landownership than California. Not many individual land grants had been made during the Spanish period, and Mexican empresario grants, such as the one given to Stephen Austin, led to fewer problems of disputed ownership than occurred in California. Texas accepted the validity of most Spanish and Mexican grants. However, some grants had been invalidated during the Mexican period, and some later claims, most made by Anglos, were rejected by the Republic of Texas. Between Texas independence and the Civil War a shifting of landownership from tejanos to Anglos began, especially in eastern and central parts of the state. In southern and western Texas, where mexicanos remained the majority, Anglo ownership of land increased more slowly, but just as inexorably, particularly after the war. Even tejano elites found their property rights challenged and some were forced to fight for their land in the courts. In many cases lands were lost because of legal stratagems or forced sales for nonpayment of taxes. Sometimes Anglo speculators obtained tejano lands for only a few cents per acre. Loss of tejano lands to Anglos was accelerated by the 1870s cattle boom.

The post-Civil War period in Texas was characterized by a number of economic developments that markedly affected Mexican Americans. The first was the great Texas cattle boom of the 1870s and 1880s, which was given impetus by increased demand for beef from the industrialized nations and by improved transportation as well as by the invention of barbed wire, which made it possible to improve the longhorn stock through controlled breeding. This cattle-based prosperity provided employment for many mexicano vaqueros, often on grazing lands originally owned by tejanos. Enclosure of lands with barbed wire tended to force out small and middle-sized ranchers, many of whom were mexicanos.

A second economic development affecting Mexican Americans in Texas during the post-Civil War period was the expansion of sheep raising. In some areas sheep took on greater economic importance than cattle. This growth was made possible in part by mexicano labor and expertise. As feeder railroad lines opened new grazing areas in the 1870s and connected them to markets for Texas wool, the sheep industry spread rapidly, especially in the heavily mexicano border region of southern Texas. This area, isolated from the rest of the state and largely outside U.S. economic boundaries, maintained strong economic and cultural ties to northeastern Mexico until the end of the century. The Nueces triangle, for example, remained essentially Mexican, and Laredo at its western end seemed to visitors to be more Mexican than American.

Economic growth was also strongly pushed in the mid-1880s by a great increase in cotton growing. Expansion of cotton acreage into south

Texas was based principally on availability of mexicano labor and led to a steadily growing stream of migrants in the 1880s and 1890s, including entire families from Mexico. The abundance and availability of this cheap labor retarded mechanization. Movement of sojourners north from Mexico, coupled with an increased flow of poor white migrants from the Old South, who brought with them their overt color prejudices, increased existing racial antagonisms. Ethnic conflict became a scarcely noticed warp of the social fabric. It spread and intensified throughout Texas, especially along the border. Toward the end of the century it was exacerbated by some overt mexicano sympathy for Spain in 1898 during the Spanish-American War.

Even though violence diminished somewhat by the end of the century, tejanos were increasingly excluded from positions of influence and power in both government and business. At the same time cities like El Paso and San Antonio, with their large mexicano populations, became important supply and processing centers. Access to cheap mexicano labor began to lure new industries from the Northeast, which in turn attracted additional workers from Mexico. The seemingly endless supply of low-skill, undereducated workers acted to hold down wages and retard improvement in their working and living conditions. As a result sharp divisions continued between mexicano and Anglo communities. By the end of the century mexicanos had become defined as cheap labor, without a claim to economic or social equality.

Because of prejudice based on race and color little or no thought was given to the social and economic well-being of Mexican Americans at this time. The majority society was unwilling to accept them as equals, and they continued to be relegated to lower economic and social positions. Nevertheless, by the first decade of the twentieth century mexicanos and tejanos shared, to a limited extent, in the growth and prosperity that Texas enjoyed. The confluence of cultures could not be halted, and a degree of acculturation was occurring in Texas as elsewhere in the Southwest. Then came the Mexican revolution of 1910, which initiated an immigrant flood that reinvigorated Mexican culture in the Southwest and postponed further acculturation for at least a quarter of a century.

6

CULTURE AND CONFLICT
IN NEW MEXICO

New Mexico, like other areas of the Southwest, experienced considerable conflict arising from the clash of two distinct and at times antagonistic cultures. From the beginning of the American period in 1848 many elite nuevomexicano landowners and merchants, often referred to as "los ricos," welcomed Anglo takeover and control. This well-to-do group was readily accepted by the new Anglo social and political leadership. From 1848 to 1912, the years of New Mexico's territorial status, it continued to have a predominantly hispano population but was dominated by a small group of Anglo and nuevomexicano politicians and businessmen. Cultural conflict developed because most Spanish-speaking New Mexicans found it difficult to understand and accept concepts of government, taxation, and land tenure based on Anglo-Saxon legal norms.

The dimensions of this contention were enlarged by the makeup of early Anglo migration into the New Mexican territory after 1848. Largely urban and middle-class, the new settlers had difficulty adjusting to the nuevomexicano class system of ricos and peones, with virtually no middle class. Misunderstanding was aggravated by the Anglo immigrants' failure to fathom the resistance of nuevomexicanos to Anglo institutions and to appreciate a culture that was deep-seated, agrarian, and Catholic. As a result, mutual understanding was difficult, and a prolonged and at times acrimonious struggle evolved.

Immediately following 1848 nuevomexicanos suffered the normal indignities of military conquest, but without the kind of economic, social, and political problems brought on by the gold rush in California or the proximity of Texas to the American South. Moreover, at the time of conquest New Mexico contained many more Spanish speakers (60,000) than California or Texas; further, their history in the area went back to the sixteenth century. In numerous small villages along the upper Rio Grande and its tributaries a distinct regional Hispanic-Mexican subculture which included local Indian elements had become deeply rooted. This subculture survived because of its adaptation to local conditions, the area's physical and cultural isolation, and the small number of Anglo immigrants during the first quarter-century of American control. Despite these factors, nuevomexicanos could not escape Anglo cultural dominance indefinitely.

The roots of conflict originated in 1846 with the takeover of New Mexico by General Stephen Kearny. Conquest had little immediate impact except to bring the United States flag and the Kearny Code. When the United States formally took over the region, most nuevomexicanos continued their cultural practices but readily acquiesced to American rule. This acceptance was facilitated by the feeling of many that they were more Spanish, or hispano in their terminology, than Mexican and thus owed little loyalty to the ineffectual government in distant Mexico City.

The apparent ease of the American takeover was deceptive. Beneath the surface there existed a deep undercurrent of bitterness and anger among those who felt they had been betrayed by Governor Armijo's failure to resist U.S. conquest. Other nuevomexicanos, especially those living near the new post-Guadalupe Hidalgo border in what is today southwestern New Mexico and southern Arizona historically had strong ties with Sonora. They therefore exhibited somewhat greater loyalties toward the mother country. Some 2,000 indicated their allegiance by crossing the border rather than accept American rule. Ironically, many of this group found themselves back in the United States when it acquired the Mesilla Valley through the Gadsden Purchase treaty at the end of 1853.

An overwhelming majority of the landowning and merchant classes remained in New Mexico and seemed readily to accept the U.S. gov-

ernment. However, for political and economic reasons some ricos opposed the Americans. Among these was Colonel Diego Archuleta, an
important nuevomexicano leader who had been second-in-command
to Governor Armijo and had failed to obtain political office in the new
government, which he believed he had been promised. He now led a
cabal of malcontents who plotted to assassinate the newly appointed
Anglo governor and oust all Americans from New Mexico. In mid-
December 1846 rumors of this intrigue reached the authorities, and
Colonel Sterling Price of the Missouri Volunteers arrested some of the
conspirators. Archuleta and other principals fled south to Mexico. Later
a rumor spread to certain U.S. quarters that the Taos pastor Father
Antonio José Martínez had masterminded the scheme. However, during
the subsequent trials of the conspirators no evidence was ever brought
forward to substantiate the gossip or to implicate the priest.

With the suppression of this Mexican and Indian plot and the trial
of the captured leaders, Americans thought that all danger was past.
Their sense of security was short-lived, however, for on January 19,
1847, Governor Charles Bent was brutally murdered and scalped at
Taos pueblo as a result of a second conspiracy. His death rekindled the
flames of nativist revolt, and in the ensuing violence many homes were
sacked and fifteen or twenty prominent landowners, all either Anglo or
pro-American, were killed. By early summer, when the rebellion was
suppressed, some 200 Indians and mexicanos had been killed or seriously wounded. The surviving ringleaders were later convicted in a trial
of dubious legality, and fifteen of them were sentenced to death. Their
being hanged for treason against a government which they did not accept
deeply shook the entire New Mexican region and left a heritage of
suspicion and animosity.

Despite bitterness felt by many hispanos over the Taos suppression,
they soon became somewhat more amenable to American control as
Texas threatened them once again. In 1848 Texas legislators attempted
to incorporate the eastern half of New Mexico as a Texas county.
Claiming that her western boundary extended to the Rio Grande, which
runs through the middle of the present state, Texas sent officials under
a Judge Spruce Baird to organize the area politically. Many nuevomexicanos remembered vividly the Texan invasion in 1841 and viewed
this renewed aggression with considerable apprehension. Frustrated by
hispano opposition, Baird finally gave up and returned to Texas in July
1849.

Recognizing the seriousness of the Texas threat, New Mexicans called a constitutional convention early in 1850. This convention, made up mostly of upper-class hispanos, drew up a state constitution which prohibited slavery. At this point the statehood issue became enmeshed in the ongoing national controversy over slavery and its expansion. After considerable debate the issue was resolved temporarily by the U.S. Congress through the Compromise of 1850, by which New Mexico became a territory and Texas was indemnified for her claim. In the subsequently elected territorial legislatures hispanos played prominent roles. For example, Miguel Otero and Father Martínez, members of leading nuevomexicano families, were outstanding leaders during the 1850s. Martínez, who earlier had served in the local Mexican legislature, was elected to the American territorial legislature and also became its first president. Even Diego Archuleta served in the territorial assembly for over a decade.

During the 1850s, slavery, which had local as well as national implications, became a divisive factor among nuevomexicanos. Many patrones were favorable to slavery because they were long accustomed to the related institution of peonage. Other nuevomexicanos approved proslavery politics in reaction to Washington's rejection of New Mexico statehood. The principal leader of this faction was Miguel Otero, whose influence on the territorial legislature led to enactment of a slave code in 1859. However, when the Civil War broke out in 1861, Otero, like many other politically active nuevomexicanos, decided not to take sides.

In spite of open solicitation by Confederate sympathizers for support most nuevomexicanos remained at least passively loyal to the Union, only dimly aware of the deep-seated economic and social reasons for the Civil War. By 1865 about 5,000 had volunteered for service in the Union Army; others served loyally in the territorial militia. Many viewed Southern troops advancing into New Mexico from Confederate Texas as simply a repetition of the 1841 Texan invasion. When they arrived, about half the frightened mexicano population of the Mesilla Valley fled across the border into Sonora. That their concern was not entirely without foundation is shown by the fact that some prominent pro-Union leaders like José M. Gallegos and Facundo Pino were placed under arrest by Confederate forces.

The Confederate invasion of New Mexico occurred in mid-1861 when a small force moved northward from El Paso and secured the southern half of the territory for the South. Early in 1862 a larger force of 3,000 Texas troops under the command of General Henry Sibley advanced up the Rio Grande and succeeded in occupying Albuquerque and Santa Fe. From Fort Union, the last stronghold in the territory held by Northern forces, an expedition was sent against the Confederates. At Glorieta Pass, near Santa Fe, Union soldiers commanded by Colonel Manuel Chávez destroyed the Confederate supply base in late March, thereby forcing the Southern troops eventually to return to Texas. This crucial New Mexican victory is sometimes referred to as the Gettysburg of the West. The Confederate withdrawal caused some difficulties for the small pro-Southern faction, which suffered embarrassment and financial losses when Union troops took over. The former Mexican governor, Manuel Armijo, and his brother Rafael, for example, lost advances of about $200,000 worth of supplies made to the Confederates, and in 1864 their store, flour mill, ranches, and other property were confiscated by Union forces.

After the Civil War conflict between nuevomexicanos and Anglos increased, principally because of widespread lawlessness that followed in the war's wake throughout the western frontier. Conditions became worse than in the disordered 1850s as desperadoes from the more settled parts of the West sought refuge in the isolated and poorly policed New Mexico Territory. Adding to the lawlessness were bands of Sonoran border outlaws that ravaged remote portions of the territory from time to time. A circular pattern of provocation and retribution developed between mexicanos and Americans. Severe racial conflict and persecution often drove Mexican Americans as well as Mexicans south of the border. Contributing further to this atmosphere of violence was the continuing disorder and agitation resulting from Indian warfare, widespread range wars between Anglo cattlemen and mexicano sheepherders, and bloody fighting by cattlemen and sheepmen against homesteaders. The Lincoln County War in 1876–78 in southeastern New Mexico was part of this frontier instability. Often mexicanos were caught in the middle of the violence.

New Mexico lawlessness in this era produced its share of folk heroes—one of them the extraordinary Elfego Baca. During a campaign for sheriff in the 1880s Baca arrested a rampaging Texas cowboy and, in the ensuing fracas, shot a Texan. A mob of Texans then decided to "arrest" Elfego for murder, and for the following thirty-six hours he fought off an estimated eighty Texans, wounding a number and killing four. Baca finally surrendered on the promise of a fair trial, surprisingly received one, and was acquitted. Later he became sheriff of Socorro County and was at one point considered a potential candidate for the governorship. He remained an important New Mexican political figure into the first two decades of the twentieth century.

The coming of transcontinental railroads to the Southwest in the late 1870s changed relations between Anglos and Mexican Americans as it had in California. The economic and political preeminence of Santa Fe and Taos declined when they were bypassed by the railroad in favor of Albuquerque. Harbingers of the rapidly industrializing economy in the United States, railroads opened new economic opportunities for businessmen with capital, especially attracting entrepreneurial Anglos. As the Southwest became more fully articulated with the national economy, the creation of empires in timber, cattle, minerals, and cotton caused extensive economic change. A heavy demand for labor ensued, especially in the mining and railroad industries, and Mexican workers were attracted from as far south as Zacatecas. Besides providing greatly needed labor, these migrants served to reinvigorate nuevomexicano culture. Meanwhile, some older hispano population centers were virtually encircled by Texas cattlemen who established themselves in the plains of eastern New Mexico.

In the 1870s improved transportation, partial pacification of Apache and Comanche Indians, rapidly expanding urban industrial populations in the East and Midwest, and other factors created a cattle boom. The ensuing large-scale cattle operations greatly expanded demand for grazing lands. Pressure for land led to Anglo acquisition of both village and private lands by purchase, chicanery, and violence. Some hispanos along the upper Rio Grande abandoned subsistence farming and moved east into the New Mexican grasslands, where they shifted to raising sheep. This expansion was accelerated by the *partido* (share) system of sheep raising. The New Mexican sheep industry grew rapidly, peaking just after the turn of the century.

In New Mexico, as in California, land constituted the basis of wealth and position. Even before the U.S.-Mexican War a few Anglos like Charles Bent and Kit Carson had acquired land through grants from Mexican authorities. After the war Anglos began purchasing land from hispano grantees who were either moving to Mexico or in dire need of cash. To determine land titles Congress created in 1854 the office of Surveyor General for the Territory of New Mexico with offices in Santa Fe. The Surveyor General was to make his recommendations to the

Secretary of the Interior, who was then to forward them to Congress for confirmation or rejection. For the next three decades the determination of land titles moved slowly. By 1886, out of a total of 205 private land claims filed, 141 had been confirmed. In Arizona, which was a part of the New Mexican territory until 1863, there were many fewer grants than in New Mexico. By 1888 the Surveyor General had examined 15 Arizona grants and recommended that 13 be confirmed. But Congress had not acted on a single one.

Although New Mexico had a limited post-Guadalupe Hidalgo influx of Anglo Americans, after the collapse of the cattle boom in the late 1880s hundreds of Anglo farmers began settling in the eastern high plains. These migrants, mostly from Texas, initiated more and keener competition with hispanos for land and water rights. In this situation local and territorial politicians used their government positions to obtain large tracts for themselves and their friends.

A loose alliance of Anglo leaders and some twenty rico families, known as the Santa Fe Ring, enabled its members to acquire large blocks of land, much of it by devious means. At times they used political and legal wiles to force grants to auction, so that Ring members, with access to capital, could purchase them cheaply. They were also able to influence legislative action and court decisions. Thus, a group of corrupt politicians, venal government officials, greedy bankers, less than scrupulous lawyers, and land-hungry nuevomexicano elites conspired to take over millions of acres. In the process many nuevomexicanos were dispossessed of lands that their families had occupied for generations.

Rivalry for desirable lands was intensified by the Forest Reserve Act of 1891, which set aside thousands of acres as national forests, much of which was village commons. A subsequent shift of national forest land from pasturage to timber, wilderness, and recreational uses affected many nuevomexicanos adversely, depriving them of access to long-used grazing lands. In time over 10 percent of New Mexican land became restricted in usage. Grazing limitation forced some to reduce their sheep and goat herds, economic mainstays in many northern villages. Herd reductions in turn seriously affected the manufacture of woolen cloth, thereby causing a depression in one of New Mexico's basic home industries.

In the face of changing conditions New Mexico's subsistence economy exhibited serious structural weaknesses by the close of the century and slowly began to come apart as villagers fought a long, losing battle against impoverishment. As the subsistence infrastructure crumbled, families were no longer able to live off the land. Overpopulated villages and underemployed villagers tried to halt the decline by seeking work outside the village in market agriculture, on railroads, and in lumber camps and sawmills. Many, perhaps a majority, were forced to become wage laborers, at least part-time.

A very different response to the loss of New Mexican lands was vigilante action by hispano groups like the Mano Negra (Black Hand) and the Gorras Blancas (White Caps). Formed in the 1880s, these terrorist organizations sabotaged the property of railroads, ranchers, and Anglo homesteaders, as the latter two fenced off lands and all three inhibited the free movement of nuevomexicano sheepherders and their flocks. Railroads and ranchers in particular suffered severely at the hands of vigilantes. In 1889 the Santa Fe Railroad had 9,000 ties cut in half during one night by about 300 masked men; the following year nine miles of barbed-wire fencing was destroyed in a single night. By the early 1890s the Gorras Blancas had become a convenient cover for lawlessness, from personal feuds to organized banditry and cattle rustling. Finally Governor L. Bradford Prince of New Mexico ordered the Gorras Blancas to disband and threatened to call out the militia and, if necessary, request federal troops. This action, plus the reaction of Anglo and Mexican Americans alike to the lawlessness, led to the decline and eventual disappearance of the Gorras Blancas.

Meanwhile, in the 1880s pressures from advancing railroads, increasing Anglo influx, the cumbersome grant confirmation process, and continuing congressional failure to act on grants made a different solution of the land issue seem imperative. These factors pushed Congress to take action, and in 1891 it created the Court of Private Land Claims for New Mexico, Colorado, and Arizona, before which all claims were to be filed within two years. This court tended to be narrowly legalistic and even less swayed by arguments of custom and usage than its earlier California counterpart.

Because of a chain of historical accidents, proving title in the three regions was particularly difficult. Many early land grant records were destroyed during the 1680 Pueblo Indian revolt; more disappeared in 1846 when Mexican troops withdrew from the area. In 1869 and 1870 much of the Santa Fe archives was sold as waste paper; twelve years later the capitol burned, destroying more documentation. In New Mexico the problem of undetermined or vague grant boundaries was more confusing than in California, partly because its land grant history began in the 1590s, when the supply of land seemed inexhaustible. Further, most New Mexican grants dated from the 1600s and 1700s and had become complicated by numerous subsequent divisions and transfers. In New Mexico the land issue was also made more complex by claims of sedentary Pueblo Indians.

In New Mexico, village commons or pueblo grants, typically referred to as ejidos, posed serious difficulties. They were the private property of the community to which they were allotted. However, the United States took the position that ejido lands belonged to the nation as successor to Spain and Mexico. After the American courts rejected town claims to ejidos in the case of *United States* v. *Sandoval* in 1897, this view held complete sway. Only about ten ejido grants were recognized.

In 1904, thirteen years after its creation, the court completed its assigned task. Out of 301 petitions claiming some 35 million acres it confirmed title to 75 grants, mostly to commercial interests which had by this time acquired the claims. The court rejected as invalid claims to 64 percent of the acreage. Many nuevomexicanos were unjustly deprived of lands, often on narrow technical grounds within the letter of the law. Possibly two-thirds of the rejections were unfair to the grantees.

The principal bases for rejection of claims were the issuance of grants by unauthorized officials, lack of documentation, and failure to occupy grants continuously. Also many grants had been made only in usufruct for lifetime grazing privileges rather than in fee simple. Though almost certainly valid, many titles could not be proved in court. On the other hand, there was much fraud and fabrication and even more attempted expansion of acreage. For example, despite an 1824 Mexican law limiting private land grants to eleven square leagues, about 48,700 acres, the famous Maxwell (originally Beaubien-Miranda) grant was confirmed for over half of the 2 million acres claimed.

Even those whose titles were confirmed had to part with many acres of their grants to pay lawyers' fees, customarily about one-third of the grant, and court costs. To achieve confirmation it cost Antón Chico claimants over sixty years, a great deal of money, and 135,000 acres. Santa Fe Ring leader and lawyer Thomas B. Catron, who had represented claimants to at least 60 grants, held title to about 2 million acres in 1894 and was part owner or attorney for an additional 4 million. Eventually Anglos came to own 80 percent of New Mexican grant lands.

Ownership of mining lands caused less conflict in New Mexico than in California. Small-scale placer gold mining had developed in north-central New Mexico late in the colonial period. New gold deposits were discovered northwest and northeast of Taos just after the Civil War, and a small gold rush in 1867 brought in many Anglos for a time. Later in the century important new gold discoveries were made in north-central New Mexico near Elizabethtown. After the Civil War some long-abandoned silver mines in southwestern New Mexico were re-opened. In the 1870s new silver discoveries were made in the Silver City and Socorro areas, followed in the next decade by a number of rich silver strikes in the southwest around Kingston.

However, the future of mining in New Mexico lay not so much with precious metals as with copper, which had been mined since the co-lonial period. In southwestern New Mexico the Santa Rita copper mines, long closed down because of Apache hostility, reopened in the 1870s when the area became more secure. Skilled Mexican miners brought from El Paso del Norte (Ciudad Juárez) early in the decade developed other copper deposits at Clifton, just across the border in the recently separated territory of Arizona. Toward the end of the century coal mining became important when deposits were discovered near Raton, Gallup, and Santa Fe in northern New Mexico. The gold, silver, coal, and copper mines employed many mexicanos from both sides of the border. Although some mining towns were considered Anglo camps, all had a high percentage of mexicano workers, and in many mines they constituted a large majority. Occasionally Mexican miners seemed somewhat disquieting, as when in 1898 they declared solidarity with Spain during the Spanish-American War.

In all mining activities mexicanos played an extremely important part, supplying techniques and skills, as well as the bulk of the labor. Nevertheless, there quickly developed a dual wage system which favored Anglos by paying them at a higher rate than Mexican miners for the same type of work. In addition to suffering from discriminatory wage practices, mexicanos were restricted largely to menial and dangerous work and were housed in segregated areas. Some worked old placers and the tailings of copper mines on their own, occasionally making a fair income by reprocessing the leavings of earlier, less efficient mining operations.

Expansion during the 1870s created additional demands for mining machinery and supplies, which in turn made freighting an important industry. Supplies, stamping mills, and other equipment were transported from northern Mexico, especially the Sonoran port of Guaymas, in long mule-drawn wagon trains. The copper also needed to be hauled to market. Men like Mariano Samaniego and Esteban Ochoa were successful teamster-operators; the latter became an outstanding southwestern leader in freighting and general merchandising. Freighting, with its numerous mexicano muleteers, remained an important adjunct to mining until replaced by railroads.

During the 1880s and 1890s New Mexico began to shift from a rural agricultural economy to a commercial, technological, and industrial one. Anglo newcomers, ignoring the Mexican custom of living in harmony with the land, sought to modify the environment to meet their needs. Many Mexican Americans, hard put to adjust to this viewpoint, rejected aspects of change such as book learning, taxation, ruthless competition, and individual political rights. Overwhelmed and bewildered by Anglo ascendancy, they withdrew from contact with Anglos to the security of their own cultural group. This withdrawal was made easier by the persistence in New Mexico of a strong folk culture which lent itself to isolationism.

Railroads had a deep impact on nuevomexicanos. They caused freighters to reduce the numbers of their teams, resulting in the discharge of muleteers, and eventually most were forced out of business. Although railroads brought about a decline of employment in freighting and carting, at the same time they provided thousands of new jobs. Railroad construction and maintenance in the Southwest was based heavily on mexicano labor, employing numerous track workers into the first decades of the twentieth century. Railroad networks fostered an economic transformation that greatly affected traditional ways.

Although a majority of nuevomexicanos persisted in their village culture, by the end of the nineteenth century a new way of life was noticeable, especially among younger people. Their changed behavior was characterized by the use of many middle-class Anglo symbols of progress, such as canned foods, iron stoves, sewing machines, phonographs, and a wide variety of factory-made goods. Acceptance of these Anglo technological innovations clearly suggests that New Mexico's Hispanic-Mexican cultural heritage was weakening and that a trend toward amalgamation with Anglo society was taking place. Another indication of this change is that by the century's end Protestant missionaries were beginning to make inroads in this overwhelmingly Catholic society.

In New Mexico the newly appointed Catholic hierarchy led to conflict for Mexican Americans. Except for a few Italian Jesuits, after Guadalupe Hidalgo immigrant French clergy controlled the church in New Mexico almost completely, treating the area virtually as a mission region. The expulsion of all Spanish-born clergy during the Mexican period left only fourteen Catholic priests in the territory at mid-century, most of them nuevomexicanos by birth. Church influence had fallen to an all-time low by 1850 when Jean Baptiste Lamy, an immigrant missionary in Ohio, was appointed vicar apostolic of the Arizona–New Mexico region. Now a part of the U.S. hierarchical system, the New Mexican church, which had been so isolated, was reorganized, and intensively organized for the first time, by the dedicated and driven acting bishop.

A French cleric of Jansenist leanings, puritanical, unfamiliar with the more relaxed Mexican religious culture, Lamy had his misgivings about the nuevomexicano clergy even before he became acquainted with them. Soon he was involved in a quarrel over tithing and church fees with the Reverend Antonio José Martínez, self-appointed and widely acknowledged leader of the nuevomexicano clergy and people. Disagreement with Father Martínez's position that giving to the church should be voluntary quickly escalated into a feud between nuevomexicano priests and the European clergy that the bishop had brought to New Mexico. Partly in reaction to Bishop Lamy's innovations Martínez resigned as pastor of his Taos parish and retired. Unhappy with his successor, Martínez began to minister to his former parishioners, without episcopal approval. This challenge caused Bishop Lamy to suspend Father Martínez, who ignored his suspension, causing the outraged bishop to excommunicate him. In the end the conflict divided not only the Spanish-speaking clergy and Bishop Lamy but also nuevomexicano parishioners and what many of them regarded as a foreign church. In spite of the disagreement, Martínez, though schismatic, remained an important religious and political leader until his death in 1867, when his schism died with him.

Another church conflict involved Los Penitentes, the lay religious brotherhood which clearly filled deep-seated spiritual and social needs. During the Mexican era this group became increasingly important as its members took over religious functions of priests who died or were forced into exile because they were Spaniards. After 1846 Penitente organizations provided cultural stability and engendered collective solidarity in the face of mounting Anglo dominance. They also acted as local courts for the isolated villagers and supplied charitable services as well.

Attempts by Bishop Lamy and his successor, Archbishop Jean Salpointe, to control the Penitentes led to increased secretiveness within the brotherhood. An obsession with painful physical penance, including flagellation, also developed. Prohibition of some extreme Penitente religious practices helped push the organization toward political activism, in which its influence was often put in the service of the Republican Party. Continued attempts by the hierarchy to bring Penitente groups under ecclesiastical control led to a bitter struggle, which ended in 1889 with the church declaring the organization disbanded and its members excommunicated. Turning to even greater secrecy because of this action and morbid tourist curiosity, the brotherhood further curtailed its religious activities. However, as a fraternal organization it continued to play an important cultural and political role in rural New Mexico.

Los Penitentes formed one influential base which New Mexican patrones used to retain political authority. A second important element sustaining their power was peonage. Although outlawed by the U.S. Congress in 1867, vestiges of this colonial institution continued to play an important role in New Mexican politics. By controlling their workers and by delivering their votes patrones were able to retain a degree of political power. With a solid base in the votes they could deliver, ricos were able to influence elections and share governing with Anglos. Because of their education and greater familiarity with Anglo institutions, many patrones found politics a natural outlet for their leadership skills.

The Otero family affords an excellent example of the patrón system's political strengths and its effects on New Mexican politics and society. Prominent in Santa Fe politics for half a century, this family produced several noteworthy leaders. In the 1850s Miguel Antonio Otero was elected to the U.S. House of Representatives for three terms, after having previously served as secretary to the territorial governor. During the Civil War he founded the important business house of Otero, Sellar, and Company, and later became a director of the famous Maxwell Land Grant Company and a vice president of the Santa Fe Railroad. His son, Miguel II, was appointed territorial governor by President William McKinley in 1897 and served till 1906. By organizing Mexican American voters and obtaining control of some federal appointments he developed a strong political machine and considerably enhanced his powers as governor.

At the end of his governorship a pattern of Anglo political dominance began to emerge although nuevomexicano membership in the legislature remained at 25 percent and above until statehood in 1912. Only in the 1930s, when nuevomexicanos were less than half the population, did it drop below 20 percent; it has stayed near that figure to the present time. During the entire territorial period members of a score of elite families took an active role in local government. They were elected or appointed to a wide variety of political offices and at times controlled the legislature. Their political power irritated many Anglos in the eastern half of New Mexico, where the latter formed a majority. In their antipathy, some Anglos even tried to have eastern New Mexico annexed to Texas.

New Mexico's long status as a territory was another factor that helped patrones retain their power. Absence of a merit system enabled the winning party to dispense political jobs at all levels. Fortunately for nuevomexicanos, territorial status also meant a weaker local Anglo power base because of greater control from Washington. After the failed 1850 attempt at statehood, repeated efforts in the second half of the nineteenth century ended in defeat because of cultural and language discrimination, religious bigotry, and political prejudice. Nuevomexicano elites themselves at times opposed statehood for a variety of reasons, not the least of which was that they had learned to use the territorial system to their advantage.

Finally, in 1912, after a long and bitter struggle that included repeated petitions by the territorial legislature and a press campaign for the "Americanization" of New Mexico through the supplanting of Spanish by English, New Mexico was admitted as the forty-seventh state. This long-overdue action came about because of national political realities rather than local aspirations. With statehood, nuevomexicanos, who still composed 60 percent of the population, finally received full U.S. citizenship.

Arizona, like New Mexico, attracted few Anglos in the early days; nevertheless, when it was granted separate territorial status in 1863 Anglos already dominated its politics. The first territorial legislative assembly counted 22 Anglos and only 3 Mexican Americans. During the entire territorial period the Arizona legislature at no time had more than 4 Spanish-speaking members, and not a single appointed official was of Mexican descent. There were some successful Mexican American businessmen like Esteban Ochoa of Tucson, who became Arizona's only nineteenth-century Hispanic mayor. Ochoa, a strong believer in education, in the 1870s donated a town lot for the first public school. Other prominent Mexican Americans like Mariano Samaniego exercised limited influence on Arizona government and politics, mostly at local levels.

From the Treaty of Guadalupe Hidalgo until the early 1880s Indian depredations remained a serious problem in Arizona. Because of persistent harassment from Apache raiders, by the mid-1850s nearly the entire population of Arizona had fled to Tucson for safety. The outbreak of the Civil War and an associated rise in Apache plundering caused some Spanish-speaking Arizonans to withdraw southward to Sonora. The arrival of Union forces in mid-1862 quickly reversed this flow. The subsequent defeat of Juárez supporters in Sonora by French invaders and their Mexican allies caused renewed migration from Sonora to Arizona, but its volume was limited by continuing intense Apache activity in Arizona.

By 1870 Tucson had about 3,000 inhabitants. Eighty percent were of Mexican descent, and a majority were recent immigrants from Sonora. During the 1860s Mexican and Anglo elites became closely interrelated, principally through marriage, because of business connections and the scarcity of Anglo women. However, by the 1880s and 1890s such intermarriage virtually ceased. Most mexicanos worked in agriculture, mining, and freighting. Because of Arizona's great dependence on Sonora freighting, the arrival of the railroad led to a long-term depression for mexicanos in the Tucson area although some were employed in railroad construction. Many left for California and for other parts of Arizona such as the Salt River valley and the numerous copper-mining centers. After 1890 mining became the number one economic activity and source of jobs; Douglas, Bisbee, Morenci, Globe, Miami, and many lesser mining towns attracted mexicanos from the border region and Sonora. From early on there was considerable segregation, both on the job and in company housing.

A congressional decision in 1910 that Arizona and New Mexico should be admitted as separate states led to calling constitutional conventions at Tucson and Santa Fe. At the Arizona convention only one of the 52 elected members was a Mexican American. In Santa Fe, hispano delegates, who constituted slightly over one-third of the total membership of 100, made a strong and ultimately successful effort to include their heritage in the document they drew up. Widespread discussion of "race" and language issues took place. The constitution they wrote reiterated the guarantees of the Treaty of Guadalupe Hidalgo and provided for the equality in law of Spanish and English. Recognizing the bilingual nature of New Mexican society, Article VIII required the legislature to make available training to prepare teachers to be capable of teaching in both languages. This provision has never been fully implemented.

Key ethnic provisions of the constitution were made virtually unamendable by stipulating that any amendments to these provisions had to be approved by a three-fourths vote in the whole state and a two-thirds vote in every county. Recognition of civil rights and the Hispanic heritage was thus made an intrinsic and virtually unalterable part of the constitution, even though they have been little observed in practice.

While the movement for statehood was reaching its climax, cultural changes were occurring which added new dimensions to existing conflict within New Mexican society. One of these was a tendency of nuevo-mexicanos to disassociate themselves from the Mexicans who began arriving at the end of the century. Considering themselves superior to the poverty-stricken who made up much of this immigration and feeling their socioeconomic position was threatened, nuevomexicanos denied having anything in common with the recent arrivals and often referred to them by the pejorative term *surrumatos*. This disassociation was buttressed also by calling themselves Spanish Americans or hispanos rather than Mexican Americans.

Another aspect of change was an increased trend among elites toward acculturation with Anglo society, a move which attenuated somewhat the conflict between the two cultures. This pattern of transition and change was suddenly interrupted at the beginning of the twentieth century by a cataclysmic event in Mexico which caused thousands of Mexicans to flee across the border into the United States. This event, which was to alter greatly the circumstances of the earlier Mexican American population of the Southwest, was the Mexican revolution of 1910.

7

NORTH FROM MEXICO

A traveler between Mexico and the United States in the second half of the nineteenth century would have found it difficult to know when he had crossed the frontier unless the boundary was marked. There was a virtually indistinguishable similarity from one side to the other, and until the last decade of the century, economic and social interaction across the border remained relatively unchanged. However, as communication and railroad transportation in northern Mexico and the American Southwest integrated the two areas more closely into their respective national economies, events in the heartland of both countries began to have greater impact on the border region. At the same time political and economic developments in the Southwest began to affect Mexico more directly. This growing interrelationship especially affected Mexican Americans as immigration from Mexico both reinforced and restructured their culture.

Some changes were brought on as a result of a regular flow of refugees from Mexico into the Southwest, particularly into Texas. One early political refugee, whose later career greatly affected the history of both Mexico and the Southwest, was Porfirio Díaz. This young mestizo officer rose to prominence during the war against the French as one of Benito Juárez's most successful generals, but later broke with his commander-in-chief. In the presidential elections of 1867 and 1871 he ran against Juárez and lost; after his second defeat he accused Juárez of electoral fraud and raised the standard of revolt, unsuccessfully.

After Juárez's death in 1872 and the installation of his successor, Sebastián Lerdo de Tejada, Díaz made another unsuccessful bid for power. Before the 1876 election, while in Texas exile, he again organized a revolt, this time successfully, to overthrow Lerdo. Believing that Mexico needed a strong caudillo to give it stability, Díaz seized control of the government and proclaimed himself president. From his assumption of the presidency in 1876 to the end of the century he became increasingly the master of Mexico, directing its economy as well as the government. Political stabilization and greater domestic tranquillity encouraged foreign investors to take advantage of railroad subsidies, of government support for mineral and oil development, and of Díaz's liberal land policy. Additional property became available to large landowners, mostly foreign speculators, as the result of legislation such as the Ley Lerdo (the Lerdo Law, 1856), which brought about the breakup and sale of Indian communal lands. Left landless, many former small landowners were forced into peonage. While debt peonage among day laborers increased rapidly, domestic and foreign investors prospered as never before. While the rich got richer, Mexico's poor suffered.

The economic policies of the Díaz government were promoted by a group of positivists, who planned and worked for a modern, scientifically run Mexico which would take its rightful place in the world. They accepted a widely held contemporary theory that certain races were less advanced because of heredity and environment; they believed that Indians and their culture were inferior and therefore not a sound base on which to build a modern Mexico. In the name of progress they set out to Europeanize Mexico's Indians. Partly as a result of positivist ideas, Yaquis and other Indians were brutally hounded, and many were sold into virtual slavery to large landowners. By the beginning of the twentieth century, as European and American businessmen extended their influence, Mexico had become known as the mother of foreigners and the stepmother of Mexicans.

As more and more land came under the control of increasingly fewer hacienda owners in the later Díaz years, scarcity of land available to rural Mexicans led to increased class tensions. To compound the land distribution problem, Mexico's population increased from 9,400,000 in 1877 to 15,200,000 in 1910, largely because of a dramatic reduction in the mortality rate, especially infant mortality, a result of improved health care. At the same time the standard of living of the Mexican peón, working for less than twenty cents a day, became even more miserable than before as the cost of corn rose. These factors motivated Mexicans, especially in the central and eastern border states, to migrate to the American Southwest.

By 1910 Mexico had 15,000 miles of railroad, built almost exclusively for the export of minerals. Five railroads connected the mines of Chihuahua, Sonora, Nuevo León, Zacatecas, Durango, and San Luis Potosí with the United States border. Peones and day laborers of northern Mexico supplied most of the labor for constructing these railroads. Discriminated against by a dual wage system, Mexican workers were paid at a substantially lower rate than their American counterparts and were also restricted to the most menial jobs. As the railroads were completed, many Mexican workers moved across the border seeking a better life in the United States. In the Southwest they worked for American railroads and mining companies. Some of them subsequently returned to Mexico with new social and political ideas engendered by American labor union experience. They wanted economic and social improvements in their homeland and their ideas contributed to the revolution of 1910 and the downfall of Porfirio Díaz.

Meanwhile, even before the twentieth century began, increasing numbers of Mexicans began to complain about Díaz's policies. Anarcho-syndicalists, who espoused the belief that all government is a form of oppression and that the product of all labor should be use, not profit, emerged as leaders in Mexican social and labor reform. This new, more militant leadership began developing what was later to become the Liberal Party, which was in fact radical. Many of its principal organizers, driven out of Mexico because of their socialist philosophy and radical tactics, sought security in Mexican American communities of the Southwest.

In January 1904, Antonio Villarreal, Juan Sarabia, and the brothers Ricardo and Enrique Flores Magón, all important leaders of the Liberal movement, fled to Texas to escape persecution. First they settled in San Antonio, where they published *Regeneración*, a newspaper that attacked Díaz as the cause of Mexico's many social and economic ills. The following year the Flores Magón brothers and other exiled Liberals fled to St. Louis, where they continued to publish *Regeneración* and organized the Liberal Party in exile. Mexican government agents followed the Flores Magón brothers into the Midwest with the implicit sanction of the American government. Persistent harassment by Díaz's agents compelled the brothers to flee to Canada, first to Toronto, then to Quebec. Ultimately, they returned to the United States in September 1906 and settled in El Paso. Using that border city as a base for their revolutionary activities, they continued to appeal to both Mexicans and Mexican Americans for help. In return for support they promised land in Mexico after they had overthrown President Díaz.

Meanwhile, other Mexican political exiles began organizing mexicano workers in the Southwest and encouraged union leaders to move toward political activism. For example, an important leader in this reform movement, Praxedis Guerrero, organized the Obreros Libres (Free Workers) in southeastern Arizona at Morenci, a leading copper-mining town with a predominantly Mexican labor force. To the south of Morenci during this same time, another Liberal leader was publishing *El Centenario* at the border town of Douglas. This newspaper and other revolutionary propaganda sheets were circulated among mexicano workers in the Arizona copper mines, as well as in Mexican mining towns across the border. Soon the activities of these exiles began to be felt in both the American Southwest and the Mexican border states of Sonora, Chihuahua, and Coahuila.

In September 1906 uprisings organized by the exiles broke out in Agua Prieta, Ciudad Juárez, and other Mexican frontier towns, but were suppressed. Captured leaders of these ill-fated attempts were jailed; however, some avoided arrest by fleeing across the border to the sanctuary of Mexican American communities. Among those who managed to escape was Ricardo Flores Magón, who fled to southern California, where he and other leaders found support among local mexicanos. In Los Angeles a group under his leadership continued to work for the overthrow of the Díaz dictatorship, publishing an anti-Díaz newspaper, *Revolución*. By disseminating revolutionary pamphlets, organizing secret cells, holding meetings, and raising funds for their activities, this movement made important contributions to the eventual overthrow of Díaz. When the revolution broke out in 1910 Mexican exiles and mexicanos were already organized to fight.

Díaz's downfall was finally precipitated by the political campaign waged against him by a member of the landed elite, Francisco I. Madero, in the 1910 presidential elections. Because Madero dared to challenge his control, Díaz had him jailed for insulting the authorities and fomenting revolution. Released from prison after Díaz's reelection, Madero fled north, seeking refuge among Mexican Americans in San Antonio, Texas. Madero recognized that it would take more than political rhetoric to overthrow Díaz and began plotting with other exiles and Mexican Americans to invade Mexico.

Farther west in El Paso the Flores Magón brothers were ready; when the Madero revolt began they crossed over into Chihuahua with about 100 men, including some Mexican Americans. Quickly disillusioned with Madero because he had reformist rather than revolutionary goals, principally "reestablishing" free elections, the brothers soon returned to the United States and again set up headquarters in Los Angeles. From there they organized a second invasion, this time into Baja California. Their ragtag army was successful in capturing Tijuana and Mexicali but was later forced to withdraw into California. In Los Angeles the Flores Magón brothers began to organize another revolutionary movement in Mexico. Ricardo became increasingly more isolated from the revolution's mainstream as he turned more radical. In 1918 he was arrested for violating U.S. neutrality laws and sentenced to twenty years in prison. He died there four years later.

Meanwhile, vigorous leadership by onetime bandit and cattle thief Francisco (Pancho) Villa, along with the landowner governor of Coahuila, Venustiano Carranza, and other followers of Madero (*maderistas*), enabled the revolutionary movement to establish a base in northern Mexico and sweep quickly southward. Díaz, soon abandoned by most of his supporters, was forced to resign in May 1911 and went into European exile. In the elections that were quickly held, Madero won overwhelmingly and assumed the presidency. Everyone thought the revolution was over; however, it had scarcely begun.

Disappointed because Madero failed to restore lands to the Indians, Emiliano Zapata, the radical southern revolutionary leader from the state of Morelos, recalled his followers to arms and again took up the destruction of haciendas, particularly hacienda records. Other, more moderate leaders followed his example in opposing the president. Early in 1913 a counterrevolutionary plot led by Madero's own general, Victoriano Huerta; Díaz's nephew, Félix Díaz; and Bernardo Reyes, a longtime Porfirian general, and assisted by the American ambassador,

Henry Lane Wilson, resulted in Madero's overthrow. His betrayal, seizure, and subsequent assassination on orders from Huerta were portents of the bloodstained years to follow.

General Huerta quickly took control of the government. However, one revolutionary leader after another denounced him as a bloody tyrant and "pronounced" against his government. In the north Venustiano Carranza initiated a movement to overthrow Huerta. He was quickly followed in this move by Pancho Villa, who led his ragged army and fearsome *dorado* cavalry in a binge of shooting and looting in support of Carranza. In Mexico's northwest Alvaro Obregón's terrifying Yaqui troops, armed with bows and arrows, also moved against Huerta; and in the state of Morelos, Zapata's continuing bloody record soon earned him designation in the press as the "Attila of the South." Within a year and a half Huerta suffered complete defeat and went into exile to Jamaica, then England, Spain, and finally in March 1915 to New York City.

From New York, Huerta entrained for San Francisco in June, but surreptitiously left the train in New Mexico. He was immediately detained by Justice Department deputies. Later he was released under bond. Reports of pro-Huerta plotting in the colonias of Galveston, San Antonio, and Eagle Pass quickly followed his release. (Elfego Baca was his U.S. representative for a while.) Refugee Mexicans who visited Huerta at this time were harassed by American officials in order to discourage counterrevolutionary activity. Later in the year, when he was jailed again, apprehension developed that members of the Mexican colonia in El Paso might try to free him. However, this concern proved baseless and he remained in custody. Huerta, who had a history of alcoholism and drug abuse, began to drink excessively, causing his health to deteriorate rapidly. As a result of inordinate dissipation he died early in January 1916, after an unsuccessful gallbladder operation.

Meanwhile, the struggle between various leaders for control of the revolutionary movement continued. As they fought for power, their contending armies looted, burned, raped, and committed other atrocities in the name of the revolution. Finally, with the assassination of Carranza and the rise of Alvaro Obregón to presidential power this gory phase of revolutionary fighting came to an end in May 1920.

The 1910 revolution, a period of incredible violence and confusion, directly affected the Southwest. Out of fifteen million Mexicans an estimated one million lost their lives in the decade of revolution, and there was a large-scale displacement of people. Thousands fled from the countryside into the larger towns and cities of Mexico; at the same time other thousands fled northward to the United States. No one knows precisely how many Mexicans were involved in this great exodus; one estimate holds that more than one million Mexicans crossed over into the Southwest between 1910 and 1920. Many of these returned when conditions in Mexico began to stabilize somewhat, especially after Obregón's ascension to the presidency.

In addition to thousands of peasants uprooted by the revolution, soldiers and supporters of revolutionary leaders like Villa, Obregón, Carranza, and even Zapata crossed over to the United States. This mass movement at times included supporters of the governments in power between 1910 and 1930. Besides government officials it was composed of politicians of various stripes, businessmen, high-ranking army officers, intellectuals, lawyers, and journalists. Because they fled from a cataclysm, the migrants of this wave came from more varied backgrounds than those of other Mexican migrations before and since. Included was a large percentage of women, children, and older persons. Many of the exiles were educated and sophisticated, but a large majority were uneducated casual workers and peones who were considered inferior by Mexican elites as well as Anglos. Mexican intellectuals strongly resisted Americanization and viewed their fellows as "mexicanos de afuera." These displaced people greatly increased the population of Mexican American border towns and barrios. Despite plans to the contrary, many ultimately settled in the United States since they found comfort and cultural security in the familiar milieu of Mexican American communities. Of those who later did return, many found that they and Mexico had both changed; consequently, many returnees eventually migrated back to the United States.

The wave of Mexican immigrants brought to the United States by the revolution included some who managed to escape with enough capital to start businesses in southwestern barrios. Among them also were landowners, merchants, and intellectuals. These last were important in creating a larger number of Spanish-language newspapers and bookstores. By 1920 this group had increased substantially the tiny Spanish-speaking middle class along the border. Moreover, as time passed, the exiled elites provided more and more leadership in the barrios. For many middle- and upper-class refugees accommodation to life in the United States was relatively easy, since they changed their geographic location, not their way of life. However, most refugees from the revolution were poor, without resources, education, or training and were forced therefore to accept menial agricultural and industrial work in order to survive. Typically they favored traditional ways and mistrusted change.

At the same time that the revolution was causing thousands of peones to migrate, the demand for workers in the Southwest was growing rapidly. The need for labor in the Southwest during this period came about because of a number of factors that coincided. Between 1870 and 1900 the total farm acreage in the American West tripled, and land under irrigation increased dramatically from 60,000 to 1,446,000 acres. By the beginning of the twentieth century sugar-beet acreage in California and Colorado had expanded greatly as a result of protective sugar rates set by the Dingley Tariff of 1897. The expansion of lands under irrigation, encouraged by the Reclamation Act of 1902, began to open up much of the Southwest to the cultivation of cotton. When the Roosevelt Dam on the Salt River in Arizona was completed, thousands of previously untilled acres became available for farming, and the Salt River valley soon became a major cotton-producing area. Elephant Butte Dam on the Rio Grande in New Mexico had a similar impact in the south-central part of that state. However, the production of these two areas did not fully satisfy the growing needs of the automobile industry for cotton used in the manufacture of millions of tires, or the Allied powers' requirements for uniforms during World War I. As a result of continuing demand, in central and western Texas cotton began to replace cattle as the primary economic base, and in Arizona and southern California farmers plowed up grazing land in order to increase their cotton acreage. This increase in cotton lands led to an expanded need for workers and to intensified recruitment of labor at the Mexican border.

While demand for more agricultural workers was mushrooming, the task of completing western railroad networks also put unskilled labor at a premium at a time when Oriental immigration dropped drastically. Chinese had formed an important part of western railroad construction gangs since their recruitment for the Central Pacific Railroad in the 1860s. When the severe depression of the mid-1870s hit the country, nativistic unions of the Pacific coast became aroused by the competition of Chinese labor. Pressured by unions and other exclusionist groups, Congress passed Chinese exclusion acts in 1882, 1892, and 1902. These acts and the 1907 Gentleman's Agreement with Japan kept out working-class Asians and by 1910 created a considerable shortage in western labor. Into this labor void the dispossessed and displaced from Mexico moved with ease.

As southwestern railroads continued to experience great labor shortages, their agents successfully recruited workers both among Mexican Americans and across the border among Mexicans. By about 1900 the Southern Pacific and Santa Fe railroads seriously began soliciting Mexican labor in El Paso, Texas. A decade later these two railroads were averaging more than a thousand recruits a month among mexicanos on the border; this recruitment reached its peak just prior to the outbreak of World War I. When that war erupted in Europe in 1914, American economic activity expanded rapidly. The United States became chief supplier to the Allies, and demand for industrial as well as agricultural workers soared. The war drastically reduced European worker immigration, while the initial U.S. response of preparedness meant that many young Americans left the labor market to enter the armed forces. To fill the labor gap Mexican workers were recruited to work in California's diversified agriculture, Colorado beet fields, Texas cotton fields, and in the copper mines of Arizona and New Mexico. They also were employed in northeastern iron foundries, in Appalachian coal mines, and on railroads all over the United States. In much of the Southwest they rapidly displaced Japanese, Greeks, Italians, and other earlier minority immigrant groups, especially after quota legislation in the early 1920s restricted European immigration.

Also modifying traditional Mexican American life was the changing socioeconomic structure in the Southwest. The change centered on Mexican Americans' relationship to the land. The new agriculture of the Southwest, based on large-scale mechanized commercial operations, required considerable capital investment in machinery as well as in land. Applying the technology of this highly competitive agriculture meant a greater investment in land leveling, extensive irrigation ditching, and other land preparation. These increased costs made it difficult for most Mexican Americans, who generally lacked capital, to remain competitive. Many were forced to sell their lands, or eventually lost them through tax foreclosures, especially in New Mexico and Arizona. Others were displaced as more dams were built and river-bottom farmlands were forever flooded.

At the turn of the century demand for workers was particularly strong in the sugar-beet industry. By the time the United States entered World War I in 1917, Colorado beet growers were using large numbers of migrants, principally Mexican Americans from New Mexico and Texas, to replace the dwindling number of Europeans. Within ten years mexicanos had become the mainstay of the industry and constituted more than half the sugar-beet workers in Colorado. In order to assure themselves of a regular and readily available labor supply, sugar companies at this time began to develop local labor colonias and encouraged migrants to settle in them rather than return to New Mexico or Texas for the winter. Also migratory workers began to winter over of their own volition, especially in larger cities in sugar-beet production areas, and gradually abandoned their annual return southward. These settlements became the bases of today's large Mexican American communities in many western cities. Denver, for example, quickly attracted a pool of Mexican American workers for the Colorado beet-growing area and soon developed into a major reservoir of agricultural workers for the entire Rocky Mountain region.

A dramatic change occurred in the Southwest as migrant mexicano labor began to replace southern tenant farmers and sharecroppers. This trend toward more extensive use of temporary workers was accelerated by the shift to large-scale agriculture and by the large numbers of migrant workers who became available between 1910 and 1920. Wage labor, though an improvement over tenancy, was still highly exploitive. Many agribusiness companies favored recruiting Mexican families and then established wage discrimination against women and children. By 1917, Arizona and New Mexico cotton growers, following the pattern set in the sugar-beet industry, were recruiting thousands of harvest workers in northern Mexico.

In California too, cotton brought about a shift to Mexican labor. Although many California farmers declared a preference for Chinese workers, whom they had traditionally used, growers in the Imperial Valley began recruiting Mexicans in Baja California and Sonora even before World War I. As wartime demand expanded cotton growing into the southern San Joaquin Valley, the resulting labor demand led to recruitment of thousands of Mexicans. At the end of the cotton harvest many of these migrants wintered in the Los Angeles area, and large worker colonias developed there, as they did in the Rocky Mountain region. By 1916 this labor force had overflowed the traditional boundaries of Mexican settlement in Los Angeles, causing a movement from old Sonoratown eastward into the Belvedere section of the city.

A majority of the workers were peasants from tiny villages on the immense central plateau of Mexico and were predominantly mestizo and Indian. They fled Mexico to escape peonage, economic servitude, and extreme poverty and to share in the economic bonanza of the American Southwest. They came not only as *solos* but also in family groups and even extended families, continuing patterns set in the latter 1800s by cotton-harvest workers in Texas. Accustomed to fierce exploitation at home, they found the subsistence wages and wretched working conditions of southwestern agriculture not only acceptable but even attractive. They were long-suffering, hardworking, and not likely to complain about their treatment. They were stereotyped by many Anglos as improvident, irresponsible, dishonest in small ways, secretive, dirty, distrustful, childishly sensitive, sentimental, gambling, hard-drinking—all adjectives applied earlier to the most recent immigrant group. Without them southwestern agriculture might have had a rather different history.

The new immigrants made productive and successful agricultural employees, but they were never able to achieve yeoman status. They remained wage workers. Their origins and nurture in small-town, rural Mexico late in the Díaz period fitted them for the role of hired hands in agricultural America. They had a dual adjustment to make: Americanization and mechanization. Few acquired land of their own. Even small-family farming, the only kind they might have aspired to, was far beyond their resources. Also, small farms were increasingly being replaced by emerging agribusiness, by factories-in-the-field.

Texas, like California and New Mexico, underwent major economic changes during this era, especially in agriculture. Farm expansion in the lower Rio Grande Valley in the early years of the twentieth century resulted from increased demand for fresh vegetables in America's large urban centers. This development, in what became known as the Winter Garden area, depended heavily on availability of cheap mexicano labor as well as irrigation and refrigerated railroad cars. Mexicanos grubbed cactus and chaparral, cleared land, planted and harvested crops, and generally made themselves indispensable to the economy of rural Texas.

They were especially important in the expanding cultivation of such labor-intensive crops as lettuce, spinach, carrots, and beans.

With the shift from tenancy and sharecropping to migratory labor, various techniques were used to tie mexicanos to specific areas. One device employed by farmers to retain a work force for the following spring was to provide migrant workers with a few acres for their personal use. Another widely adopted technique was de facto peonage, in which workers were kept from leaving by means of salary advances, debts, and outright coercion. However, low Texas wages and promises of higher wages elsewhere reduced the ability of growers to hold their labor force and led to extensive labor pirating. San Antonio and El Paso developed early mexicano labor pools, and local agricultural employers found the persistent activities of out-of-state railroad and sugar-beet labor recruiters particularly annoying.

Patterns of immigration from Mexico changed rapidly as a result of the entry of the United States into World War I. The Selective Service Act passed in 1917 served to discourage immigrants. Rumors that all immigrants would be drafted and 1917 legislation which imposed literacy qualifications and an $8.00 head tax temporarily checked the worker tide from Mexico. Soon railroads and large-scale agriculture, feeling the labor pinch more intensely because of wartime needs, began to pressure the United States government to permit extensive recruitment of workers in Mexico. In response Congress waived the new immigration requirements for agricultural workers in May 1917. A year later this waiver was expanded to include Mexicans to work on railroads, in coal mines, and on government construction projects. Also the 1885 law against importing contract labor was ignored.

Ultimately exemptions to the 1917 Immigration Act were extended until the end of June 1920. During this three-year period, approximately 50,000 Mexicans legally crossed the border into the United States on a temporary basis—that is, as bracero sojourners—and perhaps 100,000 entered the country without documents. No agreement existed between the U.S. and Mexican governments with respect to these workers, and they had no guarantees concerning employment or living conditions. Low wages and poor housing prevailed. Often employment was of short duration, but most of those who imported labor refused to accept any responsibility to repatriate Mexican nationals. As a result, there was widespread economic distress among Mexican cotton-harvest workers in the early 1920s.

The heavy influx of Mexican workers into southwestern agriculture, mining, and railroading had a domino effect on Mexican American labor in border areas. Prompted to seek work elsewhere by increased low-wage competition from immigrants and attracted by wartime opportunities in industrial centers, Mexican Americans for the first time began to migrate in numbers to midwestern and northeastern cities. Many moved into the industrial labor vacuum created by World War I. Others, less fortunate, found menial jobs in agriculture and on railroads. Mexican Americans were able to obtain steady industrial employment far more readily than Mexican nationals because they spoke English and were more acculturated than the recent immigrants.

Mexican Americans began to appear in numerous midwestern cities: St. Louis, Kansas City, Omaha, Chicago, Gary, and Detroit. Small colonias began to form as workers obtained long-term employment and brought their families. Steel plants, packinghouses, automobile factories, coal mines, and other industries recruited them to work in Pennsylvania, Illinois, Ohio, Indiana, Missouri, and Michigan. Most industrial work available to them was unskilled, hazardous, arduous, and dirty. Nevertheless, it paid better than agricultural work and tended to be regular; thus it improved their economic position. Jobs in government construction, especially in the building of military camps, also enabled many to move out of low-pay casual agricultural employment.

In 1918 several hundred mexicanos came to Detroit to work in the auto plants. By the end of World War I about 2,500 were living in the Detroit colonia, and during the winter months another 4,000 to 5,000 workers from Michigan's beet fields joined them. The Chicago colonia had about 4,000 Mexican workers at the war's end, and perhaps 50,000 were scattered elsewhere in the Midwest and Northeast. Kansas City and St. Louis had become established as worker stopover and distribution centers. In contrast to the 70,000 mexicanos located east of the Mississippi, approximately 700,000 lived in the four states of Texas, New Mexico, Arizona, and California. In addition to making available steady employment at relatively good wages in mills, factories, mines, and government construction projects, World War I afforded some of them useful experience in the U.S. armed forces both at home and overseas.

The Selective Service Act of 1917 caused many Mexicans to return to Mexico for fear they would be drafted into service. Foreign residents who had declared their intent to become citizens and all children born in the United States were legally subject to the draft. Many of this group, however, lived isolated lives, spoke only Spanish, and considered themselves Mexicans, not Americans. It is only fair to point out that many Anglos also considered them Mexicans. Thousands of Mexican Americans served valiantly in the American Army and Navy despite being urged not to join the armed forces by some leaders like Ricardo Flores Magón. Their record for voluntary enlistment was proportionately greater than that of any other ethnic group.

Although Mexican Americans proved their loyalty by excellent records in the armed services and by civilian support of the war effort, they continued to experience discrimination and racism, and their patriotism was frequently questioned. In southern Texas especially, Anglo Americans often identified them with enemies of the United States. Among the occasions for this suspicion was the revelation in March 1917 of a German offer to support Mexico against the United States. The famous Zimmermann telegram, intercepted by the Allies, promised that if Mexico joined the Central Powers, lands surrendered to the United States in the Treaty of Guadalupe Hidalgo would be returned after Germany defeated America.

Along with the implications of the Zimmermann note and German propaganda, many other matters intensified long-standing animosities between Americans and Mexicans along the border. In Texas there was widespread raiding and organized banditry as border gangs took advantage of Mexican revolutionary confusion to loot and plunder. Mexicanos were usually blamed for the pillaging, and an explosive climate was created as existing prejudices were enflamed. Border unrest and atrocities stemming from the Mexican revolution of 1910 plus indiscriminate and often criminal retaliation by the Texas Rangers and vigilantes, the unwarranted United States seizure of Veracruz in 1914, the arrest of a Mexican national in 1915 with a fantasy "Plan de San Diego (Texas)" for an insurrection which would establish an independent southwestern nation, and especially Pancho Villa's vengeful border raids in 1917 leading to General John J. Pershing's yearlong punitive expedition into northern Mexico—all contributed to increasing violence against Mexican Americans in the Southwest.

During the first two decades of the twentieth century there were widespread instances in Texas of mexicanos being subjected to threats, torture, flogging, castration, and thinly disguised murder. Many innocent mexicanos lost their lives as a result of Ranger "policing," local posse action, shootings, lynchings, and other mob violence. Some fled across the border, seeking asylum in Mexico, where they were sometimes preyed upon by local officials. By 1920 the Ku Klux Klan had become very active in southwestern mining camps, where it viciously persecuted mexicanos. Despite facing suspicion, hostility, discrimination, and prejudice during the war years, most Mexican Americans remained loyal to the United States.

World War I left a considerable residue of alienation and mistrust in Mexican American communities. In Texas the term *rinche* ("ranger") became a word used to frighten little children into being good. In 1919 Texas representative José T. Canales compiled a long list of charges against the Rangers which caused the legislature to reduce their numbers to 76 men and to place a tighter rein on the smaller force.

In the long run perhaps the most important result for Mexican Americans from World War I was that for the first time thousands of them moved out of their familiar southwestern world seeking better opportunities elsewhere in the United States. This exodus was impelled by continuing waves of Mexican immigrants who kept wages low, caused tougher competition for jobs, and reduced economic opportunity. The move weakened long-standing patterns of isolation and ethnic cohesion.

The horizons of many Mexican Americans were broadened by important World War I experiences in both civilian life and the armed services. Their levels of economic and social expectations were raised. The war also helped educate and give experience to an ethnic leadership that was vital to Mexican American organizational development during the 1920s.

8

MANDE VD., SEÑOR

Mexican immigration to the United States since 1900 is one of the great migratory movements in the history of the Americas. Between 1900 and 1990 it brought across the border two and one half million settlers with documents and a much larger, but indeterminate, number of undocumenteds. Over the years migrants have encompassed great variety; they came as permanent immigrants, legal and illegal; sojourners or commuters, daily, regular, and seasonal; temporary workers called braceros, on contract or on their own initiative; and refugees, businessmen, students, and tourists. Crossing a border that is both barrier and gateway into a country that offers bilingual accommodation, migrants have had exceptional influence on Mexican Americans in this century. Because of their considerable economic, social, and cultural impact the story of their migration requires a closer look.

Anthropologists have pointed out that this migratory movement is deeply rooted in the Mexican past. Some Chicano writers have described it as a return of Mexicans to the area of their origins—to Aztlán, the mythical northern homeland of the Mexican people. The movement was established long before the 1848 Treaty of Guadalupe Hidalgo drew a new boundary line between Mexico and the United States. Scholars emphasize that for the most part migration since the treaty was not out of one culture into another, but within a culture common to both sides of the international border. In the absence of border controls until the beginning of the twentieth century, crossings both ways continued in an informal manner with little heed for the new frontier.

From Mexico cowboys, sheepherders, miners, harvest workers, and others crossed over to visit and to take advantage of employment at higher wages in the Southwest; and, beginning in the latter days of the Porfiriato, political refugees of various persuasions from all economic levels fled to the safety of barrios in the United States. For over half a century the international boundary did little to separate Mexican American and Mexican. Until World War II they constituted a single community in the Southwest; American society seldom distinguished between the two and segregated them in the same barrio. Cultural continuity and considerable freedom to travel both ways across the border often meant that migrating to the United States involved a less than definitive commitment. In fact, an overwhelming majority of migrants initially intended to return to Mexico.

No one knows how many Mexicans migrated in the nineteenth century or how many remained permanently in the Southwest before 1900. From census reports it appears that immigration was sizable in relation to the generally sparse border population. More important than its size is the fact that this continuous northward flow established precedents and patterns for twentieth-century migration.

Distinct waves can be discerned in Mexican migration to the United States since 1900. The first significant wave, mostly from central and eastern Mexican border states, began at the turn of the century. Set in motion by population pressures and economic as well as political events leading up to the revolution of 1910, it brought as many as 100,000 Mexican nationals to the United States by 1914. The great majority went to Texas; perhaps 25,000 settled around San Antonio. Made up mostly of refugees, this first group was heterogeneous in its composition. As the revolution continued year after year, elite refugees emigrated principally for political reasons and planned to return as soon as expedient. This early wave gave a bare hint of the migration to come.

A second and much larger wave began at the outbreak of World War I in 1914 and continued through the 1920s. These immigrants, who numbered over one million, were mostly peasant farmers, small tradesmen, craftsmen, day workers, and peones who came primarily for economic reasons. Some came for religious reasons, especially during the

Cristero persecutions of the twenties. This wave most closely resembled earlier European immigrant waves. The majority, fleeing Mexico's endemic poverty, found that the burgeoning industrial Southwest welcomed them with open arms. About half this second wave came from the northeastern border states that had spawned the first group. The remainder, with California as its destination, came from the plateau of west-central Mexico.

According to census statistics, the Mexico-born population of the United States grew from about 103,000 to 1,400,000 between 1900 and 1930. The volume of the second wave provided the matrix for most present-day Mexican American communities, except in New Mexico, which attracted few from this wave. The new immigrants reinforced existing Mexican American culture and also helped to increase awareness of cultural roots.

During the 1920s important changes in immigration and settlement patterns began to emerge. By the mid-twenties Mexican immigrants began settling outside the traditional area of the Southwest. Recruited along with Mexican Americans by midwestern companies, immigrants of the large second wave fanned out in the United States; they reached Illinois and Pennsylvania in the Northeast and California, Oregon, and Washington in the West. Because of increasing employment opportunities in California proportionately more immigrants of this wave settled there than had earlier. As a result, during the twenties California had an annual increase in mexicano population of 20.4 percent; its population of Mexican descent grew to more than a third of a million by 1930. Texas, the destination of earlier Mexican immigrants, showed a yearly increase of only 7.6 percent. The sharp increase in California is undoubtedly explained by greater economic opportunities stemming from its booming agriculture and industry, compared to a slower rate of development in Texas.

The large second wave of immigration (1914–30) created great reservoirs of mexicano labor in many southwestern cities. By 1925 Los Angeles had a larger Mexican population than any city in Mexico except the national capital. Other important Mexican colonias had been established in California at San Jose, Fresno, Brawley, El Centro, Calipatria, and Calexico. The rapid explosion of southern California's mexicano population created an increasingly important source of workers for west coast agriculture and manufacturing as far north as the state of Washington and even Alaska. Little thought was given to the importance of meeting the various needs of this expanded mexicano work force.

A more modest expansion took place in Texas. By 1930 its mexicano population had grown to more than two-thirds of a million people, the majority located along the border. El Paso, San Antonio, and other large cities became transient stopping-off places for immigrant Mexicans. During the twenties 20,000 or more Mexican workers passed through San Antonio each year on their way north. Texas cities became recruiting centers for the labor needs of the North, Northwest, and Northeast and from them migration routes developed, spreading out in an arc from California to New York. The routes northward usually followed railroad lines, which provided both transportation and jobs for many migrants. By the second half of the twenties not even the southwestern labor reservoirs held enough workers. In 1926 the Arizona Cotton Growers Association began lobbying for changes in immigration legislation that would permit growers to bring in more Mexicans.

Recruitment of Mexican workers became increasingly important after the 1921 and 1924 U.S. immigration acts which greatly reduced entrance from Eastern and Southern Europe and thereby diminished the unskilled labor pool. Western railroads, particularly affected by the change, sought a new source of cheap labor to replace Greeks, Poles, Italians, and other Europeans who left menial jobs as they moved up the economic ladder. In the 1920s the Southern Pacific and other railroads were employing increasingly larger numbers of Mexicans and Mexican Americans, especially as track maintenance workers. A 1929 study showed that between 70 and 90 percent of track workers on southwestern railroads were mexicanos and that in Texas they were rapidly supplanting Negroes. The increased hiring of Mexicans by railroads led to the spread of colonias throughout the West. Often these developed from mobile boxcar work camps established along railroad routes.

Mexican railroad labor was recruited to work as far north as Michigan and as far east as Pennsylvania. The Pennsylvania Railroad brought approximately 3,000 mexicanos north to work on rail maintenance in the early 1920s, but by the end of the decade only a few hundred remained. The Baltimore & Ohio Railroad had similar attrition rates with the Mexicans it brought to the Northeast. Harsh winter conditions of outdoor work and the unfamiliar milieu in the North seem to have been important factors in discouraging mexicano workers. Within a few years most of the recruited mexicanos either had moved from railroading into other industrial work or had returned to the Southwest.

Because of post-World War I steel strikes mills began recruiting mexicano workers in the Southwest. In 1923 Bethlehem Steel brought about 1,000 Spanish speakers from Texas to act as strikebreakers in its Bethlehem, Pennsylvania, plant. In the same year National Tube Company, an affiliate of United States Steel, recruited about 1,500 Texas mexicanos for its Lorain, Ohio, plant. Illinois Steel Mills, in Chicago, also recruited Mexican Americans from the Southwest and in 1923 brought workers north from the Fort Worth area. Many were unaware that they were being hired as strikebreakers; others were willing to act as scabs to get a foothold in industry. Mexicanos were also generally excluded from Anglo unions.

As the mexicano population of Detroit increased, a Church of Our Lady of Guadalupe was founded and a Comisión Honorifica Mexicana was established to help organize Cinco de Mayo, Diez y Seis de Septiembre, and other patriotic celebrations. By 1926 there were about 5,000 mexicanos and two years later the number had jumped to an estimated 15,000, undoubtedly partially a result of the Mexican government's religious persecution of Cristero rebels during the latter twenties as well as the movement to the cities.

Chicago's mexicano population expanded from 4,000 to nearly 20,000 between 1920 and 1930, making it the largest Spanish-speaking urban area in the United States outside the Southwest. Some Mexican Americans came directly to Chicago because of industrial recruitment; some came north in a series of short moves while working on railroads; others were attracted to the city from migratory employment in nearby Michigan sugar-beet fields. From their original jobs in sugar beets, steel, and railroad maintenance Mexican Americans in Chicago later moved into menial work in meat packing, utility companies, trucking, construction, dry cleaning, hotels, restaurants, and other service industries. The new jobs posed social and psychological problems. Some Mexican Americans had difficulty adjusting to the nature and tempo of industrial work. For many adapting to a society different from that in the Southwest was also troubling.

Mexicano workers were forced to seek housing in overcrowded Chicago ghettos where they were subjected to the prejudices of second-generation Poles, Italians, Slavs, and other European immigrants. Having become partially assimilated, the European immigrants saw themselves as 100 percent American and looked down on the newly arrived Mexicans. Like the majority of Americans, they viewed Mexicans with racial hostility and considered them foreign and inferior. In this difficult situation the mexicano community sought security and support, which it found in various organizations and especially in the church. In 1923 William T. Kane, S.J., established the first Mexican Catholic parish among steelworkers in South Chicago, Nuestra Señora de Guadalupe. It grew rapidly as Chicago's mexicano population expanded and by the end of the twenties it counted 8,000 parishioners. The newcomers helped form a 75-member musical group, the Banda Mexicana de Chicago, and a number of business and social clubs, all testifying to the vitality of the Mexican American community.

While Mexicans were entering the lower ranks of industrial employment in the Northwest, this change had not reached California. Concern about the effects of continuing heavy Mexican immigration into the state after World War I caused Governor Clement C. Young to create a Mexican Fact-Finding Committee in March 1928. Headed by the directors of the departments of Agriculture, Industrial Relations, and Social Welfare, the committee made a study of Mexicans in California and the implications of their continued immigration. The committee's published report indicated that by the 1920s Mexicans had become the main source of agricultural labor in California, replacing Chinese and Japanese who had previously supplied most farm labor. Already by World War I, an increasing number of California crops were harvested by Mexican workers. The committee did not ascertain exactly how many Mexican farm workers were in the state; it reported only that they numbered in the tens of thousands. Like other casual labor, mexicano workers experienced low wages, poor living conditions, and chronic underemployment. The committee seemed to be less concerned with living and working conditions of farm labor than with the growers' labor needs.

The report further stated that about 28,000 mexicanos were employed in manufacturing (more than 50 percent in the Los Angeles area), another 21,000 in the construction and building industries, and about 3,000 in fruit and vegetable canning. Six of the larger railroads in the state employed some 11,000 Mexicans; however, the committee estimated that the total of Mexican railroad workers was considerably larger.

Most Mexicans working for the railroads, as well as other industries, were unskilled. A few were employed as electricians, molders, machinists, woodworkers, blacksmiths, upholsterers, painters, and pressmen.

Economic conditions of Mexican Americans in most of the Southwest during the 1920s were below California levels. A sharp postwar depression developed in the United States during 1920 and 1921, resulting in industrial layoffs and widespread business failures. This recession affected mexicanos because it had a severe and long-lasting impact on western agriculture. As a result, a sizable number of Mexicans were repatriated, many with financial assistance from the Mexican government. Repatriation weakened and in some cases shattered family and social ties that had developed during the returnees' sojourning years in the United States.

The cotton industry particularly was seriously battered by the twenties' recession. When the price of cotton plummeted from 38 to 18 cents a pound in 1920, many southwestern growers went bankrupt. Thousands of Mexican and other workers lost their jobs. Many were unable to collect their accumulated unpaid wages and were forced to accept charity. Angered by growers' failure to pay the wages they owed, as well as by poor working conditions, some 4,000 Mexican workers in the Salt River cotton area of Arizona walked out of the fields in June 1920. However, the strike was unsuccessful because the workers, who lacked cohesion, faced a fairly solid front of growers and law enforcement agencies. Growers used the strike to justify defaulting on their commitment to provide return transportation to Mexico for imported workers. Finally, the arrest and deportation of some strike leaders brought the strike to an end. Strikebreaking tactics set a pattern to be repeated in the Southwest.

Along with a repatriation movement that developed because of the recession, an appreciable reduction of Mexican immigration to the United States took place as the wartime waiver of immigration restrictions was rescinded in mid-1920. Because of the scarcity of jobs greater numbers of undocumented immigrants began to find it expedient to return to Mexico. While some left voluntarily as jobs disappeared and economic opportunities declined, others were officially required to leave the United States. Midwestern industries that had encouraged Mexican workers to come to the United States during World War I began to send them home in 1920; some paid for return transportation. The

Ford Motor Company alone paid for the repatriation of 3,000 Mexican workers.

By 1923 the postwar recession and its effects were diminishing and demand for workers was increasing as agriculture in the Southwest underwent significant changes. Continuing low cotton prices and increasing consumption of salad vegetables caused some Arizona Salt River valley and California Imperial Valley growers to shift from cotton to lettuce. At the same time additional acreage was being added in the Imperial Valley through the extension of irrigation, and new citrus groves began to come into production in southern California. Agribusiness began paying agents to recruit farm workers. This practice led to the rapid development of a new entrepreneur in agriculture, the labor contractor, known in Mexican American communities as the *contratista* or *enganchista*.

Labor contractors served as brokers between mexicano workers and agricultural employers, especially those hiring laborers in large numbers. Typically contratistas were Mexican Americans whose familiarity with the language and customs of la raza, as well as with the labor requirements of the farmer, enabled them to secure migrant workers. Each contratista usually owned his own truck or trucks and contracted with farmers to provide a specified number of workers for a fixed fee per head. For decades he played an important role by recruiting, transporting, and supervising immigrant and Mexican American workers. Although both Anglo employers and mexicano workers found the contractor's services useful, he was frequently viewed with suspicion, especially by Mexicans. Often he was a shrewd businessman who might exploit the workers he recruited by providing food, drink, and other necessities at excessive prices. He was accused, often with justification, of cheating on wages and contracts.

The expanded demand for farm labor which produced the enganchista also led to a rapid rise in immigration, especially undocumented immigration, from Mexico. This trend aroused concern nationally, especially in Congress. Labor unions and nativistic groups loudly demanded that the movement of Mexicans into the United States be controlled and restricted. The first indication of serious congressional concern appeared in 1921, when an attempt was made to include Mexico within the quota system established by the immigration act of that year. When United States immigration policies were overhauled in 1924, an effort was again made to place Mexican immigration under the revised quota system. Despite growing exclusionist sentiment only a general clause in the 1924 Johnson-Reed Immigration Act establishing a $10 visa fee affected Mexicans.

Although attempts to reduce Mexican immigration continued throughout the twenties, western railroads and the southwestern farm bloc lobbied regularly in Congress to retain this source of cheap labor. They were successful in maintaining a continuing flow of Mexican workers. In its concern about illegal immigration the Justice Department petitioned Congress in 1920 to make unlawful entry a punishable offense. Although this request was not acted upon until the end of the decade, in 1924 Congress did appropriate $1,000,000 to establish the Border Patrol. In July 1924 this new agency began the almost impossible task of supervising and controlling the influx of migrants along a 2,000-mile border with a staff of 450 men.

A dramatic increase in the volume of emigration from Mexico in the mid-twenties led to a corresponding rise in nativism in the United States. In 1926 fresh attempts to limit Mexican immigration by including Mexico in the quota system began with a restrictive bill introduced in the House of Representatives by John C. Box of Texas. During the following four years Mexican immigration was studied and discussed in House and Senate committees, thereby initiating the first comprehensive consideration of its implications for the United States. During the hearings representatives of the railroads, mining interests, western farmers, beet-sugar manufacturers, and cattlemen testified to their employers' imperative need for Mexican labor. These groups maintained that an end to Mexican immigration or a quota limiting it would be extremely detrimental to their businesses and might drive them into bankruptcy. The State Department also strongly opposed restrictions, arguing that the Box bill was inconsistent with traditional American policy of special relations with Latin America.

In 1928 Senate hearings on Mexican immigration brought new support for restrictive legislation from various urban-based social service agencies, teacher organizations, public health agencies, and labor unions as well as nativistic and patriotic societies and some racist groups. The coalition in support of restrictive immigration represented both extremes of the political spectrum. Although their arguments presented a window dressing of social and economic concerns, clearly most supporters aimed at restricting what they considered an undesirable ethnic group. Box himself certainly considered it so; he referred to Mexicans as peonized, illiterate, and unclean. Opponents of limiting Mexican immigration also presented their views at the hearings. Because of widespread opposition, neither the bill nor the discussion got out of the congressional committees.

Only in 1930, after the question had become moot, was there discussion of the Mexican immigration issue on the floor of Congress. William J. Harris of Georgia sponsored a quota bill in the Senate, where opponents of restriction tried, in vain, to prevent its passage by amending it to death. However, the House failed to concur with the Senate bill and therefore the quota bill did not become law. Meanwhile, the State Department had already taken steps to implement a policy to end the highly emotional conflict.

At a meeting in Mexico City in February 1929 a totally different solution to the issue was initiated. American consuls in Mexico were instructed to reduce immigration by strict application of existing legislation, such as the Alien Contract Labor Law. Later that same year the stock market crash and the Great Depression that followed accomplished what restrictionists had been trying to achieve. Not only did the depression virtually halt Mexican immigration; it also encouraged a return flow. During the thirties thousands of Mexicans returned voluntarily and thousands more were virtually forced to repatriate. With this reverse movement the second wave of Mexican immigration in the twentieth century came to an end.

———

Statistics on Mexican immigration are important, but they must be used with great caution, for they can only indicate general trends. There are large discrepancies between immigration and repatriation statistics compiled by the United States and those by Mexico and smaller discrepancies among U.S. agencies. Until 1907 U.S. data on Mexican immigration refers only to seaport arrivals; since that time the United States has tabulated each individual legal entry, so that one person crossing the border into the United States five times appears in the statistical data as five immigrants. On the other hand, Mexican government figures on emigration probably have consistently underestimated the numbers crossing into the United States. Moreover, one must clearly differentiate between gross and net immigration figures in the statistics. Net figures represent the difference between the number of Mexicans entering and those leaving the United States in a given period.

Despite these problems, certain generalizations can be made from immigration and census statistics. According to 1900 census data, slightly more than 100,000 Mexican-born lived in the United States; some 90 percent were concentrated in Texas, California, New Mexico, and Arizona, with Texas having 70 percent of the total. Although immigration records for the first decade of the century indicate that legal Mexican immigration did not exceed 40,000 net, the 1910 census listed 222,000 Mexican-born in the United States. The conclusion is obvious: in the decade 1900–10 there must have been a net undocumented immigration of at least 80,000 Mexicans.

The same technique applied to the following census period indicates that illegal Mexican entrants for the decade of the teens must have reached 112,000. However, the next decade was different. Between 1921 and 1930 gross legal immigration totaled 459,000; in addition there was considerable undocumented immigration. However, the 1930 census indicated an increase of only 155,000 Mexican-born. The explanation for this difference between 1920 and 1930 statistics undoubtedly lies in the heavy repatriation in the postwar recession of 1921–22 and again in 1929 and 1930. While precise statistics on emigration are lacking, there is some evidence of the volume of this reverse migratory movement. To aid stranded persons returning to Mexico the Mexican government in 1921–22 spent $2,500,000 for food and transportation from the border back to their native towns and villages. This large sum indicates heavy repatriation during this period.

Because of the 1910 revolution the Mexican government could not be deeply concerned before 1917 about the emigration of its nationals. In 1917 Mexico, in an attempt to implement labor provisions of its constitution of that year, requested that American employers give written contracts to immigrants and that the U.S. government ratify them. The United States, then involved in World War I, had neither the motivation nor the interest in assuming this responsibility. Disappointed at American failure to respond, in late 1917 Mexico set up checkpoints on railroads that ran to the border in a futile attempt to stop workers from going to the United States. Because emigration acted as a safety valve, Mexico made no serious effort after the end of World War I to secure American compliance.

The second wave of emigration also had negative aspects. Mexico lost a sizable part of what was probably its more able and enterprising population. In addition, serious social problems developed from the long absences of workers who were heads of families. Some men eventually deserted wives and children as a result of these long separations.

One notable aspect of Mexican immigration to the United States in the twenties was the low level of naturalization. The immigrants tended to be sojourners rather than settlers. Of the 320,000 Mexican-born who were over twenty-one years of age in 1930, only 5.5 percent had become naturalized citizens, compared to 49.7 percent for the entire adult foreign-born population. The single most important reason for this low rate of naturalization was the recency of heavy Mexican immigration; it usually took about fifteen years for an immigrant to become naturalized. Then, too, since most Mexican immigrants intended to return to their homeland after a period of work in the United States, they were not disposed to seek citizenship. Also the cultural milieu of southwestern barrios enabled them to retain their Mexican identity and caused them to remain without becoming citizens. Anglo racist attitudes toward Mexicans led to social isolation and discrimination and inevitably had the effect of discouraging them. For many, illegal entry precluded the possibility of becoming citizens. Lastly, from a pragmatic point of view Mexicans stood to gain little from United States citizenship; at this time they were still considered Mexican.

Between 1900 and 1930 more than half a million Mexicans entered the United States legally. Of these, about half ultimately became Mexican Americans. Typically after three or four return trips to Mexico most settled in the Southwest, a majority in a dozen cities close to the border. Seasonal migration and seasonal rurality became increasingly the norm for them although a movement from agricultural to industrial work was beginning. The 1930 census indicated a greater urban concentration of mexicanos supplying labor for southwestern industries. It also revealed that there were about 180,000 Mexican Americans employed in agriculture and 150,000 in common labor. Of the latter group, approximately half worked in transportation, mostly on railroads. Only about 16,000 were employed in mining, principally in the expanding copper industry.

Despite their important contributions, Mexican Americans continued to be segregated economically and socially. Since most agricultural work was seasonal, many families moved from area to area, leading a migratory life that provided little stability. Those employed on the railroads and in mining were often isolated physically as well as culturally from the mainstream of society. Nearly all received wages that provided only a bare minimum subsistence. At the same time, as cheap labor they met with growing resentment from organized labor, which refused to open union doors to them. Their economic, social, and cultural isolation continued.

The prosperity of the Southwest in the first thirty years of this century was in large measure based on Mexican and Mexican American labor. Rapid expansion and modernization could not have taken place without mexicano workers. Although the economic importance of their labor was widely recognized, they were not adequately recompensed. One could argue that much of the prosperity of the era was at the expense of mexicanos in the form of low wages and poor working conditions. In a way they thus subsidized United States agriculture, industry, and mining. They still do.

9

DEPORTING JESÚS

At the beginning of the twentieth century the Southwest was increasingly influenced by railroad networks, large-scale mining, and commercial farming based on mass markets. As the border states became more fully integrated with the national economy there were further economic changes. Railroad transportation encouraged an upsurge in dry farming, which in turn led to greatly expanded irrigated agriculture after the great drought of the mid-1880s. Brush grubbing, land leveling, and irrigation ditching all required extensive labor, as did new crops and increased acreage in strawberries, citrus, melons, tomatoes, lettuce, and early spring vegetables. These changes were among the factors that stimulated immigration of workers from Mexico.

Development of large-scale business in the Southwest was paralleled by extensive labor organizing. This trend was especially conspicuous in copper mining in New Mexico, in coal mining in Colorado and Texas, and in California agriculture. Three labor organizations led in developing unionism in the West: the Industrial Workers of the World (IWW), the Western Federation of Miners (WFM), and the American Federation of Labor (AFL). The IWW, which was sympathetic to the plight of mexicanos, tried to organize agricultural workers but was not very successful. Tough and synonymous with radicalism, by 1920 it had disappeared. The WFM, associated with the IWW for a few years in the first decade of the twentieth century, actively recruited mexicanos and played an important role in western mining. The AFL, concerned primarily with skilled workers, generally excluded mexicanos and was opposed in principle to heavy immigration from Mexico. The failure of these organizations to gain permanent improvements for workers led to strikes and violence.

By the beginning of the century railroads had become one of the major employers of mexicano labor. Mexicans accounted for about three-fourths of all railroad employees, and a majority of immigrant workers from Mexico between 1900 and 1920 were employed on the railroads, at least for a time. The Southern Pacific and the Santa Fe hired them on six-month contracts for construction and maintenance labor. Mexicanos also provided most of the labor in mining and smelting, especially in the numerous copper mines of southeastern Arizona and southwestern New Mexico and in the coal mines of Colorado and Texas. To a lesser extent they worked as lumberjacks and in Texas oil fields and refineries.

Mexicanos formed a large part of the southwestern work force and also played important roles as activists and leaders in the development of labor unionism. In 1883 several hundred cowboys in the Texas panhandle went on strike against a number of large cattle companies and won their demands for better pay. Among the leaders of this work stoppage were Mexican vaqueros. Also in the 1880s an organization calling itself the Caballeros de Labor, patterned broadly after the national Knights of Labor, was begun in the Southwest by Juan José Herrera and others. At the end of the eighties Herrera founded a closely related group, the Gorras Blancas (White Caps), made up largely of poor nuevomexicanos, which often used terrorist tactics. Recognizing that ownership of land was a more pressing issue in the Southwest than wages and hours of labor, the Caballeros and Gorras Blancas concentrated their efforts on fighting Anglo land grabbing—with only moderate success. The objectives of the Caballeros were far more political than trade unionist; as a result, it developed little influence among mexicano workers, particularly recent immigrants. By the 1890s it was all but defunct.

In the 1890s the Western Federation of Miners began organizing in the Southwest with considerably wider impact on mexicano workers than had the Caballeros de Labor. The early success of the federation stemmed in part from its ability to develop union leadership among the Mexican mining population in the Southwest. These leaders acquired experience in organizing from local mutual-aid societies (*mutualistas*) and used them as vehicles for presenting labor demands. Already in the mid-1880s strikes were reported in New Mexico's copper mines, and in the following decade sporadic work stoppages continued.

As large-scale industrial and agricultural enterprises increased in the first decade of the 1900s, more serious union activity among Mexican Americans began to appear. At Telluride, Colorado, mexicanos were involved in one of the first strikes of the new century—both as striking members of the militant WFM and as strikebreakers. At the same time labor unrest developed in Arizona as a result of organizing activities among mexicano miners. In the thriving copper-mining region of Clifton-Morenci a walkout developed in June 1903 from a conflict over reduced pay. Initiated by mexicano miners, the strike failed to receive the support of Anglo workers. It was finally brought to an end by the unusual combination of a disastrous flash flood in which more than fifty persons died and the concurrent arrest, trial, and conviction of the strike leaders. Another example of the difficulties mine workers had in unionizing was the quashing of a strike organized by the Western Federation of Miners in the Colorado coalfields. By refusing to negotiate and then importing Mexican nationals as strikebreakers—a common and long-continuing practice—the mine owners forced an end to the strike in 1904.

Mexicanos were also involved in urban industrial labor disputes early in the century. In February and April 1903 hundreds of mexicanos went on strike against two Los Angeles street railways; both strikes failed. In August 1910 there was another Los Angeles railway strike. Early in the summer mexicano and other workers walked off the job, demanding higher wages; soon the strike spread to the metal trades and to the leather and brewing industries. Support for this strike was wiped out when the strongly anti-union Los Angeles *Times*'s building was dynamited on October 1, causing the deaths of twenty-one employees. This tragedy crippled the strike and brought about its eventual failure. Again in mid-August 1919 about 1,500 mexicanos struck against the Los Angeles street railways; as before, the effort ended in defeat.

Another example of western labor difficulties was the infamous Ludlow Massacre of 1914, which occurred during a bloody thirteen-month strike against the Colorado Fuel and Iron Company in the coal-mining region around Trinidad, Colorado. Led by the United Mine Workers, the miners demanded better working conditions and increased wages. In April 1914 the Colorado militia set fire to the workers' tent camp; half the eighteen men, women, and children who died in the pandemonium that followed were mexicanos. In reaction to this brutal act, the workers took up arms and open warfare resulted. The company rejected arbitration even when it was offered by President Woodrow Wilson. Ultimately the strike failed, and a puppet company union was installed in an attempt to pacify the workers.

World War I, which broke out in 1914, led to a rapid increase in the demand for copper and therefore to expansion in copper mining. Mexican miners in Morenci and Clifton were increasingly angered by the traditional pay differential between Mexican and Anglo labor. In September 1915 mexicano workers belonging to three unions affiliated with the Western Federation of Miners went on strike over pay and other grievances. In this instance mexicano miners, who made up more than two-thirds of the work force numbering about 5,000, were joined by many Anglo workers. The National Guard was called in, but negotiations went on. After five months the strikers, still led by mexicanos, obtained an agreement that, for the first time, guaranteed equal pay rates for Anglos and Mexicans and established grievance procedures, but required the workers to give up WFM affiliation. However, wage discrimination continued in most copper towns.

Labor unrest broke out again in the Clifton-Morenci area and at Bisbee during the last two years of World War I; both mexicano and Anglo miners staged walkouts. These strikes were broken by vigilante action, wholesale deportation of Mexican nationals, and limited concessions. During the relative prosperity of the 1920s fewer strikes occurred, but as the depression settled in at the beginning of the thirties mining companies reduced wages and laid off workers. The result was an eruption of strikes. Despite injunctions and arrests, mexicanos engaged in work stoppages and strikes without benefit of organization. Unionism played a minor role in New Mexico, Arizona, and Texas and was often directed against Mexicans as cheap nonunion labor.

At the beginning of the 1930s the only Mexican American union of any importance outside California was the Sheepshearers Union of North America, an AFL affiliate. It differed from most mexicano unions in that it was a strongly cohesive and relatively well-financed organization. In the early thirties it initiated an aggressive unionization drive in Arizona and Texas. At San Angelo, Texas, it struck for better wages in 1934, but the walkout was frustrated and defeated by strikebreakers, threats, arrests, and vigilante action.

During the 1930s depression there were also a number of strikes in the San Antonio area, where the pecan industry employed thousands of mexicano workers, mostly women. In 1934 some 5,000 workers went on strike for higher wages. A wage of 15 cents an hour was established, but by the second half of the thirties piecework rates had reduced earnings to as little as 4 cents an hour. In February 1938 this starvation wage caused shellers to strike against the Southern Pecan-Shelling Company, which dominated the industry. An outstanding figure in this dispute was a charismatic young radical from San Antonio, Emma Tenayuca, who helped organize the walkout.

The strike lasted over a month, during which 1,000 or more strikers and pickets, women and men, were arrested and many jailed. It also polarized the San Antonio mexicano community, with a majority of its middle class and elites firmly arrayed against the pecan shellers. While the strikers ultimately won moderate wage increases, resort to the National Labor Relations Board proved more productive. It established a wage of 25 cents an hour in the pecan industry. The higher wage, however, caused the industry to mechanize, thus eliminating most jobs. By 1941 the Southern Pecan-Shelling Company had reduced its labor force from more than 10,000 to a mere 600 employees.

One of the important strikes during the depression was the 1933 Gallup coal miners' walkout in New Mexico. During World War I the Gallup American Company had brought in Mexican strikebreakers, and by 1930 most of its miners were mexicanos. They had been organized by the end of the 1920s into the National Miners Union (NMU), a radical adjunct to the Communist Trade Union Unity League (TUUL). In August 1933 the NMU struck for union recognition, higher wages, and an end to excessive prices in the company store. The strike lasted three months and was finally settled by compromise. However, many of the striking mexicanos were not rehired, and profiteering by the company store continued.

In New Mexico and Colorado the organizing of mexicano labor received an impetus in the next year when Jesús Pallares, a Mexican coal miner, founded the Liga Obrera de Habla Española (Spanish-Speaking Labor League). Active primarily among miners in the area around Gallup, it soon claimed a membership of 8,000 in northern

New Mexico and southern Colorado. When a strike erupted at Gallup in 1935 the newly established Liga Obrera assumed an important role. In April strikers were ousted from company housing. The evictions led to rioting in which two miners and a sheriff were killed. Murder indictments were issued for fifty-five miners and three were convicted. Eventually the other accused men were released. However, more than a hundred Mexican miners were deported, including Jesús Pallares. Others left "voluntarily." Without Pallares's charismatic leadership the Liga rapidly declined.

Mexicans and Mexican Americans tended to be set apart as cheap labor and set off from Anglo workers by union policies, job and wage discrimination, social and economic segregation, and limited educational opportunities. A significant problem of Mexican American industrial workers throughout the Southwest was the general practice of paying Anglo and Mexican American laborers at different rates for the same work. This discrimination was energetically fought by the International Union of Mine, Mill, and Smelter Workers, which had some Mexican American leadership. After 1937 the union achieved a partial redress of differential wages and other grievances through the intervention of the National Labor Relations Board.

Nevertheless, wage differentials continued to be a major problem as mining boomed during World War II. Finally the issue was brought before the National War Labor Board, which in 1944 ordered copper-mining companies to cease this discriminatory practice. However, the policy was so deeply entrenched and the companies so racist that two years later, in March 1946, the Union of Mine, Mill, and Smelter Workers had to resort to a strike to obtain compliance with the 1944 order.

California had a limited early history of Mexican American involvement in industrial unionism. However, in the early 1930s Los Angeles garment workers, three-fourths of whom were mexicano women, were being unionized by labor organizer Rose Pesotta. As the depression deepened, wages were cut and mexicanas initiated work stoppages despite court injunctions and arrests. In the end they were unable to achieve any great improvement in wages or working conditions.

In California, Mexican American leaders were primarily involved in organizing farm labor. From the beginning of the American period California's labor needs, mostly agricultural, had been met by "harvest tramps" and Oriental workers, first Chinese and then Japanese and

Filipino. Not until after 1900, when large-scale agriculture expanded rapidly as labor-intensive crops spread and Oriental immigration ended, did mexicanos begin to become an important part of the state's farm labor force.

At the beginning of the twentieth century large commercial farms linked to a mass market became characteristic of southwestern agriculture. This change was especially notable in California, where the earlier founding of large organizations like the Kern County Land Company, the DiGiorgio Fruit Corporation, and the Newhall-Saugus Land Company gave great impetus to the movement. Commercial farming by these companies and others, referred to as agribusiness, was characterized by employment of large seasonal labor forces which typically tripled or quadrupled at the peak of the harvest season. These temporary, and usually migrant, workers came increasingly from southwestern Mexican American labor reservoirs and from Mexico.

Because many crops were perishable, southwestern agriculture was highly vulnerable to labor shortages, union pressures, and work stoppages. Farmers therefore preferred an abundant supply of mobile, unorganized farm workers. Their attitude explains why agribusiness so strongly supported the unlimited admission of Mexican nationals in the 1920s and even during the depression. The latter's scant knowledge of English, their ignorance of their rights under American law, and their attitudes from having worked under exploitative landowners in Mexico made them ideal workers from the growers' viewpoint. Nevertheless, mexicano workers of the Southwest on occasion protested vociferously against mistreatment, belying Anglo stereotypes of Mexican passivity.

The spread of commercial farms employing large numbers of workers inevitably led to labor organization. In March 1903 a strike of sugar-beet workers at Oxnard in southern California took about 1,000 mexicano and Japanese workers out of the fields. After two months of strife with some violence the strikers, who belonged to the Japanese-Mexican Labor Association, won the right to negotiate directly with the grower rather than through the Western Agricultural Contracting Company. Their successful strike further weakened the stereotypical image of Mexicans as docile workers.

In the long history of American labor unionization migrant farm workers have been the most difficult to organize. During the early years of agricultural worker solidarity Mexican mutualist societies at times assumed some union functions among mexicano laborers. Sometimes labor organizations were established paralleling mutualistas. In 1911 the Mexican Protective Association was organized in the Southwest to represent agricultural workers; however, conflict between conservative and militant elements in the society led to its decline and eventual dissolution in 1914. In the following year the Industrial Workers of the World founded the Agricultural Workers Organization to unionize farm workers. It too failed. Organizing difficulties stemmed principally from the existence of sizable reservoirs of labor, the seasonal nature of the work, the centrifugal forces in migrant labor made up largely of minorities, and the workers' highly competitive rivalry. In the final analysis, however, the chief obstacle to unionization of farm labor has been the strong and aggressive opposition of farm organizations determined to keep production costs low by keeping labor costs minimal. This economic stance and the absence of social conscience or economic concern for their workers characterized many, perhaps most, growers.

An excellent example of this attitude and a major milestone in the history of migrant labor conflict was the Durst Ranch affair of August 1913. Ralph Durst operated a large hop farm near Wheatland, California. Durst, like many other farm employers, advertised for more workers than he needed to harvest his hops. He was no more inhumane than other agricultural employers, but he was not concerned with the unsanitary conditions in which his migrant employees, who included many mexicanos, worked and lived. Housing on the ranch was virtually nonexistent, and the nearly 3,000 men, women, and children who showed up for the 800 or so available jobs were provided with fewer than a dozen crude toilets. Central Valley daytime temperatures in excess of 100 degrees with extremely limited provisions for sanitation and garbage disposal, plus a lack of drinking water in the fields, created brutal conditions.

The harvest workers, led by IWW members Herman Suhr and Richard (Blackie) Ford, rose up against their subhuman treatment. In the strike's emotionally charged atmosphere a deputy sheriff fired a warning shot in the air, touching off a riot which left four dead. On the following day National Guard troops were brought in, and about 100 migrant workers were arrested. The strike was broken. Eight months later Ford and Suhr were tried, found guilty of second-degree murder, and sentenced to life in prison for their roles in arousing the crowd to riot; other leaders received long prison terms.

The widespread publicity engendered by this strike helped lead to the creation of a California Commission on Immigration and Housing. The commission's report substantiated and articulated the brutish conditions migratory workers faced, arousing widespread awareness of their treatment for the first time. In 1915 its recommendations led to state regulation of California's farm labor camps, but only minor improvements in working and housing conditions resulted. Three-quarters of a century later conditions in some farm worker camps remain deplorable, as indicated by the San Jose *Mercury-News* August 1991 exposé of conditions in El Pirul farm labor camp in the Almaden Valley, California.

When World War I broke out there was relative peace in southwestern agriculture, but toward the end of the long war several work stoppages occurred among cantaloupe pickers and citrus grove workers in the southern part of California. None of the strikes was successful. Among the strikers were Mexican nationals who had taken advantage of the wartime waiver of immigration requirements. By mid-1918 the first large-scale recruitment of workers in Mexico began, and by 1921 Mexicans dominated California's farm labor force.

Labor unrest among mexicanos working in agriculture increased during the postwar twenties. Severe declines in agricultural prices and wages caused considerable dissatisfaction and unrest among Colorado beet workers, and some began to organize under the leadership of the IWW and AFL. In 1928 tejano C. N. Idar of the American Federation of Labor directed the organizing of Mexican Americans in Colorado, Wyoming, and Nebraska and successfully formed a Beet Workers Association with a reported membership of about 10,000. However, it never affiliated with the AFL. The depression at the end of the decade and competition with nonunion Dust Bowl migrants brought about its decline.

Labor organizing among Mexican Americans in California during the 1920s was more encouraging than elsewhere in the Southwest. At the 1927 convention of the AFL held in Los Angeles, delegates discussed the impact of Mexican immigration on American labor and voted in favor of exclusionist legislation. Although the AFL conference supported American labor's rights, it made no effort to organize Mexican American workers. In November of that year a committee representing the Federation of Mexican Societies in Los Angeles took a first step in that direction. It passed a resolution calling on its affiliates to lend financial and moral support to a drive to organize mexicano workers.

As a result, a number of local unions were organized, and these then formed the Confederación de Uniones Obreras Mexicanas (CUOM) (Confederation of Mexican Labor Unions). In March 1928 this new organization wrote a constitution which declared that its purpose was to organize all mexicano workers in the United States, to achieve wage parity with Anglo workers, and to end discrimination against mexicanos. Another objective was to persuade the Mexican government to restrict the flow of Mexican immigrant labor to the United States and to take a more active role in meeting economic needs of repatriates.

A month later a general CUOM convention was held in Los Angeles at which twenty-two unions were represented. Labor unionism in Mexico demonstrated its support by sending Emilio Mújica as its representative. He served as an adviser and remained four weeks after the meeting to help organize mexicano workers. Initial enthusiasm for this effort was considerable, and by the end of 1928 the CUOM claimed to represent twenty locals with about 3,000 workers, both agricultural and industrial. However, with the depression setting in, only ten locals representing about 200 members were still functioning a year later.

Despite its rapid decline, the CUOM was important because of its clearly articulated goal of organizing mexicano workers in order to improve their economic condition. Its constitution delineated clearly Mexican American views on many issues of prime importance to la raza. It also served as a training ground for leaders who later helped to establish more successful labor organizations.

A contemporary labor dispute in the Imperial Valley illustrates clearly the difficulties Mexican Americans faced in dealing with the twin problems of an extensive labor pool and seasonally limited need for workers. In April 1928, melon pickers, with the help of the Mexican consul at Calexico, established a mutualista, the Mexican Mutual Aid Society of the Imperial Valley (MMAS), which they later converted into a union. Early in May, through this organization, they delivered to the growers a list of conditions for harvesting the cantaloupe crop, which included elimination of contratistas and acceptance of the MMAS as the representative of the workers. The pickers also demanded a small piecework raise with a minimum hourly wage of 75 cents, ready accessibility of picking sacks and crates, ice for drinking water, and improved housing. Growers were willing to accept some of these conditions but not all. As a result, cantaloupe pickers, rejecting the growers' compromise, refused to harvest the crop.

However, large-scale arrests by the local sheriff, Charles Gillett, threats to deport Mexican nationals, accusations of Communism, and use of anonymous circulars threatening to bring workers from Texas—all combined to defeat the boycott. Although the workers were forced to accept the growers' terms, they became aware of their potential power.

One unexpected result of the melon strike was that the Imperial County district attorney urged revision of the standard harvesting contract widely used by growers. The revised harvesting agreement, composed after much discussion, specified that growers rather than contratistas were responsible for wages and eliminated the common practice of retaining 25 percent of the pickers' wages in order to hold the workers until the end of the harvest season. Although use of this harvest contract form was not mandatory, its formulation was a significant victory for the workers since it had an aura of approval by a state agency and because it recommended abolition of deeply entrenched abusive grower practices. Early in the 1930 harvest season Mexican American pickers once again went on strike in the Imperial Valley for improved working conditions and repeal of a wage cut. Although the growers made concessions, they also continued their bitter opposition to unionizing.

The 1930s became a decade of farm strikes in California. Agriculture was especially hard hit during the depression, and California was the scene of half the agricultural strikes in the entire United States. There was an unusually large number of strikes between 1930 and 1935, due mainly to the fact that farm wages fell from already depressed levels of the late twenties to all-time lows. Other grievances included widespread use of contratistas, defaults on payment of wages, further deterioration of housing, and poor sanitation facilities. Radical labor organizations, capitalizing on rising discontent, won new adherents. Both the Communist-affiliated Cannery and Agricultural Workers Industrial Union (CAWIU) and its parent, the Trade Union Unity League, had some success in recruiting Mexican American workers. From the beginning of the depression, the TUUL, one of the most active radical labor groups in the West, showed considerable interest in mexicano migrants. For example, the league held a conference in 1929 at which problems of mexicano workers were discussed. It also organized a number of hunger marches; a notable one, which took place in December 1931, included many Mexican Americans from the Los Angeles area. Because the TUUL was extensively involved in western farm labor disputes during the thirties, growers often equated unionism with Communism.

In the thirties Mexican Americans throughout the Southwest became more active in organizing labor and in leading strikes. Their informal union training and experience in various government relief programs helped to provide needed unionizing skills. By mid-1934 they had organized some forty agricultural unions in California; most of these were small and short-lived. The most successful was the Confederación de Uniones de Campesinos y Obreros Mexicanos (CUCOM) (Confederation of Mexican Farm and Industrial Workers Unions), which developed out of the El Monte berry strike in Los Angeles County.

In May 1933, several thousand mexicano pickers, dissatisfied with wages that had dropped to as little as 9 cents an hour, walked out of strawberry fields at El Monte. With help from the Los Angeles Mexican consulate the workers formed a new organization around some former CUOM leaders. The strike was characterized by a struggle for control between local Mexican American leaders and outside representatives of the radical CAWIU. As the work stoppage continued, locals were organized among strawberry workers elsewhere in Los Angeles County. An agreement was reached on July 6, 1933, establishing a wage of 20 cents an hour. By that time the berry season was ending, so the workers received little benefit from the settlement. More important, ten days after the strike was settled a permanent organization, the Confederación de Uniones de Campesinos y Obreros Mexicanos was established by the workers. It quickly became the most active farm labor group in California; by the end of 1933 it had 50 locals and between 5,000 and 10,000 members. Among its organizers was Guillermo Velarde.

During 1933 many other strikes took place among migratory agricultural workers in California, and Mexican Americans were active in all of them. There were strikes by pea pickers in Hayward; cherry pickers in the Mountain View–Sunnyvale area; peach pickers at Merced, Sacramento, and Gridley; pear pickers in the Santa Clara Valley; Filipino and Mexican American lettuce workers in Salinas; fruit pickers at the Tagus Ranch, south of Fresno; and grape pickers in the Fresno-Lodi area, in which some 6,000 workers participated.

The most spectacular walkout of 1933 was the San Joaquin Valley cotton strike led by the Cannery and Agricultural Workers Industrial Union. The movement began in October at Corcoran, California, with 5,000 workers, three-fourths of them mexicanos, and soon encompassed the entire southern part of the valley. Eventually 18,000 pickers walked out, principally over demands that the rate per hundredweight of cotton picked be increased from 60 cents to a dollar. Evicted from growers' camps, cotton pickers set up a "strike city" headquarters on a rented farm. For four weeks the workers faced extremely hostile vigilante action as they picketed more than 2,000 farms along a hundred-mile front, Intense feelings were generated among the strikers on October 12 when the union hall at Pixley was riddled by rifle fire, killing two strikers and wounding several others. Tension increased when a striker was shot to death on the same day at Arvin, farther south in the valley. Because of the inflamed situation Governor James Rolf mobilized the National Guard. To calm the strikers, Mexican consuls Enrique Bravo and J. L. D. Acosta were brought in to address them. Meanwhile, the governor appointed a fact-finding commission which included San Francisco archbishop Edward J. Hannah, University of the Pacific's Tully C. Knoles, and University of California professor Ira B. Cross. The commission recommended a 25 percent wage increase, which was accepted by the growers. By the end of October most of the strikers had returned to work, and the union organization disintegrated.

Following the cotton strike the Agricultural Labor Subcommittee of the California Chamber of Commerce held a meeting in Los Angeles in November 1933 to organize opposition to farm workers' union aspirations. At this meeting a motion was approved calling for use of criminal syndicalism legislation, laws passed in twenty-four states against radical organizations and leaders, in labor disputes and passage of laws to outlaw picketing. These measures aimed to suppress union organizing in agriculture. The delegates then created the Associated Farmers of California, a powerful statewide organization dominated by big growers, land companies, food processors, and banks. They bitterly opposed unionism in general since they considered it a part of the "Red" menace. Devoted to combating unionism by "education," persuasion, and a permanent lobby at the state capital, this well-financed group in 1934 turned to more overt means of counteracting labor union activity. The Associated Farmers contributed substantially to the demoralization of Mexican American agricultural unionism in the 1930s. Generally supported by law enforcement agencies, it was responsible for much of the violation of civil rights and labor violence which characterized the period.

To fight farm worker unions the Associated Farmers specialized in the blacklist, labor espionage, agents provocateurs, vigilante action, and strikebreaking. The Cannery and Agricultural Workers Industrial Union was often the target. During a 1934 walkout at Brentwood, California, deputies and vigilantes penned up 200 mexicano strikers and later shipped them out of the county. Eight strike organizers from the CAWIU were tried and convicted under California's criminal syndicalism laws. Three years later all eight convictions were reversed by an appellate court. The CAWIU also participated in the well-known 1934 San Francisco general strike, initiated by the International Longshoremen's Union. In July the police raided the CAWIU Sacramento headquarters and arrested its leaders. Eighteen were tried subsequently under criminal syndicalism legislation and eight were eventually convicted and sentenced to jail terms. On appeal, these convictions were upheld. The CAWIU's parent organization, the Trade Union Unity League, was dissolved by the Communist Party in 1935. Its union organizers increasingly harassed by intensive police surveillance, the badly crippled CAWIU slipped into decline and inaction after the mid-thirties. Isolated from the broader trade union movement, it also lacked roots and wide support in rural areas.

As the influence of the CAWIU decreased, the Confederación de Uniones de Campesinos y Obreros Mexicanos became more active. During 1935 one-third of eighteen important farm worker strikes in California were led by the CUCOM. In a number of other disputes it was able to achieve the agricultural workers' objectives without going on strike. During this period there was a move to affiliate farm unions with the American Federation of Labor, but the CUCOM and most so-called Mexican unions felt that their members could not afford the high AFL initiation fees. Not until after World War II did the AFL, by chartering the National Farm Labor Union (NFLU), seek seriously to organize "factories in the fields."

Mexican American unions were, of course, aware of the benefits to be derived from federating small unions, as is suggested by the establishment of the short-lived Federation of Agricultural Workers Unions of America, founded in Los Angeles in January 1936. The key to this organization was the CUCOM, which supplied the leadership needed to bring together many independent Los Angeles County Spanish-speaking unions. In April this new federation called a strike in Los Angeles celery fields. Led by the dynamic Guillermo Velarde, one of the founders of the CUCOM, 2,600 strikers walked out of the fields.

The growers, mostly Japanese Americans, resorted to traditional strike-breaking techniques. Finally, in August, the strike was settled. The workers achieved a number of gains, including their principal objective, improved wages.

In June, while the celery strike was still on, the CUCOM called another strike in Orange County citrus groves. Velarde again led the workers in demanding that the California Fruit Growers' Exchange (Sunkist) recognize the union and improve working conditions. The usual methods of repression were employed by the growers: evictions, tear gas, night-riding vigilantes, and charges of Communism. One hundred and fifteen mexicanos were arrested for trespassing on a public highway. The illegally jailed strikers were detained for fifteen days, a tactic which helped demoralize the pickers. By the end of July the strike had lost much of its support and they returned to work with only a slight wage increase. In spite of difficulties encountered, mexicanos remained interested in a broader, more effective agricultural labor organization. The CUCOM and other California farm labor groups held several conferences in 1935 and 1936 in order to develop a statewide organization, with little success. The first national convention of agricultural workers, held at Denver, Colorado, in 1937, attracted delegates from most of the Spanish-speaking California unions. Many unions attending the convention joined the United Cannery, Agriculture, Packing, and Allied Workers of America (UCAPAWA), affiliated with the Congress of Industrial Organizations (CIO). However, most so-called Mexican unions eventually affiliated with the AFL; some remained independent.

As the depression eased somewhat in the second half of the thirties, improvements in agricultural employment were evident. Partly because of better conditions brought about by New Deal programs and legislation, there were few strikes among field workers in 1936 and 1937 and only two important labor disputes in California agriculture during this period. Both involved packing and cannery workers. In September 1936 the Vegetable Packers Association, an AFL affiliate, took its workers out of the Salinas lettuce fields. In response, the Associated Farmers announced that it was "against the unionization of farm labor on any basis," raised a strikebreaking fund of $225,000, and eventually crushed the strike with a citizens' army of 1,500 deputies armed with ax handles and shotguns. The following April, cannery workers struck in Stockton. Again the Associated Farmers moved quickly to suppress the walkout.

In this instance the mostly mexicano strikers were compelled to return to work largely because of the deputizing of over 1,200 farmers and a sellout by state AFL officials who accepted a compromise offered by the cannery owners.

In December 1937 the Associated Farmers met at San Jose and reorganized as the broader United Farmers of the Pacific Coast. This organization continued to oppose and repress union organizing in west coast agriculture to the end of the decade.

The last important California farm workers strike before the United States entered World War II took place in Ventura County in January 1941. Here, 1,500 lemon pickers, mostly Mexican Americans, organized the Agricultural and Citrus Workers Union, affiliated with the AFL. Rejecting union demands and refusing to negotiate, growers brought in strikebreakers. When the U.S. Department of Labor proposed arbitration, the growers refused its offer to mediate. After four months the workers gave up in defeat. They lost both the strike and their jobs.

As a result of farm labor unrest during the 1930s, particularly in California, there were six government investigations undertaken between 1936 and 1951 to determine the facts about migrant agricultural labor. The most important was by a subcommittee of the Senate Committee on Education and Labor, the so-called La Follette Committee, which held hearings in 1939 and 1940. The committee found conditions in California agriculture deplorable and degrading. It made strong and farsighted recommendations for federal legislation to assure better treatment of farm workers. Unfortunately the committee's report was not issued until 1942, when the country was intensely involved in World War II.

Unionization among Mexican Americans and Mexicans in the 1920s and 1930s took place predominantly in agriculture and mining. The Southwest spawned numerous small Mexican unions, whose energies and weak finances typically were quickly sapped by the extremely aggressive tactics of employers. The latter relied on police powers, massive and indiscriminate arrests, excessive bail, deportation, expensive litigation, savage vigilante assaults, and other forms of intimidation to end strikes and destroy unions. Although Mexican Americans gained much labor union experience between 1900 and 1940, successes were few. Their aspirations frequently were frustrated by abuse and repression; however, limited improvements were obtained in wages and working conditions.

10

UNWANTED MEXICANS

As the prosperity of the twenties turned into the depression of the thirties and jobs vanished, the Mexican migratory flow to the United States was reversed. Even before the 1920s ended, the Great Depression began to be felt throughout the United States. The number of unemployed rose from 4 million in 1930 to more than 13 million three years later. By 1933, 25 percent of the American labor force was unemployed and additional millions were underemployed. Wages dropped from 35 cents an hour to 14 and 15 cents, and as low as 10 cents. Piecework rates often brought income even lower. Weekly wages of $1.50 became common in the Southwest, and jobs at any wage became extremely hard to find.

The depression years brought economic misery and new problems to Mexican Americans. The largest minority in the Southwest, immigrants or their descendants, they lived in poor rural communities in northwestern New Mexico, in small towns along the border, and increasingly in the barrios of large cities like Los Angeles, El Paso, and Denver. Most of them experienced racism and discrimination in restaurants, cinemas, and other public facilities, as well as in employment. A small minority had achieved blue-collar or white-collar status, but the majority were employed in farming and agriculture-related activities in the cities. Generally they occupied entry-level positions with median annual incomes that were well below the poverty level. Much of their employment was seasonal, a fact which made their economic position precarious even in good times. In bad times they quickly found themselves in the ranks of the unemployed and competing, often with Anglos, for the few available jobs. Especially affected by the depression were Hispano villagers of northern New Mexico and southern Colorado and Mexican Americans living in industrial areas, mostly in the Midwest. During the thirties movement out of the Southwest by Mexican Americans virtually ceased.

As employment in meat packing, automobile manufacturing, steel, railroads, and mining declined precipitously, Mexican Americans found themselves out of work or at best working only a few days a week. Despite pontifical assurances from leaders in business and government that prosperity was just around the corner, employment opportunities disappeared. Unable to secure urban or industrial work, many tried to return to the land, seeking a way of life that no longer existed. They found that the depression had seriously affected rural areas as well, and for many the return was temporary and miscarried. Others became part of the estimated half million or more Americans who wandered almost aimlessly across the land, seeking work.

The reduction of sheep and cattle herds because of depression conditions also put many nuevomexicanos out of work. Failing to realize that economic structures had been drastically altered throughout the nation, they continued to follow earlier New Mexican economic practice, leaving their villages to seek work elsewhere. Before the depression 13,000 hispanos had successfully alleviated their rural poverty by obtaining seasonal employment outside their villages. In the thirties this traditional strategy no longer succeeded, as a study of eleven New Mexican villages published by the U.S. Department of Agriculture in the mid-1930s indicated. Before 1930 an average of 1,100 men worked outside these villages each year on railroads and in sugar beets, potatoes, and mining. However, in 1934 only 157 were able to obtain such work. Economic conditions for nuevomexicanos deteriorated further when, in April 1936, the governor of Colorado declared martial law to keep out people seeking work. Although Colorado agriculture previously had depended heavily on workers from New Mexico, now there was a large surplus of Colorado workers, and National Guard troops were ordered to patrol the border with New Mexico to bar job seekers, most of whom were mexicanos. Fortunately this use of the National Guard was declared unconstitutional, and the order was rescinded after several days.

In addition to causing a severe decline in jobs and income, the depression affected nuevomexicanos in other ways. Many were forced off their farms because they were unable to pay assessments of the Middle Rio Grande Conservancy District Project, a regional agency established in 1927 to help New Mexicans by increasing the land available for agriculture. Villagers had no voice in establishing the agency and, despite some federal government aid, many now were unable to continue paying their assessments and lost their lands. Others lost farms because they could not make mortgage payments or pay their taxes.

Some poverty-stricken nuevomexicano villagers developed strategies needed to eke out a bare living by combining subsistence farming and livestock raising with welfare aid and occasional day labor. Others, having lost their lands and thereby their means of livelihood, moved to the city to survive. Many left the villages to secure benefits of New Deal welfare programs they heard about. As the depression continued, two distinct migratory patterns evolved. One was a movement from the villages to larger urban centers of the Southwest, the continuation of an earlier widespread trend. The second was a movement from urban barrios back to rural villages.

Urban Mexican Americans also found their economic survival undermined. Even as villagers moved to urban centers, many who became unemployed in the cities were returning to their home villages, hoping to find some economic security within the extended family and a familiar culture. Since they increased an already impoverished population, their return often contributed to further deterioration of crippled village economies and to more rural poverty. Their attempts to return to subsistence living failed and subsequently most went back to the urban centers they had left, thus remaining a part of the substantial nuevomexicano migration to cities and towns of the Southwest. The ultimate result of this unequal two-way movement was a reduction of village populations in northwestern New Mexico by as much as one-third by the late thirties.

Most Mexican Americans moving to the city had only limited success in improving their economic condition. Although many did find some relief through the various welfare programs, jobs were extremely scarce. Often villagers lacked the training required for the work that was available; moreover, the depression increased job discrimination. Anti-

Mexican feelings were widespread and overt throughout the Southwest in the 1930s. Signs reading "Only White Labor Employed" and "No Niggers, Mexicans, or Dogs Allowed" were evidence of the attitudes and strong feelings of the day. The racism and discrimination experienced by Mexican Americans were the order of the times in the Southwest. Even the law was against mexicanos.

A California law passed in August 1931 prohibited employment of aliens on all public works. Elsewhere similar legislation limited work on public improvements to U.S. citizens. Contractors, like earlier gold rush Anglos, often failed to distinguish Mexican American citizens from Mexican nationals. The prohibition had the broader effect of discouraging contractors from hiring Mexican American citizens on public works projects and even on other jobs. Mexican immigrants found even pick-and-shovel work almost impossible to obtain, a difficulty shared by the American-born as well. As a result, many Mexican American families were forced to seek assistance from state and federal welfare agencies.

When depression prices for crops fell below costs of production Mexican Americans lost even low-pay, backbreaking agricultural work. The number of jobs in agriculture declined precipitously because of extremely low market prices and governmental crop-restriction programs aimed at raising prices. Large numbers of Anglo Americans competed for the limited work available, as farm families from Arkansas, Texas, Oklahoma, and other drought-ridden states abandoned their Dust Bowl acres and trekked west to join the migrant agricultural stream. Also migrating toward the "Golden State" of California were tens of thousands of uprooted southern sharecroppers and tenant farmers who similarly sought new solutions to their depression-aggravated problems.

No one knows how many Anglo Americans took to the migrant trail, but half a million is not an unrealistic estimate. Under the impact of these newcomers to the southwestern labor pool, wages and working conditions declined to even lower levels. Anglo migrants replaced local Mexican American farm workers and Mexican immigrants equally. Disastrous economic conditions and the added competition from Anglos were devastating to both groups, particularly vulnerable because of their already marginal position.

In 1934 half of California's farm labor was Anglo, and mexicanos made up no more than 35 percent of harvest workers. In Arizona more than half the cotton harvest workers came from out of state by 1937.

This competition made it increasingly difficult for local Mexican Americans to earn even a minimal living and forced many into the migrant labor circuit. In Texas alone, the depression swelled this Mexican American migrant army to some 400,000 as entire families picked cotton and harvested other crops. As a result of bitter economic competition between mexicanos and Anglos, prejudice and social discrimination against Mexicans became even more pronounced. Although both groups represented the same social class and worked equally hard, only Anglos ultimately achieved a degree of upward social mobility. Mexican Americans' socioeconomic status reached an all-time low as they became scapegoats for the depression.

Franklin Delano Roosevelt's New Deal held the then somewhat unorthodox view that government was responsible for the economic and social welfare of all its citizens. Efforts were made to alleviate the most serious problems of the 1930s with the three principal components of the New Deal program—relief, recovery, and reform. Of these three elements the first, relief, had the most direct effect on Mexican Americans. In the Southwest, as in the rest of the United States, government agencies tried both to solve depression problems and to ease the widespread suffering. In New Mexico rangeland was made available for subsistence use and an Interdepartmental Rio Grande Board was created, with the objective of giving first preference to subsistence farmers, mostly Mexican Americans.

Throughout the Southwest greatly expanded activity by federal agencies contributed to restraining ethnic conflict and ameliorating economic conditions among Mexican Americans. For example, the Farm Security Administration established permanent migrant labor camps in a score of large-scale agricultural employment areas such as the Salt River, Coachella, and San Joaquin valleys and mobile camps elsewhere during times of peak employment. These camps had facilities considerably superior to those provided by most growers. Many conservative farmers opposed the government camps as hotbeds of radicalism whose spread they were determined to halt.

In towns and cities the Federal Emergency Relief Administration also made important contributions toward alleviating Mexican Americans' immediate distress by providing critically needed employment during the winter of 1934–35. After 1935 the Works Progress Administration (WPA) provided most work relief for unemployed Mexican Americans and was both useful and well received. The WPA employed carpenters, stonemasons, plasterers, and unskilled laborers in the construction of roads, small bridges, libraries, city halls, and other municipal and state buildings. An important aspect of the WPA in the Southwest was that in addition to providing employment it also created a renewed interest in nuevomexicano folk arts and crafts as programs were undertaken to revitalize village economies. This revival helped restore nuevo-mexicanos' cultural pride and self-confidence, as the government gave validation to their ethnic skills and art.

However, many Mexican Americans who desperately needed aid were unable to obtain it because of legislative restrictions. Many were denied the benefits of various programs because they remained aliens despite many years of residence in the United States; many more were unable to meet local residency requirements. In many states such restrictions on economic assistance were greatly increased during the depression years in order to contain relief costs. This policy meant that many Mexican Americans could not obtain state relief because of their mi-gratory employment; nor could they be certified for possible employment by the WPA since that agency employed only those referred by state welfare departments. The Civilian Conservation Corps also provided work for Mexican American youths, but again employment was limited to those whose families qualified for state relief. For these reasons relief programs were often less helpful to persons of Mexican descent than to other impoverished Americans.

By early 1930 a new stereotype of the Mexican had begun to evolve, at least in the Southwest. Because of chronic underemployment and low wages, Mexicans and Mexican Americans had not been able to accumulate savings; thus, during the depression some of them (together with many other poor) had become heavily dependent on local and state relief. Added to the earlier image of a docile agricultural worker there was now a widespread Anglo perception that the vast majority of mexicanos had become public charges, a burden on American taxpay-ers. In a no-win situation, those still employed were seen as holding jobs that should go to Anglo Americans. The Mexican-born, even those who had become U.S. citizens, found themselves unwanted competitors for jobs and unwelcome applicants for relief.

Coming from a folk culture, Mexican Americans were accustomed to solving their problems without outside help. Further, because of macho attitudes most Mexican American males were reluctant to seek public help. A majority of them worked in agriculture and therefore were excluded from coverage by unemployment insurance, industrial accident insurance, and other New Deal social security programs. In addition, even insured Mexican Americans often failed to benefit fully because of unfamiliarity with claim procedures and red tape. Nevertheless, federal programs of the thirties did help Mexican Americans, especially the increasing numbers in the cities. Overall, of course, the depression had a devastating impact on them.

One of the dramatic events of the 1930s was the repatriation of large numbers of nonnaturalized Mexicans and some American citizens of Mexican descent. During the 1920s Mexicans had been encouraged to come to the United States, and hundreds of thousands had crossed the border to fill the expanding demand for workers. Objections to heavy immigration were minimized by their employers. Both employers and merchants viewed suggestions of restriction on immigration as a labor union maneuver to increase wages. In 1928 and 1929 there was a decline in Mexican immigration from previous high levels, probably the effect of farm mechanization and decreasing employment opportunities because of widespread agricultural decline. However, documented immigration for those two years still totaled nearly 100,000. Then came the 1929 crash and deepening depression. The Mexican immigration issue quickly became moot as a dramatic change in the direction of migration took place. From 1931 to 1940 inclusive, only about 20,000 Mexicans immigrated to the United States legally, and illegal entrance was discouraged. As a percentage of total immigration to the United States, Mexican immigration dropped from 20 percent in 1927 to about 3 percent in the mid-thirties.

During the depression years the cost of greatly expanded welfare rolls was among the major problems county officials had to cope with. Many southwestern government officials considered ways to reduce welfare loads and reached the conclusion that repatriation of Mexicans was the most expedient solution to their problem. Behind this thinking lay the rationale that Mexicans had always had an inclination to return to Mexico and that if their transportation costs were paid by the government, many would be happy to go back. This solution seemed ideal because transportation was relatively cheap and many Mexican immigrants had at best ambiguous claims to benefits. To a degree indigence became the measure by which Mexican nationality was judged and repatriation encouraged.

By 1930 local governments faced rapidly mounting problems of expanding relief costs and reduced tax income. Social agencies therefore began putting pressure on Mexican nationals to return to their country. Most Anglos in the Southwest considered Mexicans to be foreign, short-term labor, who had no rights to social welfare benefits. It seemed to them that the solution was simple: send the Mexican home. Apart from the ethical considerations of this solution, the civil rights violations involved were unconscionable. Legally, the situation was quite complex. Many nonnaturalized Mexicans had been living in the United States for decades and had children who were United States citizens by birth, and could not be legally deported. Even in the case of illegal entrants, deportation procedures required a public hearing and a judicial order. A surprising aspect of the 1930s repatriation is that few Americans spoke out to defend Mexican Americans' constitutional rights and the human rights of Mexican nationals. A majority approved or at least condoned repatriation.

Although there are no precise records to indicate how many Mexicans and Mexican Americans left the United States for Mexico in the 1930s, U.S. census figures clearly show the overall trend. The 1940 census counted 377,000 Mexican-born persons in the United States, while the previous census in 1930 had shown 639,000. The difference between the two figures indicates that, at a minimum, more than a quarter million Mexicans repatriated. The actual number was probably closer to half a million since large numbers of undocumented Mexicans worked in the United States and a large but undetermined number of American-born wives and children chose to accompany their husbands and fathers to Mexico. Mexican government statistics indicate that 458,000 nationals returned between 1929 and 1937; this is probably close to the real number.

Essentially there were three types of repatriates: a very small number who were formally deported; others who returned to Mexico voluntarily because they were unemployed, discouraged, or had nostalgic memories of Mexico; and the many who were threatened in various ways and left reluctantly.

Between 1929 and the end of 1931 approximately 290,000 mexicanos crossed the border into Mexico. Since most of these antedated the concerted drive to repatriate Mexicans, presumably most left the United States with a minimum of persuasion or coercion. Between 1932 and 1938 about 170,000 were repatriated, most of them probably because of organized efforts by various agencies, governmental and private, both

American and Mexican. Methods used to encourage repatriation ranged from widespread publicity announcing a campaign to return undocumenteds to offers of free transportation, to threats of reduction or termination of relief assistance, and to physical removal. A sizable number of repatriates were assisted financially by businesses, Mexican benevolent societies in the United States, and other private organizations as well as U.S. and Mexican government agencies. At times civil rights were clearly violated. On occasion naturalized citizens and American-born children were intimidated into leaving.

In Detroit the city welfare department, in cooperation with Mexican government representatives, organized repatriation to Mexico and paid fares to the border. Diego Rivera, who was painting murals at the Detroit Art Institute in 1932, participated by organizing a League of Workers and Peasants of Mexico to encourage and assist those who wanted to return. The combined efforts of local authorities, the U.S. Immigration and Naturalization Service, and Mexican officials helped 1,500 Mexicans return from Michigan in that year, most by special trains. Comparable numbers left from other midwestern states. The average cost of their return was about $15 per person.

In Los Angeles a similar process involved the Southern Pacific Railroad, which carried repatriates to Mexico at relatively low rates, approximately the cost of one week's relief payment. Because it was cheaper to send Mexicans back than to keep them on welfare, sixteen trains with over 13,000 repatriates left for Mexico from Los Angeles between 1931 and 1934 at an average cost of $14.59 per person. Denver, Chicago, and other cities with sizable numbers of immigrant Mexicans undertook similar programs.

Thousands more men, women, and children arrived by car and truck at border towns all along the frontier from Brownsville to Tijuana. Included among the repatriates were many American-born children, whose civil rights were simply ignored. When these children later wished to return to the United States, many found that they had unwittingly relinquished their citizenship by voting in a Mexican election or serving in the army. Most responsible for these injustices were U.S. government officials who failed to clearly apprise these citizens of their rights.

The largest number of returnees, at least 132,000, came from Texas; California was second and the Indiana-Illinois area third. It is interesting to note that one-half the Mexican-descent population of Indiana, Illinois, and Michigan returned to Mexico during this period. In comparison, only one-tenth of New Mexico's Spanish-speaking population was repatriated. The explanation of this disparity lies in the fact that the three midwestern states were more industrialized and therefore harder hit by the depression than were the southwestern states. Additionally, their mexicano populations had migrated there more recently and thus were likely to have a greater propensity for returning to Mexico. Some of the repatriates, having been coerced into returning to Mexico, were re-recruited by southwestern growers, many of whom disapproved of repatriation. U.S. consular reports and other sources indicate that about one-third of the 1930s repatriates had returned to the United States by the outbreak of World War II in 1939.

Despite the reverse migration, in the mid-thirties Congress continued to consider bills to limit Mexican immigration. Southwestern ranchers and growers again successfully opposed such restrictive legislation as they had in the 1920s. Many growers ignored the doubtful ethics of encouraging Mexican workers to enter the country as cheap labor and then casting them aside during the depression.

The Mexican government, also a primary force for repatriation, had been making land available to returnees since the mid-twenties and in the 1930s established a program for resettling repatriates. Returnees were met at the border by Mexican officials and directed to one of four centers—one each in the states of Guerrero, Michoacán, Oaxaca, and Chiapas. These centers, however, had limited success in relocating the returnees, and ultimately only 5 percent were settled in these communities. Conflicts arose between local farmers and some more Americanized repatriates. Later, during the recession of 1937–38, Mexican president Lázaro Cárdenas recruited Mexicans in the United States for resettlement on communal ejidal farms. A small number of repatriates were accommodated, but Mexico was unable to develop an effective repatriation program. It was ended by World War II, which completely reversed the migrant flow and largely ended repatriation.

Repatriation created much ill feeling and resentment. Welcoming Mexicans with open arms when their labor was wanted, paying them subsistence wages, and then unceremoniously sending them destitute back to Mexico when times turned difficult did nothing to enhance trust in American society and its government. It led to further disillusionment among Mexican Americans, the majority already isolated from the mainstream of American life. They became more acutely aware of their role as mere pawns in the American agricultural economy.

Before the thirties they were suspicious and distrustful of employers, labor contractors, merchants, landlords, government and school officials, and Anglos in general. By the late 1930s their suspicions and distrust had been confirmed by the government itself.

There were other aspects to the mexicano experience during the thirties. For second-generation Mexican Americans the 1930s were a time of both economic distress and a search for identity. On the positive side, events of the thirties pushed Mexican American leaders a hesitant step closer to making effective demands for equality as American citizens. The depression also led to increased U.S. interest in the problems of the poor, with special attention directed to those of Mexican Americans.

Illustrative of this awareness were President Herbert Hoover's Committee on Social Trends, the Texas State Educational Survey, and to some extent California's Mexican Fact-Finding Committee. The reports of these committees, especially the latter two, exposed the growing problems of Mexican Americans. The rising tide of social concern was manifested by the publication of scholarly studies about their problems. A leading contributor to these studies was Paul Taylor, an economist at the University of California in Berkeley, who carried out a series of detailed investigations of agricultural workers. Taylor's work called attention especially to the problems of migrant mexicanos in California and Texas.

Emory Bogardus, a prominent sociologist at the University of Southern California, focused his attention on race relations, emphasizing the importance of leadership among Mexican Americans. At the University of Texas educational psychologist Herschel T. Manuel began studying the educational obstacles encountered by Spanish-speaking children in an English-speaking environment. At the same institution historian Carlos Castañeda was beginning a career that would lead him to become the outstanding Mexican American historical scholar. In New Mexico, Lloyd Tireman studied the problems of educating Mexican American children with their dual cultural background. Also in New Mexico, Professor George I. Sánchez was beginning what was to be a lifetime of study devoted principally to Mexican Americans' educational problems, especially their being judged by ethnically slanted IQ tests. These men were on the cutting edge of the Mexican American generation. However, their wide-ranging scholarly research, conclusions, and recommendations brought about few results at the time. Published in journals of limited circulation, they did not reach America's moral conscience.

It was tragic, not only for Mexican Americans but also for American society at large, that the recommendations of these scholars were not implemented. A few attempts were made. In the 1930s New Mexico initiated some reforms aimed at accelerating the acculturation of Mexican American children. Broad changes were made in the sources and distribution of school funds in order to bring this about. Similar slight improvements occurred in California, Arizona, and Colorado. Texas, historically notorious for its anti-Mexican attitudes, lagged far behind. Mexican Americans in Texas endured the lowest levels of education, employment, health, and living conditions. In the late thirties the term "Mexican" continued to be firmly associated in the popular mind with poverty, illiteracy, and lack of ambition. To avoid being identified with this stereotype, tejanos began to refer to themselves as Latin Americans and to emphasize their Americanism; nuevomexicanos stressed their Spanish heritage and called themselves hispanos. Fortunately, World War II was to bring improvement for Mexican Americans in the Southwest, even for those who lived in Texas.

11

HEROES SECOND CLASS

World War II, even more than World War I, greatly stimulated the development of southwestern agriculture and industry. It had an especially significant impact on persons of Mexican descent in the United States. Much of this impact was broadly positive. This is not to say that they all profited from the conditions brought about by the war. However, the war reawakened hopes made dim by the depression. In both industry and the armed forces it provided second-generation Mexican Americans with new and hitherto undreamed-of opportunities for improving their economic and social well-being. Traditionally isolated and alienated from the mainstream of American life by their barrio or village culture, Mexican Americans were abruptly uprooted and thrust into the labor force and the massive U.S. war machine.

Wartime manpower needs not only motivated industry to open its doors wider to Mexican Americans; they also caused unprecedented numbers to enlist or to be inducted into the armed forces. For example, New Mexico, the state with the highest percentage of Spanish speakers, had the largest number of volunteers per capita of any state. Urged by Mexican president Manuel Avila Camacho to forget lingering animosities, considerable numbers of Mexicans living in the United States enlisted. They were also encouraged to enlist by wartime legislation which promised them citizenship in exchange for service.

For a number of reasons mexicanos tended to be overrepresented in the armed services during World War II. Mexican American communities typically had a high percentage of draft-age youths, but relatively few who had essential jobs and thus qualified for deferments. Also, because Mexican Americans generally had fewer economic opportunities than Anglos, many viewed military service as a route to acceptance, security, social equality, and adventure. However, their expectations were only partially fulfilled, for military life generally reflected civilian society and its biases.

More than 300,000 Mexican Americans served in the armed forces during World War II. Most enlisted in the army, and, based on their percentage of the total population, more Chicanos served in combat divisions than any other ethnic group. A high percentage of Mexican Americans volunteered for the more hazardous branches, such as the paratroops and marines. Their valor helped them garner proportionately more military honors than any other ethnic group. Of fourteen Texans awarded the Medal of Honor, five were Mexican Americans. By the end of the war seventeen Mexican Americans had earned the Medal of Honor. Five were awarded posthumously.

Mexican American soldiers were among the first to face the enemy —in the Philippine Islands. Toward the end of 1941 the 515th and the 200th Coast Artillery arrived at Clark Field near Manila. These two outfits were part of the New Mexico National Guard, a majority of which was nuevomexicano. After the initial attack on Pearl Harbor on December 7, 1941, Japan invaded the Philippines. Spanish-speaking Americans made up one-fourth of the combat troops defending Bataan Peninsula. After the surrender of Corregidor to the Japanese early in 1942 the infamous Bataan Death March included many soldiers of Mexican descent. Many died on the forced march, and those who survived suffered long and wretched imprisonment. Mexican American participation in these early stages of World War II has often been overlooked.

In fact, Mexican Americans took part in most of the campaigns of World War II. When the North African offensive began in November 1942, they were among those battling Panzer units of General Erwin Rommel. After Rommel's forces were defeated, the major thrust of the war shifted to the invasion of Sicily and Italy. In the Italian campaign

Chicanos formed part of two infantry units, the 88th Division and Company E, 141st Regiment, of the 36th Division. The 88th Division was made up principally of raza officers and men. In battle they quickly proved their combat effectiveness, becoming widely famed as the Blue Devils.

Company E of the 141st Regiment, a Texas National Guard unit made up mostly of Mexican Americans from the El Paso area, achieved an equally outstanding record. Company E first entered combat in the murderous invasion at Salerno in September 1943. The following January it took another vicious pummeling farther north, at the Rapido River. After fighting its way up the Italian peninsula, Company E participated in the invasion of southern France in August 1944, and ultimately pushed into the heart of Germany.

By early 1944 the Allies had won air supremacy over Europe, making it possible to launch a direct attack on Hitler's "Atlantic wall." The crucial invasion of Normandy began on D-day, June 6, 1944. On the next day the 2nd (Indian Head) Division, which included many Mexican Americans from southern Texas, landed and began to advance across northern France. In December, German forces counterattacked the Allied lines in the Ardennes. For holding back part of this German drive almost single-handedly, José López of Brownsville, Texas, won the Medal of Honor. After the war he had the unusual distinction of also receiving the highest Mexican honor given to a foreigner, the Aztec Eagle, from President Miguel Alemán.

Mexican Americans fought in the China-Burma-India theater and in the Pacific. In the Aleutian Islands, José Martínez of Ault, Colorado, became the first draftee to be recommended for the Medal of Honor. The award was made posthumously for his actions in the American invasion of Attu in May 1943. Later he was memorialized by the José Martínez American Legion Post #623 in Los Angeles and the José Martínez Disabled American Veterans chapter in Colorado.

World War II experiences were valuable for Mexican Americans. For the first time Anglo Americans in large numbers worked closely with Mexican Americans for mutual objectives. While serving actively in the ranks, the latter found little discrimination, although it persisted elsewhere. Because the army's promotional system was based on individual merit, many Mexican Americans won recognition and advancement that were hardly possible in civilian life. Few, however, became officers, largely because they lacked college education. As Chicanos became aware of their excellent military record, they developed a new sense of self-esteem and confidence.

Recruitment of Mexican Americans by west coast employers made many urban Californians really aware of them for the first time. In the Los Angeles area heightened rivalry soon brought to the surface latent tensions between Mexican Americans and Anglos. These tensions led to persecution and open racial conflict and caused serious friction between Chicanos and the police.

One major wartime incident, the Sleepy Lagoon case, as it was called by the Los Angeles press, began early on August 2, 1942, when a young gang member, José Díaz, was found unconscious on a rural road in the outskirts of Los Angeles. He died without regaining consciousness, and the autopsy showed that death had resulted from a skull fracture. No weapon was found, nor was proof of murder established, but Díaz had taken part in a gang clash the preceding evening at a nearby swimming hole. Twenty-three Mexican American youths and one Anglo who had participated in the fighting were arrested and charged with murder.

Two of the indicted youths requested separate trials and were subsequently released. The other twenty-two were tried together on sixty-six charges in the fall of 1942. The judge in the case, Charles W. Fricke of the Los Angeles Superior Court, made little secret of his bias against Mexicans, and the prosecution was allowed repeatedly to stereotype the defendants racially. The defense charged that throughout the long court proceedings the defendants were denied haircuts and change of clothing; soon they began to resemble the prosecution's stereotype of sordid Mexican hoodlums.

In January 1943, the jury, without any concrete evidence, found three youths guilty of first-degree murder, nine guilty of second-degree murder, and five guilty of assault. The other five were found not guilty. This verdict led to the creation of the Sleepy Lagoon Defense Committee, chaired by Carey McWilliams and spearheaded by youthful reformer Alice Greenfield. Organized to appeal the convictions, the committee was smeared with the charge of being a Communist front. Despite Redbaiting, the committee persisted in its efforts to secure justice for the convicted seventeen. Benefits were held to raise funds for the appeal, and about $100,000 was collected to hire lawyers. In October 1944 the California District Court of Appeals unanimously reversed the lower court's convictions and dismissed all charges for lack of evidence. This incident later formed the basis for Luis Valdez's well-known play and film *Zoot Suit*.

The Sleepy Lagoon case had widespread negative repercussions. Until the convictions were dismissed two years after the trial, it remained a focal point for extensive anti-Mexican feeling in southern California. The Los Angeles press, including the L.A. *Times*, and the Hearst newspapers exploited the situation with sensationalist journalism emphasizing alleged mexicano criminal activity. This "crime wave" in the newspapers put strong public pressure on police departments, which responded with systematic roundups of Mexican American teenagers and other repressive measures. Police harassed Mexican American youth clubs and overpoliced barrios; there were extensive arrests based on race and the vaguest suspicion. Concerned with Latin American relations, Washington pressured the newspapers to stop labeling suspects as "Mexican." The press responded with code words like "pachuco" and "zoot suit" to suggest negative racial designations.

At the time of World War II, Los Angeles had a large second-generation Mexican American teenage population, children of the large immigrant wave of the 1920s. Some of these found a sense of belonging or status by joining barrio gangs whose male members often affected a distinctive "uniform" known as the zoot suit, consisting of a flat-crowned, broad-brimmed hat; lengthy draped coat; and high-waisted, baggy-legged trousers with tight-fitting pegged cuffs. Long duck-tailed, squared-off hair and a long, elaborate watch chain usually completed the outfit. Chicanos had adapted this dress from a widespread style associated with jitterbugging, a dance fad originating in the East.

In April and May 1943, a few months after the convictions in the sensationalized Sleepy Lagoon case, some minor incidents between zoot-suiters and Anglo military personnel took place in Los Angeles and Oakland. Typically these fracases developed from quarrels over girlfriends. It was ironic that while Anglos and Chicanos were fighting side by side in the armed forces, military personnel roamed the streets of Los Angeles seeking out and attacking zoot-suiters. Rapidly mounting tensions soon led to tumult in Los Angeles during the first days of June when serious clashes broke out between zoot-suited Mexican American youths and hundreds of restless Anglo sailors and soldiers. Streetcars and buses were stopped, and zoot-suiters were pulled off; theaters were entered, lights turned on, and zoot-suiters dragged out. Many were assaulted and had their clothes ripped off, their long hair cut. These vicious attacks quickly became virtually an undeclared war on all young Chicanos by roving bands of unrestrained servicemen. The conflict reached a peak on June 7, when fleets of taxis filled with sailors cruised the streets of Los Angeles seeking victims. To make matters worse, officials responded to these attacks by following the cabs at a distance and then arresting the victims.

In this emotion-laden situation the conservative Spanish-language newspaper *La Opinión* called for a cooling off and asked Mexican American youths to forgo their rights of self-defense in the face of these criminal attacks. However, retaliation by gangs of adolescent Mexican Americans was inevitable. Fists, rocks, clubs, and on occasion knives were the language of response. Meanwhile the Los Angeles English-language press fomented further trouble with sensation-mongering headlines, inflammatory stories, and strident editorials against the servicemen's victims.

What had begun as a series of street brawls quickly turned into a full-fledged race riot incited by the press and condoned or ignored by major law enforcement agencies. Rioting also broke out in Pasadena, Long Beach, and San Diego. This violence triggered similar racial attacks against Mexican Americans in Chicago, Detroit, and Philadelphia during the summer of 1943. Throughout the country there was strong reaction to these outrages, and *Time* magazine later called the Los Angeles violence "the ugliest brand of mob action since the coolie race riots of the 1870s."

Eventually, the Mexican ambassador in Washington, Francisco Nájera, requested that the State Department investigate the Los Angeles incidents. This pressure, along with reports that the riots were being used in Axis propaganda, caused the State Department to insist that military police take steps to bring servicemen under control. Consequently, overnight passes and leaves were canceled and strict controls were instituted. As a result, the assaults quickly tapered off and order was restored by mid-June. At the height of the trouble several thousand people were involved; a few were seriously injured, no one died. However, fear of racial disorder persisted during the rest of the summer, and some southwestern cities experienced street brawling in 1944 and 1945.

Several official committees that investigated the riots failed to find ethnic tensions as a major factor in southern California. City and county officials seemed more concerned about bad publicity than with ascertaining the causes of the rioting. The official version of the Los Angeles violence was that the soldiers and sailors had acted in self-defense and that there was no element of race prejudice involved. However, a citizens' committee appointed by Governor Earl Warren and headed by Catholic bishop Joseph McGucken of Los Angeles found that, while the causes were complex, the riots were principally the result of racial antagonism stimulated by inflammatory news reporting and discriminatory police practices. Because the press exploited the prejudicially used term "zoot suit," guilt was often determined by length of hair and cut of trousers rather than by evidence of wrongdoing. The matter reached such ridiculous proportions that on June 10 the Los Angeles City Council seriously debated an ordinance that would have made it a punishable offense to wear a zoot suit.

In the long run the Sleepy Lagoon affair and the zoot-suit rioting had a few positive, though limited, results. Greater attention was focused on conditions in the Los Angeles Mexican American community. Open grand jury hearings on the problems of Mexican Americans were held and produced—at least temporarily—some Anglo concern about society's treatment of Mexican Americans. For example, in 1944 a Los Angeles Commission on Human Relations was set up to develop programs designed to improve mutual understanding between Anglos and Mexican Americans. For the next two or three years considerable interest was shown in what was referred to as the "race question." Los Angeles also expanded its educational and recreational budget for heavily Chicano East Los Angeles, and various committees and programs were set up to improve communication between officials and the Mexican American community. Many meetings, institutes, workshops, and teachers' conferences were held on the problems of la raza. Another by-product was the Civic Unity Council, which came in part out of the zoot-suit committee headed by Carey McWilliams. This grew out of demands by liberals for an agency that would give ethnic minorities greater representation in civic matters. Unfortunately, the Civic Unity Council became increasingly conservative and ineffective and disappeared in 1948. However, politicians continued to pay lip service, at least, to the concept of fair treatment and political representation for Mexican Americans. Among Chicanos the zoot-suit riots continue to have emotional relevance.

Another facet of the Mexican American experience during World War II in the Southwest was the intrusion of *sinarquismo* from Mexico.

Sinarquismo, an extremist right-wing political philosophy with Spanish and German Fascist connections, developed during the latter 1930s in precisely those areas from which most immigrants to the United States had come, especially the state of Guanajuato. In Mexico it claimed 500,000 adherents. Its ideology strongly emphasized Mexican nationalism and opposed both Mexican and U.S. involvement in the war against the Axis powers. During World War II, an attempt was made to spread its teachings to barrios in the United States, especially in centers of heavy mexicano population such as El Paso and Los Angeles.

In Los Angeles two local members with connections in Mexico, Pedro Villaseñor and Martin Cabrera, provided leadership for southern California, in part by publishing *El Sinarquista*. This newspaper carried various rumors intended to discourage Mexican Americans from actively supporting the war effort and tried to create distrust of the government. Sinarquistas preached the return of the Southwest to Mexico, a proposal which was consonant with the way some mexicanos viewed the Southwest. This movement was taken seriously by the United States and Mexican governments. Mexican Americans overwhelmingly rejected its divisive appeal, even though some defended the organization's right to present its views. Throughout the Southwest sinarquismo probably at no time attracted more than 3,000 or 4,000 members, although it claimed ten times that many in southern California alone.

Sinarquismo's appeal to Mexican Americans was further weakened by improved economic opportunities. Wartime employment in the new industrial centers of the Midwest and the west coast caused many Mexican Americans to move from rural areas and villages of the Southwest, especially New Mexico and Texas, to urban centers throughout the country, where they obtained higher-paying regular employment and acquired union membership on a much wider scale. Family incomes rose substantially because of higher wages and the fact that several family members were now employed. For the first time Mexican American wives abandoned traditional roles and found work outside the home. This new socioeconomic pattern brought dramatic changes in Mexican American familial relations.

In New Mexico the war years saw considerable development of federal defense agencies. Most important was the atomic energy project at Los Alamos; this and other programs provided many nuevomexicanos with higher-paying industrial and other urban employment. Between 1939 and 1942 about one-half of all working-age males left the rural villages of New Mexico. Although some remained in agriculture, many were able to obtain defense and war industry work thanks to skills acquired during the depression years in various federal programs for unskilled workers. When the war began, the New Mexico Department of Vocational Education greatly expanded these training programs. By September 1942 some 3,500 nuevomexicanos had been taught such critically needed wartime skills as welding, mechanics, and basic electronics. These trainees were able to obtain jobs in new industrial plants throughout the Southwest, especially in California, where airplane factories, shipyards, and other war industries created great demands for skilled and semiskilled workers.

Although some employers still showed reluctance to hire Mexican Americans during World War II, the federal Fair Employment Practices Committee's efforts enabled many to secure work commensurate with their new skills. Strongly supported by influential Senator Dennis (Dionisio) Chávez of New Mexico, the FEPC undertook numerous investigations of discrimination in the Southwest. Even though most Mexican Americans were little aware of the committee's existence, it helped them obtain industrial employment. Most performed well on the job and opened the door wider to others who followed. However, when a peacetime economy returned, many found themselves the first to be laid off.

Generally Texas had less wartime industrial development than other parts of the Southwest, but the oil industry expanded greatly between 1940 and 1946. As a result, Mexican Americans were able to establish a foothold as petroleum workers. Other tejanos moved to Chicago and Detroit to take jobs in war industries and to Kansas City and Denver to work in meat packing and beet-sugar refining. Meat packing in Texas also opened its doors to Mexican American workers during the war. Although most unionized plants generally treated workers equally, many nonunion plants discriminated; wage differentials existed, job opportunities were limited, and promotions were few. The copper-mining industry in Arizona and southwestern New Mexico was long noted for discrimination against Mexican Americans, one-third of its employees.

Wherever they worked, mexicanos were apt to encounter prejudice. To cope with this continuing problem, President Franklin D. Roosevelt appointed the well-known historian Carlos E. Castañeda of the University of Texas as a special assistant on "Latin American" (the Texas euphemism for Mexican) problems. As assistant to the chairman of the

Fair Employment Practices Committee, Dr. Castañeda helped to improve opportunities and working conditions for Mexican Americans. Early in 1945, as part of its war against discrimination, the FEPC ordered the Shell Oil Company to revise its work contracts in order to comply with the Fair Employment Practices Act.

World War II also brought into sharp focus the economic and social plight of Mexican Americans outside the workplace. As a result, federal and state governments took steps to improve the situation. Attempts were made to reduce prejudice in public schools by curtailing segregation of Mexican American children and by trying to foster appreciation of both Mexican and general Latin American history and culture. In January 1944 the Texas Supervisory Committee on Inter-American Education recommended setting up teacher-training institutes to implement these objectives. Summer workshops were established for public school teachers. These workshops encouraged teachers to develop more open attitudes toward Mexican American students and to respect their civil rights. Curriculum materials and teaching units were prepared. Although these tentative moves to help Mexican American children were only partially effective, they were at least a first step— recognition that problems existed.

One interesting effort to improve relations between Anglos and Mexican Americans during World War II was the Spanish-Speaking People's Division in the Office of Inter-American Affairs. The office was not created to deal specifically with problems of Mexican Americans, but its coordinator, Nelson Rockefeller, received numerous suggestions that it focus its attention on them. Consequently the Spanish-Speaking People's Division was set up in April 1942, with Carey McWilliams in charge. This division sought to eliminate discrimination against Mexican Americans and to develop educational programs that would enable them to participate more effectively in American life. It supported creating community action programs, particularly to train community leaders. It prepared cultural materials for teachers and generally tried to stimulate cultural awareness. Although the plan was never completely implemented, important conferences and institutes were held in the Southwest during 1942 and 1943. The division also organized a number of teachers' workshops to encourage the teaching of Spanish and to develop sensitivity to Latin American cultures. It also helped states establish vocational training programs and provided scholarships for Spanish-speaking students.

By the end of World War II the economic status of Mexican Americans showed some improvement. Many industries and jobs that had earlier been almost completely closed to them now provided employment. There was a lower incidence of discrimination, greater access to union representation, and more opportunities in the semiskilled and skilled trades. Small-business ownership had increased. More Mexican American children were getting better educations than ever before. More were completing elementary school, and many were going on to high school. Nevertheless, compared to Anglos they continued to be handicapped by inferior education and unequal educational opportunities. Constraints on Mexican American social progress persisted in part due to deep-seated institutional racism and endemic personal prejudice.

After mustering out of the service many Mexican Americans returned home with new aspirations and ambitions. The GI Bill made available to veterans opportunities for higher education, job training, and business and home loans, none of which had earlier been accessible to most Chicanos. Many veterans shed their traditional parochialism and became eager to improve their social status. Some used the law's provisions to go into business for themselves; others took advantage of the educational opportunities. New self-confidence led these veterans later to establish important organizations like the American GI Forum, the Mexican American Political Association, the Community Service Organization, and the Political Association of Spanish-Speaking Organizations, among others. Returning Mexican American soldiers took the lead in renewed efforts to secure civil rights, thereby infusing traditional attitudes with a new spirit of hope and activism.

However, most Mexican American veterans, even heroes like José López, found that little had changed in the way the majority society viewed them. Medal of Honor winner José López was denied service in a Texas restaurant. Sometimes even in death Chicanos were set apart. In 1948 the remains of Félix Longoria, who had been killed in the reconquest of the Philippine Islands, were returned to the United States for reburial. A bitter dispute arose in his hometown when the only mortician in Three Rivers, Texas, refused to have services for Longoria in his chapel. The story quickly made national newspaper headlines. Most Americans disapproved of the mortician's decision, and the Texas Good Neighbor Commission, appealed to in the case, declared that his refusal was discriminatory. Lyndon B. Johnson, just having won his first election to the U.S. Senate, intervened in the situation and obtained burial for Longoria in Arlington National Cemetery. This was just one of many racist incidents which provided the Mexican American community with dramatic reminders in its continuing battle for civil rights.

World War II had a deep impact on Mexican Americans. It uprooted many and provided higher economic and social goals, new and often broadening experiences, technical training, and expanded job opportunities. Nonetheless, in most areas access to white-collar and supervisory jobs remained limited. In some Texas towns motion-picture theaters, restaurants, and hotels excluded mexicanos until the 1950s, and barbershops and beauty parlors became open to them only in the late 1960s. Not until the 1970s were swimming pools and cemeteries desegregated. The war also provided Mexican American families with new sources of income. Armed services allotments considerably reduced bleak family poverty and the feeling of hopelessness that existed in the 1930s. Money sent to families by nuevomexicanos had a substantial effect on the economic welfare and stability of New Mexican villages. The move to the cities also enlarged incomes, but sometimes resulted in increased racism and conflict, as in the Sleepy Lagoon and zoot-suit affairs.

Changes brought on by the war led to the beginning of greater self-awareness. The war tended to weaken the traditionally close-knit Mexican American family structure and accelerated Americanization. Rapidly expanding urbanization, new skilled employment, and military service tended to distance Mexican Americans further from traditional Mexican life and values. There was a move from a peasant mentality with strong parochial elements to a more egalitarian, working-class, and capitalist culture. Clearly, World War II, like World War I, greatly boosted the acculturation of Mexican Americans.

By 1940 there were more American-born Mexican Americans than immigrant Mexican Americans. Wartime experiences worked changes in the attitudes of the former, but had less effect on their elders. The latter, mostly immigrants culturally conditioned to deprivation, tended to retain the traditionalism and limited aspirations characteristic of peasant societies. Continuing links to home villages in Mexico, as well as Spanish-language newspapers, magazines, and radio stations, helped to preserve a Mexican village culture.

On the other hand, younger Mexican Americans were increasingly motivated to attain higher economic and social positions. They moved to more desirable employment in towns and cities, where their urban experience tended to further weaken traditional Mexican values. Deepened in their sense of citizenship, they began to form political pressure organizations to advance and reinvigorate their struggle for civil rights and to develop political power.

12

BRACEROS: WORLD WAR II
AND AFTER

The Mexican term *bracero* comes from the Spanish word *brazo* ("arm") and has a number of meanings. In its widest sense it is roughly equivalent to the English "hired hand." It is used here to refer to Mexicans recruited as temporary contract workers under several U.S.-Mexican arrangements. Brought into the United States for seasonal employment, braceros normally returned to Mexico at the end of their contracts. However, some stayed over to the following year; others returned to Mexico and came back in succeeding years—often to the same area and the same employer. Ultimately many of them—possibly 350,000 —shifted from bracero to immigrant status. Braceros have been a conspicuous part of recent Mexican migration to the United States. They may be viewed as initiators of the third immigrant wave.

This governmental bracero program in the United States can be divided into three periods. The first, during World War II, began in August 1942 and ended in December 1947; the second ran from February 1948 to 1951; and the third, from 1951 to December 1964, was initiated largely because of labor needs during the Korean War. While the first period was very important for the American war effort, it was relatively small in scale and brought in fewer than a quarter million braceros in five and a half years. In this first phase Mexican workers were recruited under executive agreement and Public Law 45, passed by Congress in 1942. During the interim second period, arrangements for braceros were less formal, and fully two-thirds were undocumented workers already in the United States who were legitimated in order to provide them some protection. The third period, as we shall see, was far more important both to Mexico and to the United States, since it lasted fourteen years, during which some four and one-half million Mexicans were recruited.

These programs had their faint beginnings during World War I, when the Mexican government in 1917 requested the United States to guarantee contracts of immigrant workers, a petition which the American government ignored. A second step toward the bracero programs took place during the heavy immigration of the mid-twenties, when the Mexican consul general at San Antonio, Enrique Santibáñez, proposed an organized program of seasonal migration, supervised by the two governments. This suggestion went unheeded by both governments. Subsequently, however, the Mexican Congress in 1931 passed labor legislation designed to regulate foreign employment. It specified that all contracts must include certain basics, such as housing, medical service, and half pay during illness, and that contracts for temporary agricultural employment of sixty days or more must be in writing. These safeguards for Mexican workers abroad proved ineffective since they could be implemented only with United States cooperation, which was not forthcoming. The United States had its own agricultural problems during the thirties: midwestern drought and massive unemployment.

In the mid-1930s Dust Bowl migrants began to contribute significantly to the makeup of America's harvest labor force; by the latter part of the thirties they comprised about 50 percent of all migratory workers in western agriculture and 90 percent in California. These migrants greatly reduced the demand for foreign workers. When World War II broke out in Europe in 1939, domestic workers continued for a while to meet most U.S. needs for farm labor. However, increasingly agricultural workers were lured away by the higher wages of rapidly expanding defense industries, especially in west coast cities. As a result, by 1941 the American government made its first informal inquiries to Mexico about the possibilities of contracting farm workers. The Mexican government responded that workers might be obtainable if the United States would guarantee employment conditions and supervise the program.

This response and the entrance of the United States into the war in December 1941 after Pearl Harbor marked the beginning of an organized bracero program. Early in 1942 California sugar-beet growers asked the United States Employment Service (USES) for permission to bring in Mexican workers. Immediately thereafter, the citrus industry and railroads made similar requests. However, the USES first undertook recruitment of domestic labor, and only in mid-May 1942 did it certify a probable need for 3,000 Mexican agricultural workers. Growers wanted an open-border policy such as had existed during World War I, when they simply hired individual Mexicans who had crossed the border. Texas and California growers especially badgered the government constantly for Mexican workers under some such informal arrangements. Mexico, disquieted by memories of the recent repatriation of thousands, was not enthusiastic about supplying workers. However, when she declared war on the Axis powers in late May she indicated willingness, as an ally, to supply braceros to the United States.

A U.S.-Mexican committee began working out details of a worker importation program, incorporating some ideas of the noted Mexican anthropologist Manuel Gamio, who had made a major study of Mexican workers in the United States during the 1920s. Gamio had proposed the concept of regulated migration, which would not only provide the United States with workers but would also, he hoped, lead to improvement in Mexico's agricultural practices and in her overall economy.

In July 1942 an executive agreement was signed by the two governments, and the accord was ratified at Mexico City two weeks later. It included minimum guarantees governing wages and working conditions, pay at the prevailing rate for at least 75 percent of the contract period, and the right of individual workers to request contract termination at any time. This agreement emphasized the temporary nature of the arrangements, but set no specific time limit to them. Either government could terminate the pact on ninety days' notice. To a considerable degree the United States was assenting to the 1917 position of the Mexican government. The arrangements to safeguard workers' rights were considered to be excessively protective by growers but were accepted, albeit reluctantly, because of their need for labor. Subsequently modifications of bracero program policies were determined, often through purse-string controls, by a Congress sensitive to the views of agricultural interests.

One example of agriculture's influence was Public Law 45 of April

29, 1943, which, among other things, authorized spending public funds to implement the agreement with Mexico. Under its provisions Department of Agriculture agents determined prevailing wage rates and interpreted details of policy virtually without restriction. After June 1943 direction of the bracero program was turned over to the War Food Administration. There, grower interests dominated even more, and some reversion to earlier patterns of treatment of foreign workers occurred. Mexico's attempts to obtain fair treatment for braceros seldom succeeded completely; a gap always seemed to exist between American promises and worker reality. The bracero agreements did not eliminate exploitation; they merely set limits to it.

Between 1942 and 1947 more than 200,000 braceros were employed in twenty-one states. The program began in 1942 with 4,000 men; the number quickly rose to 52,000 the following year, peaked in 1944 with about 62,000 workers, and then diminished to about 30,000 in 1947. More than half the braceros were employed in California agriculture; the remainder worked principally on southwestern railroads and agribusiness farms. In the 1944 harvest season, braceros made up 9 percent of all agricultural labor in the Pacific states and in that year worked 10 million man-days of farm labor, harvesting crops estimated at $432 million. Their labor made it possible to fill wartime demands for food. Growers favored braceros because they were dependable, able, and cheap and because they enjoyed draft-free status.

Generally, the bracero program in agriculture was successful. Unquestionably, had it not been for the program there would have been greater food shortages during the war. The cost of the program to the federal government amounted to more than $450 per bracero, for a total of more than $113 million. This partial payment of labor costs by the United States government was in effect a subsidy to large-scale agricultural enterprises and railroad companies, the employers of most braceros.

Many thousands of World War II braceros worked for railroads transporting crops and other supplies needed at home and by the armed forces. Late in 1941 the Southern Pacific Railroad requested permission to bring in Mexican nationals for track-maintenance work. The government took no action on the application. After an eighteen-month effort to obtain sufficient American labor by urging retirees to return to work, recruitment of railroad workers began in Mexico in May 1943. Thirty-two railroads requested and secured Mexican workers under an agreement which included a minimum wage and a guarantee of 90 percent employment during the six-month contract period. Eventually, about 80,000 Mexican braceros worked for railroads, over half of them for two companies, the Southern Pacific and Santa Fe lines.

Texas did not participate in the wartime bracero program. Texas growers and ranchers strongly advocated the open-border concept which had functioned profitably for them since the late 1800s. The open-border policy was, of course, contrary to the bracero accord. Nevertheless, Mexicans were recruited outside the agreements by private labor contractors, and on May 11, 1943, the Immigration and Naturalization Service (INS) authorized issuance of one-year work permit cards, which in effect provided Texas with a federally sanctioned open-border policy. Some 2,000 workers entered Texas before the border was again closed—because of protests from the Mexican government. This flouting of the U.S.-Mexican compact and Mexican national feelings was only one part of Mexico's complaints against Texas. In June 1943 the Mexican Secretary of Foreign Affairs, Ezéquiel Padilla, announced that no braceros would be authorized for work in Texas because of numerous complaints from Mexican consuls in the state about discrimination against Mexicans.

Responding to Mexico's refusal to supply workers, Texas leaders reassessed the consequences of prevalent racial attitudes and practices. As a result, on May 6, 1943, the Texas legislature passed the Caucasian Race Resolution, which endorsed the concept of equal rights for all Caucasians in public places of business and amusement. (Mexicans had been officially classified as Caucasians by the U.S. government.) Of course, the resolution did not have the force of law. In mid-June, Texas governor Coke Stevenson informed Secretary Padilla that measures were being taken to reduce discrimination, and he promised enforcement of the recently passed resolution. Governor Stevenson also told Padilla that he intended to create an antidiscrimination commission (however, Stevenson did not appoint this commission until September). Padilla responded simply that the action promised was unequal to the magnitude of the problem. Texas obtained no braceros during 1943.

In 1944 and 1945 both Padilla and Mexican president Manuel Avila Camacho considered allowing braceros to work in Texas; however, they feared that once Texas received approval for braceros, antidiscrimination efforts would cease. Many other Mexican officials shared this belief, which was substantiated and reinforced by the Texas legislature's failure to pass a 1945 bill to prohibit racial discrimination in restaurants. Meanwhile, Texas filled her labor needs during the later war years by hiring high school and college students, more undocumenteds, and even prisoners of war and by recruiting Mexican Americans.

The absence of braceros in Texas during the war benefited American workers, but only to a limited extent. In order to attract more domestic farm labor a program was initiated in January 1945 to improve working conditions, worker housing, and educational opportunities. In the following spring some Texas farm communities even prepared reception centers to welcome migrant workers. As a result, Texas migrants, most of whom were Mexican Americans, found conditions improved over previous years, but generally the measures were unequal to meeting the extensive need for improvement.

In September 1943 Governor Stevenson created the Texas Good Neighbor Commission to counter poor treatment and widespread discrimination. During its first years the commission stressed educating people about the evils of discrimination rather than supporting antidiscrimination legislation. The commission claimed that it brought about improved Anglo understanding of mexicanos between 1943 and 1947. In 1947 it was made a permanent state agency. Governor Beauford H. Jester, who succeeded Stevenson, had a different view of the commission's function, and it became largely ceremonial. Within two years the agency, which seldom included more than a mere handful of Mexican Americans, had completely redirected its focus, its activities centered on entertaining visiting Mexican dignitaries. After oilman Neville Penrose was named chairman in 1950 the commission concerned itself even more with being a goodwill diplomatic agency. On balance, Texas efforts were probably less effective than the bracero program in improving Anglo-Mexican understanding.

Although the bracero program was generally received favorably on both sides of the border, it had a different impact north and south of the Rio Grande. Whatever the reservations of Mexican officials, the average Mexican had only high expectations about working in the United States; financially he usually fared considerably better than he would have in Mexico. Recruited at first in central Mexico, braceros came from a wide range of economic backgrounds; the typical bracero was an unmarried male who grew up in a fairly isolated rural village and had moved to a larger Mexican town. In his prime working years, he became a bracero because of endemic unemployment and underemployment in Mexico. He was barely literate in Spanish, and able to speak only a few words of English.

Bracero experiences in the United States were not uniformly agreeable. However, since employment in Mexico was scarce, pay frequently below subsistence levels, and treatment often shabby, workers usually wanted to return to the United States and its much higher wages. They could expect to earn three to four times as much per hour as the average Mexican agricultural worker. Braceros were willing to endure long separation from family and possible hardships for the financial reward. By the war's end repeaters comprised about 70 percent of the braceros. Many veteran braceros returned year after year with the hope of working for the same companies or growers. To a degree this attitude may have reflected a patrón-peón relationship.

Criticism of the bracero program came from both sides of the border. However, it was never serious enough for either country to terminate the program. Although a majority of growers preferred bracero workers, many of them resented the guarantees stipulated in the program, especially the minimum wages advocated by the Mexican government. On the other hand, United States labor complained that growers used braceros to hold down agricultural wages. It may be pointed out that cotton wages in Texas, which obtained no braceros, rose 236 percent during the war years, while in California, which used more than half of all braceros, cotton wages increased only 136 percent. Moreover, at the growers' request, in 1943 the War Food Administration set wage ceilings in asparagus, tomatoes, grapes, and cotton—all crops extensively using bracero labor.

Braceros had their own complaints, some reflecting their exaggerated expectations or disillusioned hopes, others the harsh conditions of their work. These included prejudice and discrimination, substandard housing, poor food, physical mistreatment, undue exposure to pesticides, unjust deductions from wages, unreasonable charges for room and board, and low net earnings. Weekly earnings at times were below the cost of shelter and board, which usually came to about $12. The average annual income of wartime braceros did not exceed $500. In the 1950s it began to rise and by 1960 it had reached nearly $900.

The most frequent complaints, although not the most serious, concerned the food provided in farm labor camps. Braceros had little or no choice about housing and food, and charges for room and board were deducted from their pay. They complained that food, provided by concessionaires, was often foreign to Mexican tastes, of low quality, and poorly prepared. More serious were the complaints about housing, which generally was shabby, often pest-ridden, and substandard to the point of providing barely minimal shelter. At first braceros were often housed in dilapidated farm structures, decrepit trailers, railroad cars, and even in modified chicken coops. However, government construction of ninety-five farm labor camps by the end of 1943 improved the situation. While braceros' complaints did not stress discriminatory treatment, perhaps for fear of being sent back to Mexico, the Mexican press carried considerable criticism of discrimination as well as poor working conditions and lamented the manpower loss to Mexico. Protections written into the U.S.-Mexican agreements often proved difficult to enforce even though violations were verified and documented by contemporary investigators like Dr. Ernesto Galarza and Carey McWilliams.

Victory over Japan early in September 1945 brought World War II to an end. A year later, on November 15, 1946, the U.S. Department of State notified the Mexican government that it wished to terminate the bracero agreement. Employers, however, pleaded a continuing need for braceros, arguing that the need for agricultural workers remained acute and that they required time to adjust to their former labor sources. In an effort to continue the wartime supply of workers, a bill was introduced in the House of Representatives in January 1947 to extend the bracero program to the end of June 1948. This bill was amended and passed in June as Public Law 40, which provided for the program's termination and repatriation of all braceros by the end of the year. The statutory basis for the program ended at that time.

However, expiration of the program did not bring an end to the importation of Mexican workers. Only the special legislation authorizing the wartime program was abrogated. The pattern and rationale for hiring braceros remained an important element in southwestern agriculture. Between 1947 and 1951 workers continued to be brought across the border as agribusiness returned to prewar practices. Labor contracting was undertaken directly by agricultural organizations and farmers without any arrangements between the two governments and with extremely limited supervision, by Mexico only. In addition, thousands of Mexicans without documents were hired on the north side of the border without any controls or oversight. These undocumenteds were commonly referred to as *mojados*, or "wetbacks," because they presumably swam the Rio Grande to enter Texas.

After the war the United States and Mexico were both concerned about the rapid increase in undocumented workers in the Southwest and widespread indications of worker abuse. In early 1947 they worked out an agreement that included the legalizing of undocumenteds and a promise of sincere efforts to reduce illegal entrance. Texas growers responded to this arrangement by obtaining certification for a 25-cent-an-hour wage for braceros, despite higher prevailing rates in the Southwest, including Texas. In April 1947, Pauline Kibbe, executive secretary of the Texas Good Neighbor Commission, strongly criticized the low certified wage. Her statement brought her into direct conflict with powerful agricultural and ranching interests and later forced her resignation from the commission. Dissatisfied with the Texas growers' position on wages and their failure to live up to other agreements, Mexico in September 1947 stopped legalizing undocumenteds and again put Texas on her blacklist.

In January 1948 importation of alien workers was transferred from the Department of Agriculture to the Department of Labor and a month later the United States and Mexico again reached an agreement on agricultural workers which retained few wartime bracero guarantees but once more stressed the importance of reducing illegal entrance. Then the United States Employment Service established 40 cents an hour as the prevailing wage in the Rio Grande Valley, despite complaints of Texas growers that it would bankrupt them. Agribusiness interests, however, then used the 40-cent wage scale as a yardstick, extending this wage to include not only imported labor but also local, mostly Mexican American, labor.

In the fall another wage dispute developed as the Texas cotton harvest approached. Growers, still fighting for minimal wage rates, agreed on a maximum of $2.50 per hundred pounds, although the going rate was $3.00. Responding to this arbitrary grower wage setting, the Mexican government said that without a $3.00 rate Mexican workers would not be available. Early in October the INS was informed that the cotton would rot in the fields without braceros to pick it; as a result, the Texas border at El Paso was opened to Mexican nationals from October 13 to 18. Despite Mexican government efforts to prevent its citizens from crossing into Texas, including the use of troops, nearly 7,000, lured by jobs even at $2.50, streamed across the border. As they crossed, they were placed under technical arrest by INS representatives and "paroled" to local United States Employment Service centers. Loaded into trucks of the growers' agents with the approval of the USES, they were then taken to labor camps. Strong protests against this legal but unethical maneuver were made by the Mexican government, various labor organizations, and many Mexican American groups. A few days later Jaime Torres Bodet, Mexico's Secretary of Foreign Relations, declared the February bracero agreement abrogated because of the American action. Subsequently, the United States, after taking several muddled positions, expressed regret for this El Paso incident, but only after the cotton crop had been picked!

For the next nine months there was no U.S.-Mexican arrangement on braceros. However, both governments continued to be concerned about the rapidly increasing undocumented flow across the border and undertook further discussions, which finally led to a new agreement on braceros in August 1949. This accord emphasized the suppression of illegal entrance and included a denial of braceros to growers hiring undocumenteds. It also provided for the legalizing of mojados already in the United States and recruitment at the border.

As a result of this new agreement, 87,220 undocumented immigrants were legitimated as braceros in 1949, and in the following year an estimated 60,000 more were legalized, as Mexicans continued to enter the United States without papers. From 1947 to 1950 undocumented workers already in the country formed the majority of contracted braceros. As the legitimating continued, Mexico became increasingly unhappy with America's failure to respect the spirit of the "drying-out" arrangements and complained of worker ill-treatment and violations of contracts by growers, especially in Texas and Arkansas. Her complaints were ignored.

The Korean War, which broke out in 1950, marked the beginning of the third period of the bracero program. American manpower needs led to a return to stricter controls on the importation of Mexican labor. The Mexican government notified the United States that if large numbers of workers were wanted as in World War II, it would be necessary to reestablish guarantees agreed upon during that war. Because of this strong stand by Mexico, President Truman appointed a Commission on Migratory Labor, which included Archbishop Robert Lucey of San Antonio, a longtime supporter of mexicano goals, to study the problem.

As a result of the commission's report and demands by the Mexican government, on July 12, 1951, a migratory labor agreement, Public Law 78, was passed by Congress as a temporary two-year Korean War measure. Its supporters assured the country that it would end the problem of undocumented Mexican immigration.

Public Law 78 outlined a new bracero program, in effect making the Department of Labor the labor contractor and detailing provisions for close administrative control. Under this legislation the Secretary of Labor certified the need for workers, authorized their recruitment in central Mexico, transported them from recruiting centers to labor camps in the United States, and guaranteed that all contractual terms would be met. Public Law 78 specified that braceros were to be contracted for periods of six weeks to six months, during which they were guaranteed work for 75 percent of the time and would be paid the prevailing wage established by the Secretary of Labor.

In August 1951, Mexico and the United States signed an accord formalizing Public Law 78 as treaty. This agreement led to a sharp rise in the importation of braceros; the number hired in Mexico jumped to 192,000 in 1951 and 197,000 in 1952. The popularity of this program with growers caused negotiations to be undertaken in 1953 to renew the law's provisions for two more years. While the step was debated in the United States, Mexican government officials threatened to cut off this labor supply unless bracero wages were raised. In a coercive move the United States announced, in January 1954, a temporary policy of recruiting at the border outside the bracero agreement. This action paralleled an earlier effort by the Associated Farmers of California to recruit South Korean workers under Section H-2 of the McCarran-Walter Immigration and Nationality Act of 1952, when it seemed that Mexico might refuse to extend the two-year 1951 agreement. The new border-recruitment policy led to an incident similar to the one at El Paso in 1948. Despite the Mexican government's efforts to restrain her nationals from crossing the border, about 3,500 of them entered the United States at Calexico, were certified, and assigned to growers—with complete disregard for Mexico's protests. This border recruitment ended early in February. At the same time, many illegal immigrants were "dried out" by the technicality of recrossing the border and returning immediately to the United States as braceros. In March the Mexican government agreed to recruitment at the border, insisted upon by growers.

Public Law 78 was extended for two-year periods in 1954, 1956, and 1958, kept alive by a coalition of conservative Republicans and southern Democrats, all representing farm states. Between 1955 and 1959 the average number of braceros entering the United States per year approached 430,000. The postwar bracero movement reached its peak in 1956, when some 445,000 Mexicans were processed. There were approximately 193,000 in Texas; 151,000 in California; 30,000 in Arkansas; 22,000 in Arizona; 20,000 in New Mexico; 7,000 each in Colorado and Michigan; and 15,000 elsewhere. Over Public Law 78's fourteen-year history its four and one-half million braceros constituted roughly 25 percent of all seasonal farm workers hired in the four states of Texas, California, Arizona, and New Mexico. Their numbers testify to their significance in the southwestern farm economy.

Prompted by criticisms of inhumane bracero treatment from various socially conscious American groups such as the California Migrant Ministry, the National Catholic Welfare Council, and Mexican American leaders like Ernesto Galarza and César Chávez, the Labor Department in 1958 initiated a two-year study of Public Law 78. This Eisenhower administration investigation substantiated most charges made by critics and led to minor improvements in working and housing conditions for some braceros. Controversy and criticism surrounding the program led to a bill in the House of Representatives to phase out bracero workers. However, it failed to pass.

When Public Law 78 came up for renewal in 1960, a seven-month debate ensued, ending finally in a compromise six-month extension. This long discussion made Americans more fully aware of the use and abuse of Mexican labor. The National Council of Churches of Christ in America, the National Catholic Welfare Council, the National Consumers League, the Agricultural Workers Organizing Committee of the AFL-CIO, and other organizations urged strongly that the bracero program be terminated. At the same time a number of factors served to make bracero labor less attractive to agribusiness. Establishment of a $1.00 hourly minimum wage for braceros in 1962 by Secretary of Labor Arthur Goldberg, fought bitterly by growers, reduced the benefits of using Mexicans. As "cheap labor" became less cheap, increased mechanization, especially in cotton and tomatoes, and a prohibition against using bracero labor on power machinery were added factors contributing to diminished bracero employment by the early sixties. Lastly, some decline in the power of agricultural interests in Washington caused Congress to take a more critical view of the program.

Influenced in part by the civil rights movement, in May 1963 the new 88th Congress voted down a bill to extend Public Law 78 for a period of two years. However, in December it voted to renew the program for one year with an amendment specifying that this was the final extension. This congressional stipulation forced growers to begin seeking other sources of labor. At the end of December 1964 Public Law 78 finally expired amid dire predictions that its end would mean a billion-dollar crop loss each year and a great decline in southwestern agriculture. Neither occurred.

Since termination of Public Law 78 various attempts have been made to revive the bracero program, but these efforts have had little effect. In May 1964, even before its expiration, a major effort was initiated by the National Council of Agricultural Employers, organized to undertake the task of lobbying for braceros. Early in 1965 growers demanded the privilege of employing braceros, arguing that not enough domestic workers were available for their needs. Although President Lyndon Johnson's Secretary of Labor, Willard Wirtz, did not accept this argument, he approved use of Section H-2 of the McCarran-Walter Act to bring in about 20,000 temporary Mexican workers. In the same year pressure from agribusiness interests caused Governor Ronald Reagan of California to make prison labor available in agriculture. Since then, the braceros' place in southwestern agriculture has been filled from a variety of sources, especially undocumented aliens, Mexican and others.

Between 1951 and 1965 a total of four and one-half million braceros worked in the United States—plus a similar number of undocumented workers. A majority of both groups were repeaters, so it is impossible to know how many individuals were involved. As the years passed, the bracero program attracted a more diverse Mexican constituency. As a group, third-period braceros tended to be older than the World War II braceros and more of them were married. Perhaps 350,000, 8 percent of the gross number, ultimately settled in the United States. These third-wave braceros had considerable impact on Mexican Americans since they often competed with the latter for jobs.

13

THE SLAVES WE RENT:
UNDOCUMENTEDS,
GREEN CARDERS, COMMUTERS

In the years immediately after the end of the second bracero program (the third period) in 1964, there were a number of attempts in Congress to revive it. The braceros' place in the U.S. economy was quickly filled by undocumented workers, H-2 guest workers, permanent-visa immigrants, and commuters. H-2 workers, so called because their importation was authorized by section H-2 of the McCarran-Walter Immigration and Nationality Act of 1952, averaged 35,000 to 40,000 annually within a decade. Permanent-visa Mexican immigrants, often referred to as "green carders" after the color of their documentation, more than doubled in ten years to 70,000 annually. The number of commuters, those who cross the border on a daily, weekly, or other regular basis to work in the United States, also rose sharply. Many of them were "white carders," entering on temporary visas, but there were also green carders and U.S. citizens among the commuters. Lastly, there was a large, rapidly increasing, and seemingly endless influx of undocumented Mexicans.

After World War II the United States and Mexico reached an understanding to reduce illegal entry. However, political and community pressures often interfered with the work of the INS and its agency, the Border Patrol. Deferential to southwestern farm interests, the INS was often less vigilant when workers were needed, particularly at harvest time. Employer clout was also indicated by changes in Border Patrol funding. Some public officials used undocumented workers in their private businesses; border-area congressmen sometimes took the lead in reducing Border Patrol appropriations, for example in 1952 and 1954. At times border patrolmen have been threatened by growers or their agents, their vehicles occasionally disabled, and patrolmen were given annual leave at the height of the cotton harvest.

There is considerable evidence that the bracero programs tended to stimulate illegal crossing. Many returning braceros described enthusiastically the comparatively high wages in the United States. The bracero's expenses, the frequent necessity of a bribe in order to be chosen, and bureaucratic red tape persuaded many Mexican workers to cross the border without papers. However, the widespread availability of legal braceros until 1965 held the undocumented flow in check to some degree.

The postwar years saw undocumenteds replacing Mexican Americans in the work force, at first particularly in Texas. As time went on, various factors encouraged Mexican undocumenteds. Among these were the absence of legal penalties, insufficient border control, a heavily mexicano rural Southwest, the increase in border and transborder recruiters, and widespread lack of public concern. Undocumenteds were also encouraged by migratory traditions that had become institutionalized over the years. This institutionalization was the result of strong ties, partly set up by the bracero program, between particular Mexican towns or regions and specific American labor markets.

At the end of World War II new factors came together to increase greatly the number of undocumenteds moving into the Southwest. The consolidation of small landholdings in central Mexico and a widespread increase in capital-intensive, irrigated cash-crop farming in northern Mexico brought large numbers of workers from central Mexico to the north and to border cities. Because the northern Mexican labor supply was constantly being drained off, employers recruited more workers than they actually needed. Many of these, attracted to the United States, crossed over, at first usually for relatively short stays. The regional need for labor on both sides led to rapid expansion of border cities, especially those on the Mexican side. Between 1940 and 1950 the population of Ciudad Juárez jumped from 48,881 to 121,903; twenty years later it reached 407,000. Matamoros, Mexicali, and Tijuana all experienced substantial population increases.

The push northward of these unemployed or underemployed workers on the Mexican side of the border was matched by a rapidly rising demand in the American Southwest for farm workers as the integrated production of corporate farming increasingly predominated. Between 1945 and 1955 some 7,500,000 acres of newly irrigated farmland came into production in seventeen western states. Demand for workers at the beginning of the harvest season skyrocketed as growers tried to move their crops to market as quickly as possible at the beginning of the season in order to obtain the higher prices prevalent during that very limited time. A rapid rise in the number of undocumented Mexican workers crossing the border resulted.

The smuggling of undocumenteds, which previously had been important only in Texas, became a thriving and lucrative business along the entire border between Mexico and the United States. Those who did the arranging, *coyotes*, plied their trade from Matamoros to Tijuana. Some coyotes headed highly organized systems which might include small fleets of trucks or buses, secret hideout camps, counterfeit documents for the workers, and guides, called *pateros* or *polleros*, to take illegals across the border. Despite frequent inhumane treatment—being stuffed in automobile trunks, locked in closed vans, hidden in false compartments, or tied to the undercarriage of vehicles—undocumenteds continued to use the coyote's services. No one knows how many crossed into the United States, but in the nine-year period from 1947 to 1955 more than 4,300,000 Mexicans entering the country without papers were taken into custody and returned to Mexico. How many discrete persons were involved is not known, since eventually nearly all who tried to enter continued to try until they succeeded. Most statistical estimates are of gross, not net, undocumented inflow, and seldom are departures from the United States, deaths, or changes in immigrant status taken into account.

For all practical purposes the United States and Mexico have become linked in a single labor market since World War II. Structural economic differences between the two countries have fostered continuing migration, especially of undocumented workers because of increasing difficulty in obtaining visas. The pattern of migration has become deeply embedded in Mexican society. Institutionalization of these networks, especially during the 1950s and 1960s, made the journey across the border possible for virtually everyone, including women and even the poorest class of day workers. At the end of the official bracero program in 1964, these migration networks routinely continued to bring Mexican workers to the United States in ever-larger numbers as employment opportunities in Mexico declined significantly.

As more undocumenteds moved into the lower Rio Grande Valley, local Mexican American labor, unable or unwilling to compete with low-wage Mexican workers, sought better opportunities through seasonal out-migration northward and northwestward, thereby swelling the annual migrant stream from Texas. During the early postwar years Texas paradoxically became both the largest importer and the largest exporter of harvest labor; in some areas as many as half the local workers moved out, at least temporarily, when undocumenteds were hired in large numbers. Many moved into areas where their presence had previously been minimal. In Arkansas, for example, by 1948 about 13,000 Mexican Americans and Mexican nationals had largely replaced African Americans in the cotton fields. In 1960 the San Joaquin Valley tomato harvest employed 8,530 braceros, but only 860 Mexican Americans. Opportunities coming out of World War II also enabled many Mexican Americans to move out of central and southern Texas to seek jobs in urban centers of the state and elsewhere, especially California. This migration after World War II has had major significance in present-day Mexican American patterns of settlement, perhaps equal in importance to the waves of migration which resulted from the 1910 Mexican revolution. It has sometimes been referred to as a "brain drain."

Had the drying-out process in Texas after World War II been successful in reducing the undocumented flow, it might have helped Mexican Americans achieve better socioeconomic conditions. However, it was not. The United States and Mexico hoped that extensive legalization would reduce illegal border crossings and agreed to make greater efforts to end crossing by undocumenteds. These expectations were clearly not realized. Indeed, the possibility of legalization via drying out may have encouraged illegal migration.

Nor did the Korean War bracero program have the promised effect of reducing the flow of undocumenteds; to the contrary, Border Patrol interceptions increased. There is evidence that many employers deliberately discouraged local workers and used low-pay undocumenteds as much as possible. To make that easier, in 1952 Congress passed the so-called Texas Proviso, which specified that hiring undocumenteds was not illegally harboring them. The purpose of the law was to discourage the smuggling of undocumenteds without interfering with hiring them. Moreover, not all illegal aliens were employed in agriculture; according to INS statistics the nature of the jobs undocumenteds sought was changing.

In 1953 immigration authorities were picking up 2,000 undocumenteds per month in industrial occupations, and by mid-1954 this figure had increased to 3,500. As more illegals moved into industrial work, opposition from organized labor increased. At a Mexico City meeting in December 1953 the AFL and CIO joined Mexican labor groups to protest that undocumented workers were detrimental to the welfare of both United States and Mexican union labor. Only in the recession of 1953–54 and the near-doubling of U.S. unemployment (1.8 million, or 2.9 percent, in 1953 to 3.5 million, or 5.5 percent, in 1954) did many Americans and the government begin to view Mexican workers as a threat to U.S. labor. One result of this perceived menace was Operation Wetback in 1954. For a variety of reasons it was followed by reduced levels of undocumented immigration until termination of the second bracero program a decade later.

In June 1954 the U.S. Attorney General, Herbert Brownell, Jr., ordered a massive deportation drive. The rapidly increasing use of undocumented rather than contract Mexican labor was abruptly checked by this sudden and intensive concentration on more rigorous enforcement of immigration laws. Brownell cited the possible illegal entrance of political subversives as a chief reason for his action; however, labor union concern about the increase in undocumented workers was unquestionably also a factor, as was the diminishing political power of southwestern agribusiness. Operation Wetback was widely publicized beforehand in California and Texas in order to discourage employers from hiring undocumented workers and also to encourage illegal immigrants to leave the United States voluntarily, as many had in the early 1930s. Allegedly 1,075,000 illegal entrants were rounded up and sent back to Mexico in 1954 by a special mobile force organized along military lines by the Attorney General's office. Many deportees had been living in the United States for a long time—some for ten years and more. Touted in the media as the solution to the problem of illegals, the drive was often merciless and sometimes abusive.

In implementing Operation Wetback the civil liberties and human rights of deportees and their families were often callously ignored, and physical treatment of deportees was sometimes marked by intimidation, harshness, and contempt. Of the approximately 3,700,000 undocumenteds returned to Mexico between 1950 and 1955 only 63,500 were expelled as a result of formal deportation proceedings. Many left the country "voluntarily." In its 1955 annual report the INS confidently announced that the "wetback problem no longer exists," although, in fact, its causes had not even been addressed. The roundup did not end illegal border crossing and it had only a short-term effect in reducing undocumented immigration.

Operation Wetback did have limited beneficial results for Mexican Americans, especially in southwestern agriculture and to a lesser extent in industry. Included among these benefits were expanded job opportunities and some improvement in pay, working conditions, and housing. Texas cotton wages offer one specific example. Before Operation Wetback, Texas cotton growers were paying as little as $1.50 per hundred pounds of picked cotton. After Operation Wetback in Texas the wage rose to $2.05—a 36 percent increase almost overnight. Similar increases took place in other commercial farm and truck-garden crops. However, the operation was at best a mixed blessing.

Operation Wetback had a limited effect on the economic lot of Mexican Americans, but its results in social terms were more ambiguous. One negative aspect of the 1954 operation was the way in which it affected families. Families were broken up when heads of households were deported, often leaving wives and children to fend for themselves and ultimately to become financial burdens on society. Although some wives and many children were United States citizens, the majority chose to leave the country in order to remain with husbands and fathers. As a result of these heartbreaking experiences, and others, many Mexican Americans have negative or cynical attitudes toward government agencies and programs.

After a decade of considerably reduced levels of undocumented immigration, there was a rapid rise in illegal entrance beginning in the second half of the 1960s. During the seventies an average of 721,000 Mexicans without papers returned to Mexico each year; in the eighties the figure rose to more than a million per year. Most experts see undocumenteds basically as sojourners rather than settlers; however, as more found employment in service industries and manufacturing, they left a residue of permanent Mexican immigrants without documentation. The 1980 census counted 2.1 million Mexican nationals without documents; perhaps as many as 150,000 to 200,000 were added each year in the 1980s. As undocumenteds spend more time in the United States, they become more comfortable and tend to develop economic, social, and familial ties that bind them to El Norte.

With the increase in illegal border crossing and the rise of apprehensions during the seventies, Mexican undocumenteds acquired high political visibility. They became a national issue and the target of an intense anti-alien movement spearheaded by the Federation for American Immigration Reform (FAIR). Strongly favoring restriction of immigration from Mexico, in the 1980s FAIR entered into a dialogue with INS officials which aimed at greater militarization of the border. Inspired by FAIR's rhetoric, a group of Texas vigilantes captured and detained undocumenteds at the border in 1986. In California motorists organized "Light Up the Border" rallies, and San Diego teenagers in camouflage clothing hunted down undocumenteds at the border.

In a depressed economy undocumenteds were perceived by many to be unfairly taking jobs from American citizens and to be a financial drain on social services. Nativists also saw them as a threat to the linguistic and cultural unity of the country. Undocumenteds have become victims of coyotes, contratistas, crew leaders, employers, landlords, and government officials. Some have been victimized by unscrupulous legal advisers and by purveyors of counterfeit documents. Because of their illegal status they lead a clandestine existence, constantly fearful of deportation and often forced to accept employment below standard in working conditions, pay, and housing. They form an underclass which has become the particular concern of the INS.

In late April 1982, with unemployment nearing 10 percent, undocumented workers were targeted in selective INS raids in nine cities—Chicago, Dallas, Denver, Detroit, Houston, Los Angeles, San Francisco, New York, and Newark. Labeled Operation Jobs, the raids removed undocumented aliens from "high-paying jobs" in the expectation that they would be replaced by unemployed Americans. The raids seemed to be aimed predominantly at Mexican, or at least Hispanic, workers. Of the 400 aliens arrested in about forty businesses in the San Francisco Bay Area during the sweep, all but a handful were Spanish-speaking. Employers reported that raiding officers ignored workers who did not appear to be Latino. As a result of a class-action lawsuit and amid charges of racism, the INS suspended further raids. Spot checks two months after the raids revealed that a large number of the aliens, some now with legal papers, were back on the job.

In the 1970s and 1980s raids in factories and on farms, sweeps in barrios, arbitrary detentions in shopping centers, and roadblocks have led to no long-term reduction of the undocumented population, but they did harass and abuse many mexicanos. The raids, with helicopters, patrol cars, and dogs, have increasingly become accepted by the public as necessary to establish control of immigration. The INS has contributed to public fear of immigrants by publicity which refers to them in emotional terms like "invasion," "flood," "surge," "crusade," "dangerous erosion" (of border control), etc. Again the object of these searches and sweeps seems to be primarily Mexican nationals. As a result of the class-action suit against the INS, in January 1992 the agency assented to a court order that prohibits stopping or detaining people solely because they appear to be Hispanic. However, the ruling is legally binding only in northern and central California.

An important aspect of the situation may be that the Border Patrol focuses on numbers. While Mexican undocumenteds represent less than two-thirds of all illegal entrants, they make up approximately 90 percent of all illegal aliens apprehended by the INS. Statistically an undocumented daily commuter from Ciudad Juárez is equivalent to a Nicaraguan or a Guatemalan at the end of a 1,000-mile journey, or an Irish national, after an even longer trip. Since the Border Patrol can easily apprehend great numbers of illegal commuters, less effort is directed at stopping immigrant-smuggling activities.

In recent years more than one million Mexican undocumenteds have been apprehended annually and returned to Mexico. Over 90 percent cross at five Mexican border cities: Tijuana, Mexicali, Nogales, Ciudad Juárez, and Nuevo Laredo, and approximately 50 percent enter the United States through the sixty-six-mile sector at the Tijuana–San Diego crossing, despite a recently erected six-mile ten-foot-high steel fence and barrier. Most of these, when apprehended, presumably cross again and again until they succeed. The same individual may be apprehended several times and be counted as three or four people in INS statistics. Most students of undocumented immigration believe that increasing the size of the Border Patrol and other proposed remedies will do little to deter illegal immigration; reducing economic disparities between Mexico and the United States is fundamental to a permanent solution.

No one knows how many undocumented aliens there are in the United States, but the best-informed estimates at the beginning of the 1990s range from one to two million. Of these between 55 and 65 percent are Mexicans, mostly males between eighteen and thirty-five years of age with five years of schooling. A majority are unmarried and come to the United States by themselves (*solos*), but family migration is on the rise, bringing more women and children. This change has been more noticeable in the late 1980s after the Immigration Reform and Control Act went into effect. Although the trend in recent years has been toward greater dispersal throughout the country, over half of undocumenteds, as well as of legal immigrants, come to California. Establishing themselves mainly there and in Texas, they form at least 10 percent of the population of Mexican descent in the United States.

There were other changes in Mexican immigration during the second half of the 1980s. More of the new undocumenteds, increasingly from larger Mexican cities, are skilled workers who seek industrial and urban employment rather than jobs in agriculture. Many work in hotels, restaurants, health-care centers, laundries, and car washes. Although less than 25 percent work in agriculture and related employment, they make up the largest single ethnic group in that field. One result of the new trend is a marked reduction in seasonal fluctuations of migrants. Border Patrol apprehensions are almost as numerous in November, December, and January as at the height of the summer harvest season.

The Mexican government initiated its own program to reduce the number of undocumented workers, especially commuters, crossing into the United States. It created districts in which foreign companies could establish in-bond factories for labor-intensive manufacturing. The economic rationale behind this response was that goods, not workers, would be moved back and forth across the border. By 1970 over 200 of these bonded factories, called *maquiladoras* or *maquilas*, had been established and were employing about 19,000 workers. The 1970s and 1980s saw amazing growth in this sector. Between 1980 and 1989 the in-bond industry sales rose from less than 3 percent to nearly 11 percent of total Mexican manufacturing sales. By the end of 1990 there were 1,948 maquiladoras with half a million employees. In the next year maquiladoras became Mexico's largest source of foreign exchange after petroleum.

This innovative approach to a long-standing problem has had considerable economic success but it has also met with criticism. American labor has been strongly opposed to the program. The Mexican government finds that border-zone industries attract job seekers from central Mexico, so the objective of reducing the labor pool at the border has not been realized. Nor have the maquilas reduced the northward flow of undocumenteds. In fact, they may stimulate illegal entrance by attracting many more workers to the border region than there are jobs. Only about 10 percent of the employees are male.

The maquiladoras have attracted large numbers of young women to the border cities, where they seek employment. A considerable increase in the number of Mexican women entering the United States without documents has resulted. This development is also a result of the 1986 Immigration Reform and Control Act, which has encouraged family reunification. Recently observers along the border have reported that women, a large majority of them under thirty, now make up between 20 and 35 percent of the undocumented aliens who enter the country.

Another important sector of the southwestern labor force has always been the permanent-resident immigrants from Mexico. In 1850 the United States had a Mexican American population estimated at 87,000 to 118,000; during the next half-century 13,315 Mexican immigrants with visas arrived by sea. No one knows how many crossed the unsupervised land border. After 1900, with southwestern border immigrants included after 1907, documented immigration rose rapidly. As a result of this influx, Mexican immigrants outnumbered Mexican Americans from 1910 until the 1940 census. In the past decade approximately 1,000,000 entered the United States, not counting those given amnesty under the 1986 Immigration Reform and Control Act (IRCA). In recent decades legal immigration has contributed heavily to the growth of Mexican American communities. The volume of this immigration, primarily from lower socioeconomic classes in Mexico, has swelled and somewhat unbalanced the social and economic basis of the Mexican American population.

LEGAL MEXICAN IMMIGRATION

1901–1910	49,642
1911–1920	219,004
1921–1930	459,287
1931–1940	22,319

1941–1950 60,589
1951–1960 299,811
1961–1970 453,937
1971–1980 640,294
1981–1990 .... ca. 1,000,000

Total legal Mexican immigration from 1821 to the implementation of IRCA in 1988 was about 3 million; in 1988 the total Mexico-born population was 2,985,000. These statistics do not take into account the number of documented immigrants who returned to Mexico—estimated at 35 to 50 percent. Statistics on the immigration of Mexicans to the United States vary somewhat from source to source, including U.S. government agencies, and must be used with a degree of caution. The reader should be aware that even U.S. census statistics are not strictly comparable, since decennial censuses have used varying criteria to identify Mexican Americans.

Permanent-visa immigrants, possessors of I-551 cards (I-151 before 1978), the so-called green card, are legally and permanently admitted immigrant aliens who may, therefore, live and work anywhere in the United States. A green card is valid indefinitely unless the possessor is absent from the United States for more than a year, is unemployed for more than six months, or is involved in strikebreaking. Enforcement of these regulations is often lax, and green carders are allowed to equate employment with the residency requirement.

Mexicans with a green card straddle two economic and social worlds. Even after a decade in the United States, with ties that bind the settler to American society, the location of their permanent home may remain ambiguous. Since migration to the United States may be for the Mexican a process recurring over years rather than a single event, the differentiation between settler and sojourner (and commuter) is often not clear-cut. For a variety of reasons some Mexican green carders are not interested in living permanently in the United States. A substantial number of these become commuters.

Commuter status has no basis in law, and although the INS accepts and uses the concept it does not identify commuters in its statistical reports. A commuter is defined as someone who lives in Mexico (or Canada) and crosses the border on a regular basis—daily, weekly, even seasonally—to work in the United States. Commuters, therefore, may be green carders, temporary-entrant white carders (form I-186), U.S.

citizens living in Mexico, or undocumented border crossers. With the elimination of the bracero program in December 1964, a noticeable increase in the employment of commuter workers took place, and they took over many jobs performed earlier by braceros. In some border areas commuters dominate certain fields of employment; overall they make up about 16 percent of the U.S. border work force.

Efforts in the U.S. Congress during the late sixties to restrict (green card) commuting failed in the face of strong opposition. Since then no serious effort has been made to limit commuting. Nobody knows how many commuters there are. A recent study of nine large metropolitan border areas estimated that there were about 160,000 daily commuters. A 1987 estimate held that there were between 150,000 and 300,000 green card commuters alone.

The economic impact of commuters, especially undocumenteds, has long been discussed and disputed. What is the nature of their role in the U.S. economy? Do they take jobs that would otherwise go to American citizens? Or do they take work that most Americans refuse to accept? Are there large numbers of undocumenteds in certain jobs because the work is low-pay, low-prestige, hard, and dirty? The answers are not clear. Undocumented workers are employed in a wide variety of jobs. A 1984 sampling of apprehended employed undocumenteds indicated that 72 percent earned more or less the then legal minimum wage of $3.35 per hour; 28 percent earned $4.25 or more per hour.

In the debate about the economic impact of commuters and undocumented workers one view sees the effect as overwhelmingly negative. Supporters of this interpretation argue that commuters take jobs which would normally be filled by American citizens. Because they are willing to work for lower wages, they crowd out border-area American workers, mostly Mexican Americans, who then seek employment elsewhere. They also tend to prevent or delay improvement in wages and working conditions, and they make it difficult to organize workers into unions. Lastly, commuters are recruited as (sometimes unwitting) strikebreakers. In addition, it is alleged by some that they contribute to crime and give Mexican Americans a bad name.

The opposing view admits the truth or partial truth of many of these assertions but responds that the overall impact is positive. Commuters create jobs as well as take them. Besides, defenders say, a majority of the industrial jobs they take, if not taken by them, would not remain in the United States but would be transferred to Haiti, Hong Kong, or

South Korea. Commuters are described as an indirect subsidy to American business, offsetting competition from low-wage foreign companies. Obviously the net economic impact is debatable.

What of the impact of commuters and undocumenteds on social services? Do they pay their own way or are they a tax drain? A 1975 INS study would seem to show that they "cost" the United States $13 billion annually, and journalistic reports frequently give the impression that they abuse the social welfare system. However, empirical findings, including a 1985 Rand Corporation study in California, have concluded that the average undocumented paid more in taxes than he/she received in services, except for education. Focusing on short-term school costs obscures the long-term benefits that accrue to the nation when the children of undocumenteds are educated. A 1989 survey commissioned by the California legislature interviewed 5,000 IRCA amnesty applicants. The results showed that they rarely used government assistance programs and that 70 percent were employed full-time the month previous to the survey. Commuters, it is contended, make relatively little use of social services because they fear that to do so might jeopardize their employment. Recent trends toward family immigration might result in greater demands on social services, especially food stamps and Medicaid as well as education. Some local communities with high concentrations of immigrants might pay a disproportionate share of public service costs. A 1985 Urban Institute study concluded that most negative concerns about Mexican immigration were generally unfounded.

Overall, while undocumenteds and commuters may have a negative impact on Mexican Americans in the local job market, their employment may result in an increase in total employment. Lower labor costs may have saved some marginal industries such as sportswear manufacturing for American workers and almost certainly have resulted in lower prices for consumers. All in all, studies by the Urban Institute, the Rand Corporation, and the Council of Economic Advisers, as well as a broad consensus, indicate that the impact of undocumenteds on the economy is modestly positive rather than damaging, but the issue remains a matter of dispute. Fundamentally the objection to undocumenteds is social and political rather than economic.

14

A NEW BREED

Mexican Americans' efforts to organize for their protection and advancement have their roots in the nineteenth century. Ever since the Treaty of Guadalupe Hidalgo they have fought for their lands, sought equal justice, taken important roles in labor organizing, participated in politics where possible, and formed groups for mutual protection. Mutual-aid societies, commonly referred to as mutualistas, existed at the time of the treaty but increased considerably toward the end of the century. These organizations, mostly local in scope, pooled the limited resources of many to provide a small measure of security in a difficult environment. Basically they provided burial insurance and a variety of emergency services. In addition, they supplied a focus for barrio life, promoting social and cultural activities like plays, lectures, discussions, and celebration of Mexican and American holidays. They also provided experience for future leaders of labor and civil rights groups that came later. Generally members came from the working class, although some were clearly from the middle class. These early regional organizations had names like Sociedad Mutua Hijos de Hidalgo, Sociedad Mutualista Benito Juárez, and Unión Patriótica Benéfica Mexicana Independencia. After World War I they began taking English rather than Spanish names.

Among these late-nineteenth-century societies was the Alianza Hispano-Americana, founded in Tucson in 1894 in the hope that it would provide typical mutualista security and regain some of the status la raza had earlier enjoyed. Although overwhelmingly middle-class, its leaders announced that they welcomed working-class males. The Alianza was organized into regional lodges, each with a considerable degree of autonomy. Members participated in both social activities and sickness and death benefits. At a time when there was no government social security program the benefits attracted an extensive membership.

Initially mutualista in format, in the 1900s the Alianza became additionally concerned with economic issues. In the Clifton-Morenci copper-mine strikes it supported militant demands for pay equal to that of Anglo miners. During the 1920s it turned toward civil and legal rights and provided legal counsel to poor mexicanos. After World War II the Alianza sought better schools, developed a scholarship program to further its educational goals, and set up a civil liberties department. During the sixties internal dissension caused a decline in membership, and its badly managed finances were reorganized. Finally, at the end of the decade it went into receivership, from which it failed to recover.

Of a somewhat different nature than the Alianza was the Primer Congreso Mexicanista, a onetime organizing meeting which arose early in the second decade of the twentieth century out of the continuing deterioration of tejanos' socioeconomic position. In 1911 newspaper editor Clemente Idar began calling for a convention to address the problems facing tejanos: discrimination, commonplace lynching of mexicanos, and the decline of Mexican culture and language. The Congreso, which met in Laredo in mid-September, had representatives from most Texas mexicano groups. Stressing Mexican nationalism, it created the Gran Liga Mexicanista. An interesting aspect of the Congreso was its concern with the public role of mexicanas, which led to the founding of a second organization, the Liga Femenil Mexicanista. Neither organization survived.

A full decade after the beginning of the Alianza another mutualist and fraternal society, the Liga Protectora Latina, was founded in Phoenix, Arizona. During the Arizona copper-mine strike of 1917 it played a central role in uniting Mexican American and Mexican miners in a struggle for higher wages and equal treatment with Anglo workers. At the same time it staunchly supported the United States war effort and condemned the disruptive tactics and radicalism of miners belonging to the Industrial Workers of the World. Vigilante violence, a few concessions, and deportation of Mexican leaders ended the strike. Plagued by internal bickering and weakened by other factors, the Liga went into a decline in the 1920s and finally disappeared during the depression of the thirties.

Heavy immigration of Mexicans to the United States during the decade of the Great Revolution led to new societies having mutualist and social goals, but strongly emphasizing Mexican nationalism. More important in the long run, an organization called the Comisión Honorífica Mexicana was set up in the Southwest at the beginning of the 1920s. First established in Dallas and Los Angeles by the Mexican consular service, its purpose was to aid Mexican nationals until help could be obtained from the nearest consulate. Numerous chapters were established subsequently and much broader goals were developed. Since World War II local Comisión organizations have directed more attention toward Mexican Americans and centered their concerns on education, particularly on providing scholarships for college-bound students. During the late sixties and early seventies some chapters acted as a conservative counterforce to militant Chicano leadership in the movimiento.

The experience of military service in World War I helped lead to an important early-twentieth-century organization, Sons of America. Some veterans, perceiving a bitter irony between their responsibilities as American citizens and their treatment as a minority, began to demand their full rights as citizens. Imbued with ideas of educating fellow Mexican Americans about these rights, they developed organizations for this purpose. Founded in San Antonio in 1921, the Sons of America was the first consciously Mexican American organization. It was one of the first groups to turn to English, rather than Spanish, organizational names. Its basic objective was to assist Mexican Americans in achieving acculturation and integration through political action. Generally it limited membership to Americans of Mexican and Hispanic background, and it strongly urged its members to learn English and to become citizens. It hoped to end prejudice against Mexican Americans, to achieve equality under the law, to obtain greater educational opportunities, and to acquire political representation at all levels. Concerned about the widespread exclusion of Mexican Americans from jury service and firmly committed to the goal of political power, it stressed voter registration.

The Sons of America quickly expanded to seven councils throughout Texas. The councils were semi-independent and varied in both philosophical viewpoints and emphasis. Conflict soon developed, causing the San Antonio council to reorganize as the independent Knights of America. This separation prompted Benjamín Garza, a Corpus Christi council leader, to call for a unity convention of southern Texas community leaders. In August 1927 a meeting held in Harlingen, Texas, discussed Mexican American problems and especially the need for a unifying organization. Representatives at the convention decided to reorganize the Sons, and invited the other councils to participate. The invitation was rejected. Finally, after considerable discussion and controversy, the delegates created a new organization, the League of Latin American Citizens, with objectives very similar to those of the Sons of America.

Under Garza's influence the Corpus Christi council in February 1929 voted to withdraw from the Sons of America and called again for a convention to unite all Mexican American organizations. Ten days later representatives from the League of Latin American Citizens, the Knights of America, and the Sons of America met in Corpus Christi and formed the League of United Latin American Citizens (LULAC). In the following May, LULAC adopted a constitution which stressed its middle-class goals of economic, political, and social rights for all Mexican Americans.

LULAC's mission was to "make living conditions better for future generations of Mexican Americans" by concentrating its efforts on civil rights, education, and employment. Its declared objectives were: to bring to an end mistreatment and discrimination; to obtain equality before the law and in education, government, and the business world; to promote the training of more Mexican American doctors, lawyers, engineers, and other professionals; to champion ethnic pride; to encourage proficiency in English as a way to greater equality; and to develop active and effective political participation as the heart of citizenship. Its constitution clearly indicated the move from mutualista viewpoints to a primary concern about acculturation and full civil rights. Up to the time of United States involvement in World War II, LULAC was the principal organization in the search for an American identity.

Representing the middle class, LULAC sprang from the modernizing process that swept the Southwest between World War I and World War II. Its goal was to enable Mexicans to embrace American society while retaining a sense of their ethnic origin. In the barrio it served the Mexican immigrants who had come to the United States expecting change but also wanting some continuity. It sought a middle-class balance between legal and nationalistic Americanism and cultural Mexicanism. At times its voice for cultural pluralism was misunderstood and interpreted as an unwillingness to integrate.

Its program clearly outlined, by the early 1930s LULAC began to demonstrate considerable influence in Texas through its eighteen councils. From Texas it soon extended to urban centers with sizable mexicano communities in the Southwest and elsewhere. As a founder and national president from 1930 to 1931, Alonso Perales, an articulate and forceful tejano attorney, inspired Mexican Americans to push for their political and civil rights. In 1932 women's auxiliaries were incorporated and later in the decade a junior LULAC emerged. World War II caused a decline in membership as young men went into the armed services, but LULAC chapters continued their strong support of the war effort.

After World War II, LULAC became a particularly effective political broker on behalf of Mexican Americans. Viewing education pragmatically as a means to upward mobility and better jobs, it stepped up its struggle for equality of educational opportunity, achieving two notable successes. In 1945 it initiated legal action against four Orange County, California, school districts, claiming de facto segregation of mexicano students. This lawsuit, *Méndez* v. *Westminster School District*, led to a landmark decision in favor of the complainants; a federal court enjoined the school district to discontinue segregation. Two years later the circuit court upheld this decision. In 1948 LULAC was also successful in fighting a case of intentional segregation in Texas. Victory in this suit, *Delgado* v. *Bastrop Independent School District*, resulted in evasive tactics by local school districts until the 1960s. Although the court decisions in these two cases, and others, clearly established the illegality of segregation, they by no means ended it. The struggle for equality of education, though partially successful, continued.

In 1957 LULAC initiated a preschool English-language program called the Little School of the 400, which was later taken over by the Lyndon Johnson administration as Project Head Start. By 1975 LULAC had established a national scholarship fund which awarded more than $5.6 million to about 11,000 students in the next sixteen years. During the postwar years LULAC expanded from a regional to a national organization of some 200 councils with about 15,000 members from

California to Washington, D.C. By the late seventies it had reclaimed organizational leadership in the community and by 1980 its struggle had begun to bear more fruit. In 1979 it celebrated its fiftieth anniversary, having become a Hispanic organization by including Puerto Ricans and Cuban Americans among its more than 100,000 members.

In the three decades between 1930 and 1960 a new generation of community leaders arose in the barrios and colonias of the Southwest. Mexican American veterans of World War II, having had their hopes raised, refused to submit to the discrimination of the prewar era. Often denied their civil liberties and excluded from full participation in American life, they were determined to address issues of cultural, racial, and economic prejudice that had held them in subjugation. To achieve this objective their leaders organized the first large-scale Mexican American movement for civil rights. They struggled for meaningful political representation, ethnic tolerance, and cultural pluralism, and rallied fellow Mexican Americans to their cause.

In the Midwest, particularly in Greater Chicago with its sizable mexicano population, efforts to organize date to the war years of the 1940s. Among the groups founded in this decade were the Mexican Civic Committee and the Spanish-Speaking People's Council. In the following decade there was also the Mexican American Council and the Comité Patriótico Mexicano. Sometimes with support from local Catholic leaders, these organizations opposed discrimination and helped recently arrived rural mexicanos cope with the city. Creation of local umbrella organizations like the Spanish-Speaking People's Council and the Pan-American Council which embraced all Latinos were very frustrating because each member group had its own agenda. There were also problems of rivalry among the various leaders.

As we have seen, during the late twenties and early thirties a working-class movement organized numerous labor unions. In 1938, at the end of intense unionization activity, a radical labor-oriented organization was founded in southern California. This Congreso del Pueblo de Habla Española, the brainchild principally of Luisa Moreno, Josefina Fierro de Bright, and Bert Corona, also included some academicians as well as businessmen. It spearheaded a major effort of the Mexican American left to secure basic civil rights for la raza. Emphasizing a commitment to trade unionism, it was the first organization to envision a broad movement which would unite Mexican Americans, Mexicans, and other Latinos. The Congreso aimed at national coverage, but at its peak counted only about 6,000 members, mostly in southern California. During World War II it made a decisive commitment to wartime unity in the fight against fascism; on the home front it took an active role in combating sinarquismo and was active in the Sleepy Lagoon Defense Committee. Radical reformist rather than revolutionary, the Congreso practiced direct confrontation and public protest. As a result of internal discord over its wartime stance it declined rapidly after 1943 and soon disintegrated.

A decade after the establishment of the Congreso another radical organization emerged. Founded in 1949 by liberals and leftists who had participated in the Amigos de [Henry] Wallace movement during the 1948 presidential election, it was intended to be a permanent nationwide organization to fight for Mexican American rights. This new political organization, the Asociación Nacional México-Americana (ANMA), came out of the leftist International Union of Mine, Mill, and Smelter Workers. It was supported by various liberal and radical groups, including the Communist Party, as were many unionizing efforts in the 1930s.

ANMA became deeply involved in the fifteen-month (1950–52) copper miners strike at Bayard, New Mexico, made famous by the film *Salt of the Earth*. It also strongly protested the mass deportation of undocumented Mexican workers during Operation Wetback in 1954. In that same year the Attorney General added it to his list of subversive organizations. Harassed throughout its life by the FBI, which labeled it a Communist-front organization, ANMA lost community support and became a casualty of the McCarthy Red scare and the Cold War. At its peak it had thirty chapters in the Southwest and claimed 4,000 members.

At the end of World War II organizing activities were quickly renewed. Unwilling to accept second-class status, Mexican Americans, or Chicanos as some now preferred to call themselves, led a pragmatic assault on the barriers that restrained them. Direct action and energetic participation in the political process were characteristic of the movement. As a result, the postwar years witnessed the creation of various organizations that accepted cultural diversity and rejected the melting-pot analogy. Early expressions of these concepts and of the new down-to-earth mood were the Civic Unity Leagues and the Community Service Organization (CSO), founded on unique community-organizing ideas promoted by the Chicago-based Industrial Areas Foundation, a brainchild of social activist Saul Alinsky.

The first Civic Unity League was established in 1947 by Ignacio López, militant editor of the southern California weekly *El Espectador*, to continue his long crusade for Mexican American rights. The Unity Leagues publicized incidents of flagrant discrimination against mexicanos and advocated use of the boycott and courts as tools to obtain redress. They were successful in several lawsuits over segregation and elected some Mexican Americans to local offices in the forties and fifties. Much of the Civic Unity Leagues' early success was due to López's adroit leadership. Later he was also active in the CSO and the Mexican American Political Association (MAPA).

The Community Service Organization was begun in 1947 to support the candidacy of public health educator Edward Roybal for the Los Angeles city council. Roybal had been defeated in an earlier bid for a seat on the council. The CSO's initial task, therefore, was to create a voting bloc. The chief organizer was Fred Ross, Sr., an Alinsky disciple who had earlier assisted in establishing Civic Unity Leagues. With the active support of the CSO and its membership Roybal was elected by an overwhelming majority, 20,000 out of 32,000 votes cast. Since its principal goal had been achieved, the CSO found it necessary to generate new objectives. While continuing voter-registration and citizenship drives, it turned to a wide variety of civic actions dealing with concerns of the Mexican American community, especially civil rights violations.

Focusing on police brutality and integration through naturalization and acculturation, the CSO quickly spread from Los Angeles to other urban centers, especially in California and Arizona. By stressing voter education it expanded Mexican American participation in the electoral process and attracted a wide following. In the early 1960s internal conflict arising out of the CSO's relation to the Industrial Areas Foundation led to the withdrawal of some dynamic members, among them César Chávez. However, it quickly recovered and by the second half of the sixties claimed a membership of over 50,000 in twenty-two chapters, but then declined as a result of various factors: especially greater competition from new Mexican American organizations and the more activist mood of the times, as well as internal dissent. When Chicano activism slowed down during the late seventies the CSO regained some of its lost membership, but it has remained essentially a California-based organization. It was one of the first grass-roots organizations and acted as a bridge to Chicano participation in the civil rights movement during the 1960s.

The 1948 Longoria case in Three Rivers, Texas, illustrated the new postwar style of Mexican American leadership. Chicano veterans protested loudly when the mortuary there refused to conduct reburial services for Félix Longoria. A bitter public quarrel followed. Angered by this racism, Mexican American veterans held a meeting the following March at Corpus Christi to discuss what they might do to protest discrimination as well as poor service in the Veterans Administration hospital of that city. Their meeting led to the establishment of the American GI Forum (AGIF), under the leadership of Dr. Héctor Pérez García. Dr. García, a World War II combat surgeon with a distinguished military record, had taken an active role in the Longoria affair.

Although the Forum was organized in response to immediate specific problems, it quickly developed broader goals. Initially it sought to inform Mexican American veterans about their rights under the GI Bill; it then expanded its services to inform the community about available government services. It sought to develop Chicano leadership and to reach raza goals through extensive participation in political, civic, and community affairs. The AGIF strongly stressed political action in a nonpartisan stance. It was (and is) active at all levels of the political system but opposed confrontational tactics. It held voter-registration drives during the fifties and filed lawsuits over civil and social discrimination, especially against Texas school segregation. Employing patriotic rhetoric and symbols, it created a secure position from which to defend Mexican American civil rights and to demand reforms in a decade when anything considered foreign was suspect. Many leaders of its 150, mostly Texas, councils were prominent during the 1960 presidential election in organizing Viva Kennedy clubs.

After stagnation and some membership decline in the 1960s, the Forum revived and expanded in the late seventies as college-educated businessmen and professionals infused the organization with new blood. The AGIF has spread throughout the Southwest and beyond. At the beginning of the 1990s it had a membership of more than 20,000 in thirty states and the District of Columbia; it remains one of the largest and most important Mexican American organizations. Its heavily middle-class membership has given it a voice and influence with many government officials, particularly in recent more conservative Republican administrations. The longevity of the Forum and of LULAC is seen by some observers to be the result of their tactical flexibility. Both organizations provide a vehicle for Mexican Americans who want to contribute to the community within a clearly defined middle-class framework.

Because most Mexican Americans since the 1930s have traditionally voted Democratic, the widespread voter-registration and political activities of the American GI Forum, the Community Service Organization, and other raza groups helped increase Democratic Party strength. However, it seemed to many politically minded Chicanos that the party took their support for granted and resisted integrating them into the party structure and leadership. These feelings led a group of Chicano activists headed by Bert Corona, Edward Roybal, and Eduardo Quevedo to meet in 1959 at Fresno, California, to consider how they might better promote Mexican American political interests. After prolonged discussion they decided to form a new political organization, the Mexican American Political Association (MAPA). MAPA's emphasis was political, ethnic, and nonpartisan. It supported Mexican American candidates in both major parties. It took public stands on issues affecting la raza, it lobbied with public officials for Mexican American interests, and it carried out political-education programs in the community. MAPA initiated a new stage in Mexican American political activism.

From its inception the Mexican American Political Association had a loose organizational structure because of serious differences between militant and moderate factions. Initially it generated widespread enthusiastic interest among southwestern Chicanos and was paid the supreme compliment of imitation. Early in 1960 a group of tejano political leaders formed Mexican Americans for Political Action, sometimes called Texas MAPA. Overshadowed in the election year by the more charismatic Viva Kennedy clubs, it soon faded. California MAPA, on the other hand, continued to influence state politics in the early 1960s and successfully fielded raza candidates. With MAPA support in 1962, Edward Roybal won a seat in the U.S. House of Representatives, a position from which he retired in 1993 at the age of seventy-seven. As MAPA factionalized in the late 1960s and early 1970s it declined, then revived, only to lose strength again in the early eighties. In 1983 Fernando Chávez, César's son, was named president of MAPA in a divisive election that brought accusations of improper activities on the part of the United Farm Workers. Suffering from factionalism and growing conservatism, it has remained essentially a California organization, despite efforts to expand nationally. It has been in the forefront of efforts to increase political representation of California Mexican Americans.

After John F. Kennedy's election in 1960 the goal of a nationwide political organization continued to have attraction for Chicanos. Representatives of California MAPA, Texas MAPA, the CSO, LULAC, Viva Kennedy clubs, and other groups met in Phoenix, Arizona, to create an organization with a national membership and broad Hispanic concerns. MAPA's early successes made it a natural model for such an organization. The elections had shown the importance of the Mexican American vote and indicated that Anglo political control was vulnerable. A national organization could consolidate raza power. Under the leadership of Dr. Héctor García and others the Political Association of Spanish-Speaking Organizations (PASSO/PASO) was formed after some rancorous discussion. Dr. García was elected its first president.

Serious differences in philosophic outlook caused California MAPA and the CSO to withdraw their support from PASSO. Its membership, therefore, was limited largely to activists in the Texas Viva Kennedy clubs. It failed to become the national organization that had been envisioned; instead, it largely replaced Texas MAPA. It has been active mainly in that state and has concentrated on civic education and direct political action. Its most notable success was at Crystal City, Texas, where, in conjunction with the Teamsters Union, the Catholic Bishops' Committee for the Spanish Speaking, and other groups, it led a campaign in 1963 to elect an all-Mexican American town council. However, the Crystal City campaign was also divisive and led to a falling-out in PASSO; most of Héctor García's followers later withdrew. With this split-off of moderates and in keeping with the mood of the late 1960s PASSO turned somewhat more militant.

During the early 1960s PASSO attempted to establish chapters in Arizona. Instead this move led to the founding in Phoenix of the American Coordinating Council of Political Education (ACCPE), based on PASSO but adapted more closely to the political needs of Arizona Chicanos. A nonpartisan organization, the council had some successes in electing Mexican American candidates to town councils and city school boards, but it was never successful at county or state levels. Although it spread to most of Arizona and at its peak had ten chapters with about 2,500 members, it remained a fairly lusterless reflection of

PASSO. The political impact of these organizations, though limited, was clearly evident by the mid-sixties; Mexican American voters in the Southwest found themselves regularly courted by candidates for public office as both major parties took greater notice of their political potential, their needs and aspirations.

During these years Mexican Americans were exposed to the militant black civil rights and the Black Power movements and to strident anti-Vietnam War demonstrators. As they moved to the cities during and after World War II various civil rights issues had greater importance for them. In the countryside, in a largely self-sufficient agricultural economy, civil rights issues arose infrequently. In an urban environment it was more obvious that, while all men might be created equal, some were more equal than others. All of this led to a further step in the Mexican American awakening.

Central to this new perception were four new Chicano leaders deeply concerned with the denial of civil rights. Beginning in the second half of the 1960s, César Chávez, Rodolfo "Corky" Gonzales, Reies López Tijerina, and José Angel Gutiérrez spelled out their goals for la raza. Each created an organization to achieve the objectives he set for Mexican Americans. The most widely known of these leaders, and the first to attract national attention, was César Chávez, whose initial goal was to organize migrant agricultural workers.

As we saw in Chapter 9, early efforts in the 1920s and 1930s to organize agricultural workers had limited success. Efforts in 1936 and 1937 to organize California field, packinghouse, and cannery workers in the American Federation of Labor met with rebuffs from state AFL leaders and strong opposition from the Associated Farmers. In the late forties the National Farm Workers Union (NFWU) was formed in the Central Valley of California. Under the leadership of Ernesto Galarza and others it called a strike against the DiGiorgio Fruit Company that lasted from 1947 to 1950. The strike failed. Nearly a decade later the United Packinghouse Workers of America organized field workers, who struck unsuccessfully in the second half of the fifties. At the end of the decade the AFL-CIO established the Agricultural Workers Organizing Committee (AWOC), which recruited members in the Imperial Valley of southern California. During the 1950s César Chávez Estrada, a longtime director and organizer in the CSO, became convinced that his mission in life was to organize harvest workers, a majority of them mexicanos. In 1962 he left the CSO to develop the National Farm

Workers Association (NFWA). This ultimately became the United Farm Workers (UFW), an AFL-CIO affiliate.

Faced with low harvest wages in California vineyards, in September 1965 the NFWA joined with about 600 Filipino members of the AWOC led by Larry Itliong in a strike against San Joaquin Valley table-grape growers. Chávez believed that the strike had a chance for success because the bracero program had terminated nearly a year earlier in December. He quickly came to dominate the strike and to determine its course, dramatizing *la huelga* (the strike), as it became widely known, as a broad, nonviolent crusade for human dignity and civil rights. The cry "huelga" became a greeting, a challenge, a movement—"la Causa." With help from lieutenants Dolores Huerta, Fred Ross, Sr., Jim Drake, and many others, the charismatic Chávez was able to arouse and organize the ill-used migrant workers. The Delano Grape Strike combined support from labor unions, civil rights groups, student activists, the Catholic Bishops' Committee for the Spanish Speaking, the California Migrant Ministry, and state and national political leaders with Gandhian nonviolence and the symbol of the Virgin of Guadalupe. However, success did not come quickly or easily.

After a 250-mile march from Delano to Sacramento in 1966 to call attention to the strike, Chávez's twenty-five-day fast in the following year to reinspire the strikers' commitment to nonviolence, and a nationwide 1968–70 table-grape boycott, in July 1970 the union finally obtained a series of favorable three-year contracts with most Central Valley table-grape growers. This successful conclusion to the long strike, achieved with the help of the Bishops' Committee, was a testimonial to César Chávez's ability to inspire, organize, and lead. It also indicated overwhelming support from mexicano farm workers. When the contracts expired in 1973, most grape growers did not renew them and instead signed up with the Teamsters union. This reverse was temporarily offset by the 1975 passage of a state Agricultural Labor Relations Act, which provided field elections that enabled the UFW to win back many of its contracts. However, the benefits of the act for the UFW disappeared when the grower-dominated California legislature ended its funding.

The 1970 success in the Delano grape strike led to the next organizing target for the UFW, the lettuce industry in California's Salinas Valley. Here the Teamsters Union was well established and worked closely with the large lettuce growers. Despite picketing, boycotts, lawsuits, and repeated efforts to come to an understanding with the Teamsters about jurisdictional apportionment, Chávez was unable to repeat in Salinas his success in the Central Valley vineyards. In February 1978 the UFW called off the lettuce and grape boycotts and intensified its efforts to expand the union in Texas and Florida.

Earlier organizing efforts by Chávez's disciples in Texas led to a series of agricultural strikes from mid-1966 to 1969. At the end of June 1966 a march from Rio Grande City to the state capital at Austin failed to pressure Texas governor John Connally into supporting the UFW. The lack of in-depth organization, the absence of widespread liberal support, some leadership bickering, plus strikebreaking help from local government agencies, including the Texas Rangers, perhaps foredoomed the effort to failure. Its only positive result was to spotlight Mexican American civil rights groups in Texas. Although its success in the fields was limited, UFW ideas and influence spread in the Southwest, and even to Florida.

However, during the late seventies the parent organization was weakened by internal dissent in UFW ranks, especially over Chávez's use of the Synanon Game, a harsh personal encounter technique that caused defections. At the beginning of the 1980s there was widespread criticism of the UFW's activities in state politics and Chávez's domination of the union. During the 1980s he hoped to reverse declining national support for unionism and the loss of UFW contracts by using direct mailing and computerized lists. He initiated a third grape boycott in 1984 to protest excessive and negligent use of dangerous pesticides by growers and to call attention to the emasculation of California's Agricultural Labor Relations Act. In August 1988 Chávez undertook a thirty-six-day fast to revive flagging support for the four-year-old grape boycott. Although his fast received much media publicity, it seemed to have little practical impact.

At the beginning of the nineties the UFW had a membership of about 10,000 and perhaps 100 contracts in vegetables, citrus, and other agricultural staples. Mechanization and the continuing oversupply of undocumented workers were important factors in its decline. An inexhaustible cheap labor pool has been institutionalized by the Replacement Agricultural Workers (RAW) section of the 1986 Immigration Reform and Control Act (IRCA). A victim of active hostility from agricultural interests and of changing societal concerns, the UFW has also suffered from amateurish administrators and factionalism. Finally, as the UFW has become less relevant to urban Mexican Americans their support has declined.

Late in 1992, the 1984 grape boycott and the campaign against careless use of pesticides were still in place, although few people seemed aware of them. To fulfill the desire for union representation a covey of smaller, local associations have arisen. These organizations were formed in response to specific, usually local, problems as farm workers' wages dropped to less than $5.00 per hour. Some of these groups are limited to a specific crop, while others, like the Border Farmworkers' Union, are delimited by area. In April 1991, in order to pool their expertise, ten of these groups joined to form the Alianza Campesina. This limited development is seen by agricultural labor leaders as a "Band-Aid" solution to serious economic problems continuing to confront harvest workers.

Unquestionably, over the years Chávez and the UFW have had a considerable impact on agricultural wages and working conditions. For both Mexican Americans and Anglos, César Chávez became a symbol of social justice. He was a galvanizing force in making Americans aware of the many injustices Mexican Americans have suffered and still live with. He won a remarkable victory in the vineyards of the Central Valley, although by 1990 its benefits seemed mostly symbolic. As the leader of a civil rights and labor organization he developed the widest appeal, both in the United States and abroad. In November 1990, Mexican president Carlos Salinas Gortari awarded César Chávez, along with folklorist Américo Paredes and sociologist Julián Samora, the Aztec Eagle, the highest honor given to a foreigner. Chávez died on April 23, 1993.

During the late 1960s César Chávez's activities were frequently eclipsed in the press by the more sensational militancy of Reies López Tijerina and his followers in New Mexico. Like Chávez, Tijerina had grown up on the migrant harvest circuit and had limited formal schooling. At seventeen he became a convert to the Assembly of God, a fundamentalist Protestant group. After training in a small Texas Bible school, he then engaged in missionary work along the Mexican border. A decade later Tijerina broke with the sect over matters of church discipline.

By the mid-1950s social justice, rather than his religious creed, had become Tijerina's primary concern. Against vicious local Anglo opposition he spent two years in Arizona trying to establish a utopian cooperative community, Valle de la Paz. In 1960 he moved to New Mexico, where he had already begun to investigate the land-grant issue. Gradually he became convinced that all nuevomexicanos' problems derived from loss of their lands—particularly the town ejido grants. Regaining these land grants became his goal. In 1963 he began to recruit followers in an organization he called Alianza Federal de Mercedes (Federal Alliance of Grants), which, after May 1967, became the Alianza Federal de Pueblos Libres (Federal Alliance of Free Towns).

While recruiting members, Tijerina first turned to the courts to establish the validity of nuevomexicano land claims. By the time of the Delano grape strike the Alianza claimed 20,000 members. Legal appeals having proved fruitless, in 1966 it initiated direct action designed to draw public attention to its claims. The failure of a march from Albuquerque to the state capital in July was followed by more confrontational tactics such as an attempt in October to take over Echo Amphitheater in Kit Carson National Forest, which Tijerina claimed to be part of the San Joaquín de Chama ejido grant. The following June, Tijerina and Alianza members, aliancistas, descended on the Rio Arriba county courthouse in the small town of Tierra Amarilla in order to make a citizen's arrest of the district attorney, Alfonso Sánchez. The incident culminated in a shoot-out between aliancistas and local officials and touched off a massive manhunt with planes, tanks, and helicopters.

Arrested and charged with numerous offenses in connection with both events, Tijerina acted as his own attorney and in a series of trials and appeals won some "not guilty" verdicts. While his cases were in the courts, he visited university and college campuses, giving provocative speeches. He also took a leading role in the 1968 Poor People's March to Washington, D.C., where he vainly demanded a meeting with Secretary of State Dean Rusk to discuss the Treaty of Guadalupe Hidalgo. In the following year he continued his aggressive tactics, attempting a citizen's arrest of Supreme Court nominee Warren Burger, New Mexico governor David Cargo, and other prominent figures. In January 1970 he was convicted in connection with the courthouse raid and sentenced to prison.

After serving more than two years in federal prison Reies Tijerina was paroled in late July 1971 with the condition that he hold no office in the Alianza for the next five years. Following his release he turned to the theme of "Brotherhood Awareness." At the El Paso La Raza Unida Party (LRUP) convention in the following year, he played the role of elder statesman while Corky Gonzales and José Angel Gutiérrez contended for leadership. A month later, in October 1972, he lost many young followers when he angrily walked out of the Tierra y Cultura Congress, which he had called, because it voted, over his objections, to support the LRUP in the November elections. He returned to northern New Mexico land-grant concerns, and when his five-year parole period ended in 1976, he reassumed the presidency of the Alianza.

During Tijerina's imprisonment and parole the Alianza declined considerably. It lacked a strong organizational structure and was handicapped by uncertain and erratic funding. Also, it had always depended heavily on Tijerina's charismatic and energetic leadership. During the second half of the seventies and the early eighties, Tijerina, a legend but now the leader of a considerably weakened organization, made great efforts to interest Mexican presidents in supporting the Alianza on land-grant issues because of the Treaty of Guadalupe Hidalgo. He failed to move them. Mexican government policy has been to take no public position on problems facing Mexican Americans except to criticize denial of their civil rights.

During the seventies and eighties Tijerina attracted less national attention, partly because of his more restrained activities. His support declined and was ultimately reduced mostly to older grant claimants of the Rio Arriba region of northwestern New Mexico. In June 1987 a twentieth anniversary celebration of the Tierra Amarilla "raid" drew fewer than 200 participants to listen to Tijerina's rambling accusatory and at times anti-Semitic diatribe. It was ignored by the national press.

By dramatizing the land-grant question for the entire Southwest and by focusing attention on the deep poverty in rural northern New Mexico this complex man played an important role during his two decades in the limelight. He also rekindled nuevomexicanos' pride in their culture, language, and ethnic identity. Tijerina attracted a mixed following of conservative older nuevomexicanos, most of them descendants of grantees, and of young Chicano activists, mostly students, in a nationalist, irredentist alliance. By the 1980s history had passed him by, and he no longer influenced the course of southwestern events.

To the north of Tierra Amarilla a staunch advocate of Chicano nationalism, Rodolfo Gonzales, commonly known as Corky, set up a civil rights organization in 1966. He based his Cruzada Para La Justicia (Crusade for Justice) on a Denver group called Los Voluntarios, which he had founded earlier. His vague Chicano nationalism never went beyond rhetoric and emphasized Mexican Americans' need for ethnic pride, identity, self-determination, and economic and political autonomy. Ex-GI Forum member, ex-Golden Gloves boxing champion, and ex-Democratic political leader, he envisioned himself as heading a civil rights movement to fight police violence and judicial race hatred toward young Chicanos. The Crusade's center was an old Denver church complex which he converted into classrooms, a library, gymnasium, meeting hall, and social center. This multipurpose base enabled Gonzales to encourage family involvement in the Crusade.

Gonzales was one of many Mexican American leaders who boycotted President Lyndon Johnson's White House Conference on the Mexican American when it met in October 1967 at El Paso. The following summer he participated in the Poor People's March on Washington, D.C., playing an important but secondary role to the flamboyant Tijerina and the black leader Ralph Abernathy. In Washington he issued "Demandas de La Raza," for education, housing, employment, civil rights, and land reform. Meanwhile, to politicize young Chicanos he also gave impassioned talks at college and university campuses. His Plan of the Barrio program and enormously popular poem "I Am Joaquín" added to his stature and to his youthful following. Among Chicano youths his Crusade furnished much of the direction and motivation for the movimiento's politics of protest from 1966 to the mid-1970s. His emphasis on cultural nationalism and political activism attracted a large following among Chicanos of high school and college age, drawn to him by his idealism and rhetorical vigor. During the last years of the sixties and the first of the seventies his Crusade for Justice was arguably the most influential movimiento organization.

In March 1969, Gonzales's first Chicano Youth Liberation Conference, held in Denver and attended by 1,500, developed the Plan Espiritual de Aztlán. The plan's strong nationalist ideology marked a sharp break with earlier assimilationist attitudes of groups like LULAC and the GI Forum. Setting a goal of cultural nationalism, it promoted the concept of Aztec Aztlán, identified with the Southwest, as the Chicano homeland. At the second annual conference the following March, Gonzales called for the organizing of a Chicano political party as well as the establishment of Aztlán. He also announced he was forming a Colorado La Raza Unida Party.

In September 1972, La Raza Unida Party held its first national convention in El Paso. Delegates engaged in vigorous debate over the party platform, political tactics, and leadership. Chávez was effectively excluded; Tijerina attended, but had no leadership to offer. Supporters of Gonzales and followers of José Angel Gutiérrez, founder of the Texas LRUP, dominated the meeting and vied for control. The convention supported much of Gonzales's vaguely socialistic program; however, Gutiérrez won the leadership struggle, emerging as the party's spokesman. LRUP's provocative rhetoric gratuitously alienated many Mexican Americans who usually voted Democratic and might have supported it.

Gonzales's defeat at El Paso marked the first step in the Crusade's decline, as Mexican Americans, reflecting a national conservative trend, turned away from his verbally extremist nationalistic stance. However, he continued to maintain the Crusade's Denver complex with its social services and to defend the civil rights of Colorado Chicanos. As he became increasingly alienated from the Mexican American mainstream, he lost power at the national level. During the late seventies he returned to boxing, training amateurs at first and then professionals. In October 1987 he was severely injured in an automobile accident from which he made a very slow recovery.

While other leaders were involved in dramatic confrontation, José Angel Gutiérrez, a graduate student in political science at St. Mary's University in San Antonio, was organizing fellow students into the Mexican American Youth Organization (MAYO). MAYO's principal objective was to achieve social change by creating Chicano political power in a state dominated by conservative rural Anglos. Gutiérrez was elected its first president. The son of an immigrant Mexican physician who settled in Crystal City, Texas, he returned there to implement some of his ideas for organizing Mexican Americans politically. As a pragmatic politician he recognized that most Mexican Americans would not support the revolution that some radical Chicano ideologues were proposing. Widely known for his rhetorical radicalism, he never went beyond left-wing liberalism in his actions. Partly because of his rabid rhetoric he was denounced by Democratic tejano politicians who viewed MAYO as a threat to their positions and the limited gains already achieved.

Following raza difficulties with the Crystal City school board which caused a high school walkout late in 1969, Gutiérrez organized local Mexican Americans into La Raza Unida Party. In the April 1970 elections Gutiérrez and two other Chicanos won seats on the school board. Two Mexican Americans were also elected to the city council, and

LRUP candidates won city council and school board elections in several nearby towns. In the same year, LRUP was organized in both California and Colorado, and several regional conventions were held in the next two years.

Local electoral success created considerable pressure on La Raza Unida to go national in the 1972 presidential elections. At the El Paso convention Gutiérrez's pragmatic position of working within the two-party system won out over Corky Gonzales's demand for a national third party LRUP ticket. In subsequent elections local La Raza Unida candidates had some success, but it soon became clear that LRUP influence had already peaked. Nevertheless, La Raza Unida showed sufficient strength so that the two major parties subsequently nominated raza candidates in districts with large Chicano populations. LRUP was unable to extend its grass-roots organization beyond southern Texas or to develop a permanent presence even regionally. Its failure to obtain enough signatures to qualify for the ballot in California and Arizona was a major setback. In the 1974 election LRUP candidates in California failed to achieve incorporation of East Los Angeles, a measure they had made the heart of their campaign. It was a mortal blow.

As rhetorical militancy subsided in the late seventies, moderate Mexican American views predominated. LRUP became fragmented and finally collapsed from internal conflict and lack of grass-roots support. Attacks by conservative Anglo leaders in Texas also contributed to the party's demise. Although Gutiérrez was elected judge in Zavala County in 1974, constant difficulties with the Anglo-dominated legal establishment caused him to resign seven years later. He then turned to college teaching. José Angel Gutiérrez's pragmatic political attitudes appealed to many second- and third-level Chicano leaders working within the U.S. political structure. Although his often strident rhetoric attracted youthful activists, it frightened many Anglos and alarmed moderate Mexican Americans.

These four leaders were an important part of la raza's long struggle for full rights. They appealed to the varied segments of Mexican American society. Each emphasized specific aspects of its many problems. Each gave his followers a set of specific goals and renewed hope. Each worked for social justice and stressed the need to establish and guarantee civil rights. Each played a major role in making American society more aware of its injustices to la raza. All were significant in the evolution of the movimiento.

15

EL MOVIMIENTO

The movimiento of the 1960s and 1970s was a direct consequence of successful organizational goals and efforts of the forties and fifties. It was possible because of the incremental improvements in educational, economic, and social mobility that the generation of the sixties and seventies had access to. It began in reaction to Anglo discrimination and racism and from its beginnings demanded civil rights and equality of opportunity in a more pluralistic American society. There was a gradual move from early protests against denial of civil rights to advocacy of a militant cultural nationalism that sometimes spoke of separation and independence. Incremental reform was no longer enough; now students demanded—a favorite word of the movement—Chicano power.

The movimiento was comprised of both groups and individuals with various agendas and strategies to achieve them. It ranged from traditional conservative economic and social protest to cultural nationalism and violence, from reform to revolution. On the left it included Marxist ideology. As it became more politicized, it radicalized for a time much of the usually conservative Mexican American middle class, and it evolved into what many referred to as Chicanismo.

Chicanismo, like the movement, had different meanings for different people. It cut across the boundaries of class, place of origin, gender, and generation. It visualized Mexican Americans unified by common experiences and by pride in their heritage and culture, rather than by economic status, education, or class. Generally it was indifferent to assimilation or acculturation. It argued that Chicanos had a right to cultural autonomy and self-determination. It regarded Mexican Americans as cut off from their roots and dehumanized as they were transformed by their employment into an economic commodity. It agonized over identification and felt it was necessary to develop a true Chicano identity, culture, and history.

Over the years Mexican Americans have been held down by poverty, inferior schools and teachers, language and cultural differences, employment as migrant labor, demographic concentration in the Southwest, and continuing heavy immigration from Mexico. Historically all too many Americans viewed the educating of Mexican Americans as a way to "teach" them their proper role as cheap labor. "Mexican" schools were notoriously shabby, overcrowded, poorly staffed, and underfinanced. The July 1931 Lemon Grove, California, affair illustrates early raza reaction. Mexican American parents called a boycott because the school board arbitrarily decided to build a separate school for mexicano students. Their lawsuit arguing that the school was inferior was the first successful legal challenge to school segregation.

Between 1930 and 1940 the Mexican American school population doubled as children of the large 1920s immigrant wave reached school age. Despite some improvement, at the end of World War II many schools attended by Mexican Americans were in worse condition than they had been during the Great Depression. In the 1960s renewed demands for equality in America and a clearer realization of education's importance in achieving it led to an educational revolt among Chicanos. As their elders campaigned for civil liberties, many young Chicanos became directly involved in pressuring society to respect Mexican Americans' right to equality in education. Initially they worked within a liberal reform framework. Encouraged by a nationwide movement for economic and civil rights in the 1960s, they quickly escalated their expectations and demands.

The nationwide student movements in the 1960s were made up of individuals born after World War II. As more Chicano students entered upper levels of the educational mainstream, they became increasingly concerned with curricula and quality in both secondary schools and colleges. In high schools they employed walkouts, sometimes called "blowouts," and boycotts to promote their demands for educational quality and equality, more relevant social science courses, bilingual and bicultural education, more raza teachers, counselors, and school board members.

At colleges and universities various techniques were employed: mass protest demonstrations, sit-ins in administrative offices, and other direct-confrontation tactics—usually accompanied by emotional rhetoric and sometimes by attacks on university property. Some faculty members joined the students in demands for incorporating Chicano history and culture into social science courses, admitting more raza students, creating Chicano studies programs, and increasing Chicano representation on faculties and governing boards.

Influenced and in some instances directly guided by adults like Corky Gonzales in Denver and high school teacher Sal Castro in Los Angeles, student militants led walkouts in secondary schools all over the Southwest. The boycotts began early in the spring of 1968 at Wilson High School in East Los Angeles and quickly spread. In March 1968 nearly 10,000 students walked out of five Los Angeles high schools. School authorities responded initially by calling in the police, who attacked student meetings and made mass arrests. In many instances protesting students were treated with unnecessary roughness and sometimes with brutality. Many were briefly jailed. Eventually the walkouts compelled administrators to acknowledge the dismal conditions of East Los Angeles schools, and they met with students to discuss remedies. The underground Los Angeles press published student complaints and helped spread the movement. Similar demands and walkouts followed in many cities of the Southwest before the end of the 1967–68 school year.

The youthful exuberance of activists who quickly came to dominate the student movement added drama to the decade from 1965 to 1975. Ignoring the passive role prescribed by custom and usually by their elders, these young Chicanos provided both leadership and strong support in the fight for raza rights. Heeding the example set by four charismatic figures of the sixties, Chávez, Tijerina, Gonzales, and Gutiérrez, youthful urban Mexican Americans now began organizing their fellow students. Prompted by idealized mental images of charismatic revolutionaries like the Mexican Emiliano Zapata and the Argentine Ernesto "Che" Guevara, they quickly developed militant student organizations throughout the Southwest.

Focusing on ethnicity, self-identity, and alienation, these new student pressure groups used the loosely defined concept of Chicanismo to interpret the Mexican American experience. Formed during the late sixties and energized by the civil rights movement, these groups concerned themselves with the quality of their education. Thousands of Chicano students, by challenging the system and sometimes their more moderate and reticent barrio elders, acted as a goad to school administrators and community leaders. Most student demands were eventually supported by Mexican American communities and by existing organizations like MAPA, LULAC, and the GI Forum.

Student organizations developed most successfully in California. In 1966 the Mexican American Student Association (MASA) was founded at East Los Angeles Community College, and United Mexican American Students (UMAS) seems to have arisen from a meeting held at Loyola University in Los Angeles. UMAS, with representatives from various MASA chapters, tended to be service-oriented and to maintain close ties with the community. During the 1968 Los Angeles student walkouts UMAS supplied much of the leadership. In the San Francisco Bay Area, the Mexican American Student Confederation (MASC), founded at this same time, stressed college educational programs and was inclined to be more politically oriented and also more militant in its program and leadership than UMAS in the south.

In Texas, the Mexican American Youth Organization (MAYO) was officially organized in 1967 at St. Mary's College (now University) by José Angel Gutiérrez and other student leaders. Active in a wide variety of community concerns, its principal goals were aggressively political. It spread quickly to other college and high school campuses in Texas. Campus visits by Corky Gonzales and Reies Tijerina served to further MAYO's efforts to arouse student interest and involvement. Early in 1969 MAYO issued a Del Rio Manifesto protesting discrimination, racism, and injustice and affirming Mexican American cultural identity.

In New Mexico, the Chicano Associated Students Organization (CASO), at first called the Spanish American Students Organization, succeeded in persuading Highlands University authorities in Las Vegas to institute multicultural courses. It then climaxed its efforts by getting for the university the first Mexican American president in the United States, Dr. Frank Angel. In the high schools the Chicano Youth Association (CYA), centered in Albuquerque, was concerned mostly with discrimination in the schools, the limited number of Chicano teachers and counselors, and the neglect of important Chicano educational needs.

The rapid growth of student organizations led to the calling of a conference in 1969 at the University of California at Santa Barbara to bring together the various university and college groups under a single umbrella organization. The name chosen for the group, the Movimiento Estudiantil Chicano de Aztlán (MEChA), clearly rejected the appellation "Mexican American" and served to spread the use of the term "Chicano" in the Southwest. Among the organizers of MEChA were Alberto Urista (the poet Alurista), Juan Gómez Quiñones, and Moctezuma Esparza. The conference drew up the Plan de Santa Bárbara, a comprehensive approach to developing Chicano college programs. It included a description of MEChA's ideology as well as course descriptions and sample degree programs. MEChA ultimately replaced most earlier student groups, particularly in California.

Quarrels among the movement's impetuous young leaders sometimes interfered with effective organizational functioning. Not all leaders were clear-thinking, and some followers believed that organization and leadership were inherently elitist and therefore suspect. For some, spontaneity was to be preferred over planning and organizing. Some barrio youths felt that unless one were poverty-stricken and spoke street-wise Caló one could not be considered genuinely Mexican American and certainly not Chicano. Student militants confronted and denounced those community leaders they saw as middle-class and therefore outmoded. As a result, some important movimiento efforts suffered.

Not all Mexican Americans welcomed this youthful militancy. Many older Mexican Americans saw the Chicano movement as a brash, upsetting, and polarizing offensive that ultimately might undermine their precarious accommodation to American society. Some conservatives were quick to denounce it as too aggressive, too strident, and ultimately as divisive. Political leaders like tejanos Henry González and Eligio "Kika" de la Garza labeled various Chicano activist groups as reverse-racist and un-American. Others saw the student movement as unsophisticated, naive, unprofessional, and ultimately counterproductive. Still others were unwilling to endorse the Chicano movement without qualification but recognized the pressing need to publicize Mexican American grievances.

By the end of the 1960s the Chicano movement had made a substantial impact on southwestern high school, college, and university campuses. As a direct result of student activism there were staff, curricular, and policy reforms in most schools. Indirectly the protests also caused other schools, not faced with walkouts or other disruptive tactics, to accept many of what were ultimately, if reluctantly, recognized as legitimate demands, including courses in ethnic studies, recruitment of minority teachers, and sensitizing school faculty and staff to the educational needs of Chicano students.

At the college level, departments of Chicano studies and ethnic studies were created, and courses in Chicano history and sociology were legitimated. In a number of institutions Chicano studies and ethnic studies were recognized as major or minor fields of study, and at San Jose State University in California a graduate program was initiated. Equally important, for the first time serious efforts were made to enroll Mexican American students and to recruit raza faculty. However, because of long-standing deficiencies in educating Mexican Americans, at times there were not enough qualified minority teachers to implement the curricula.

A major drawback for Mexican Americans has been their lack of an institutional academic base, such as blacks have had since the Civil War—for example, Howard University in Washington, D.C. Such a base serves to identify and train leaders. During the 1970s efforts were made to develop Chicano university bases, but they were only partially successful. In Austin, Texas, the Juárez-Lincoln University was organized, and in northwestern Oregon, Mount Angel College became Colegio César Chávez. In California at the beginning of the seventies, a former army base near Davis became Deganiwidah-Quetzalcoatl University (DQU), shared by Chicanos and Native Americans. A decade later the National Hispanic University was founded in Oakland by a group headed by Dr. Roberto Cruz, a former university professor and administrator. In 1990 under his leadership the National Hispanic University moved to nearby San Jose with its large Mexican American population, but kept its Oakland property as a satellite campus. Among the problems faced by small private institutions is securing accreditation and the external financial support that often depends heavily on being accredited.

The student movement had extraordinary importance, especially among urbanized Mexican Americans, in providing encouragement and support for education. As a result, Mexican American students have made some modest gains, as 1990 Bureau of Census statistics indicate. The number of those 25 years of age and over with fewer than five years of schooling has dropped to 15.9 percent (compared to 1.6 percent for the non-Hispanic population), while the number of Chicanos between 25 and 34 who have completed high school has increased to 50.5 percent (compared to 89.2 percent for non-Hispanics). The annual dropout rate remains an unacceptable 10.5 percent. Generally Chicanas had lower levels of formal education than Chicanos; on average they completed 8.8 years of schooling.

The 1990 census statistics also show that the number of Hispanics completing four years of college has risen appreciably; however, it was very low to begin with. Although the number completing college has about doubled over the past two decades, it has barely reflected the increase in the Mexican American population. Of the 2,658,000 Mexican Americans between 25 and 34 years of age, 7.4 percent, or about 196,700, completed four years of college (compared to 25.2 percent for non-Hispanics). A total of about 400,000 of those over 25 have completed college.

By underscoring pride in culture and history the movement helped develop a generation of scholars as well as activists. Each year from 1985 to 1990 about 600 Hispanics have earned doctorates. A whole generation of young Chicano historians, political scientists, and sociologists poured out of American universities in the seventies and eighties and began researching, writing, and publishing as well as teaching. Increasingly raza students chose the sciences, engineering, education, and other professional schools. Nevertheless, even in the Southwest less than 5 percent of teachers are Mexican Americans, while la raza makes up more than 17 percent of the student body.

Despite progress, Mexican Americans still lag behind Anglos in educational achievement. Although the quality of many barrio schools has improved, Mexican American children continue to be handicapped by inferior schooling and unequal educational opportunities. In the primary grades language seems to be a major problem and poverty is a critical factor for high school and college students. For many Mexican Americans secondary and college education must give way to the struggle for survival. Survival may mean that a son quits school to work for food on the table or a daughter works or stays home to care for her younger siblings while both parents work. Poverty is the largest single obstacle to improvement in higher education for la raza. It accounts for low educational levels, which in turn continue the cycle of poverty.

Other Chicano organizations besides campus groups were concerned about education for Mexican Americans. School walkouts led to organizing within the community; an important group, especially during the high school walkouts, was the community-based Brown Berets, composed mostly of youths of high school age. The paramilitary Berets undertook the task of defending students and the community from police harassment and other repression. Many identified their activities as part of the Third World movement for liberation.

In 1969 the Brown Berets joined with other groups, especially MEChA, to form the National Chicano Moratorium Committee in order to protest the high percentage of Chicano casualties in the Vietnam War. An initial rally in December was followed the next August by a national moratorium march in Los Angeles as a climax to demonstrations throughout the Southwest. The march attracted between 20,000 and 30,000 participants from most of the fifty states. In the course of monitoring the march some 500 police and deputies descended on the participants in Laguna Park, creating a chaotic scene of brutal intimidation and mass arrests. In the turmoil three people were killed, many were injured, and some 400 were arrested, including Corky Gonzales, who had been invited as a speaker. Rubén Salazar, a prominent and popular Los Angeles news and television reporter, was killed in the Silver Dollar Bar after the "riot" by a high-velocity tear gas projectile that should never have been fired. The coroner's inquest did not indict the officer responsible for Salazar's death and he was never brought to trial. Most Chicanos and many Anglos felt that the police had greatly overreacted to the march and that the inquest into Salazar's death was seriously flawed.

The Brown Berets had special appeal for barrio youths of limited education and they manifested some suspicion toward businessmen, professionals, and even college students. Factionalism and discipline problems which led to adverse publicity, plus intense police intimidation, caused the group to lose the support of some barrio moderates. In 1972, David Sánchez, founder of the Brown Berets, disbanded the organization because of factional violence and police infiltration. It served an important function in the community by arousing and politicizing many uncommitted moderate Mexican Americans.

In Texas, the Mexican American Cultural Center (MACC), founded in San Antonio in 1969, and the Catholic parish-based Communities Organized for Public Service (COPS) had a similar function of ener-

gizing the community. Both were in part the result of Bishop Patricio
Flores's interest, but they also reflected movimiento influence. The two
groups lobbied and worked successfully for raza economic and political
concerns. COPS publicly challenged the established political and economic powers, a bold departure from earlier organizations of a similar
cast. MACC provided leadership and organizer training programs for
community workers from all over the Southwest.

The Catholic Church as well as the educational system came under
pressure from the new Chicano activism. Although Catholic Mexicans
brought with them to the United States strong religious convictions,
many also felt considerable distrust of the church as an elite institution.
Moreover, they found that U.S. Catholicism, led by clergy and hierarchy with a European orientation, did not provide the ethnic comfort
that many missed.

There existed a dilemma within U.S. church thinking. Generally,
its policy was to foster Americanization among immigrants, even while
realizing that it would eventually lead to loss of some adherents. As
they assimilated, second-generation Mexican Americans' attachment to
the faith could be expected to weaken. Partly in order to reduce this
likelihood, during the 1940s and 1950s the church pushed the development of the Catholic Youth Organization (CYO) and an excellent
parochial school system was created. Many Chicano leaders of the 1970s
and 1980s saw their early parochial education and CYO experience as
extremely important to their later success.

Before 1945 the church hierarchy paid little attention to Mexican
American socioeconomic problems. In January of that year the bishops
of Los Angeles, San Antonio, Santa Fe, and Denver met in Oklahoma
City and organized the Bishops' Committee for the Spanish Speaking
under the direction of San Antonio's archbishop, Robert E. Lucey.
With this leadership some clerics and nuns participated in UFW activities during the Delano grape strike. In 1970 the Bishops' Committee
on Farm Labor played the paramount role in bringing the Delano strike
to a successful conclusion. Four years later the Bishops' Committee
moved to Washington, D.C., and became the Secretariat for the Spanish Speaking, with broad objectives of furthering social justice for Hispanics. In the absence or weakness of other supportive institutions the
church has remained important to Mexican Americans' search for
justice.

Militancy within the movimiento swept away earlier inhibitions, and for the first time Mexican Americans looked critically at the church. An activist Chicano group in the Los Angeles area, Católicos Por La Raza (CPLR), in the early seventies assailed the hierarchy for neglecting Mexican American Catholics. Especially irritating was the fact that some churches in the Southwest still practiced segregation. CPLR demanded attention and reforms, punctuating its activism with a militant Christmas Eve church service demonstration that led to arrests and jail sentences. Undoubtedly partly in response to nudging by the movement, during the 1970s the Vatican appointed about ten Mexican American bishops, and greater efforts were made to recruit Latinos for the priesthood. By 1990 there were two dozen Hispanic bishops in the United States who could articulate in hierarchical circles the concerns of la raza, from education to immigrants' rights.

Meanwhile, at the end of the sixties a group of Chicano priests began an organization to demand greater church concern for Mexican Americans. Named Padres Asociados Para Derechos Religiosos, Educativos, y Sociales (PADRES) (Priests Associated for Religious, Educational, and Social Rights), it also promoted among parishioners a greater awareness of their power to bring about social and economic change. A broadly similar organization of nuns and Catholic laywomen, named Las Hermanas (The Sisters), is more narrowly religious in nature. Founded in Texas in 1970, it is now a national organization; its major goal is to involve Chicanas in active ministry.

In recent years Mexican Americans have become the object of intensive proselytizing by Protestant groups. Of late, evangelical fundamentalists have been particularly aggressive and successful in establishing storefront churches in the barrios. To encourage conversion a number of sects have muted their lack of enthusiasm for some Mexican Catholic practices, particularly devotion to the Virgin of Guadalupe. This toleration of Mexican socioreligious cultural traditions in some cases also includes music and prayers. Multifaceted in their approaches, Protestant churches have dealt with economic and political as well as religious concerns of Mexican Americans. In the Delano grape strike the Migrant Ministry of the National Council of Churches took a prominent role and Protestant clergy were often in the forefront of UFW supporters.

Although movimiento leaders failed to develop a political umbrella organization nationwide, they did have some successes at the national level. Most important were the National Council of La Raza (NCLR), the Southwest Voter Registration Education Project, and the Mexican American Legal Defense and Education Fund (MALDEF). Assisted by a $2.2 million grant from the Ford Foundation to help it through its first five years, MALDEF was established in 1968. As an advocacy agency its preeminent goals were to protect the statutory rights of Chicanos and to help more enter the legal profession.

MALDEF's national governing board initially established offices in Los Angeles and San Antonio. Five years later its financial basis and concerns were appreciably enlarged during the presidency of Vilma Martínez, a dynamic Chicana lawyer and civil rights leader. In the mid-seventies it won suits against various Texas school boards that continued segregation practices despite the courts. Vilma Martínez was replaced as president by Joaquín Avila at the beginning of the 1980s, and he in turn was followed by Antonia Hernández. Under their vigorous leadership MALDEF has continued to stand out in defense of Mexican American rights. During the eighties MALDEF won an important political victory in its Watsonville, California, suit to end at-large elections. Since the passage of the Simpson-Rodino Immigration Reform and Control Act of 1986, investigating and litigating complaints of discrimination resulting from the law has become one of its priorities. With offices in five southwestern cities and in Washington, D.C., it has come to be recognized as the most important advocacy agency for Mexican Americans.

The Southwest Council of La Raza began with broad objectives not unlike those of MALDEF. With a Ford Foundation grant, it was initiated in 1968 in Phoenix, Arizona, as a coalition of two dozen Chicano groups. In 1972 the council moved to Washington, D.C., and one year later was metamorphosed into the National Council of La Raza (NCLR) as it expanded its activities under the able leadership of Raúl Yzaguirre. During the seventies the council developed close ties with more than 100 community organizations as it supported them with advice, know-how, and technical assistance in fund raising, program development, and operation. As the politics of confrontation and radical rhetoric subsided in the mid-seventies, the council's reputation in the Mexican American community grew.

Closer to MALDEF than to the council in its basic concerns is the Southwest Voter Registration Education Project, founded at San Antonio in 1974. Its principal concern is voter registration and election participation. The project works with community groups to encourage

Mexican American citizens of voting age to register and take an active part in politics. With the help of Voting Rights Act amendments in 1975 and 1982, it has had a major part in more than doubling the number of Mexican American voters registered. Despite uncertain funding, it also has helped elect Mexican Americans to public office.

In addition to the achievements of these prominent national and regional organizations, gains have been made by hundreds of other regional and local groups which formed a part of the Chicano movement. Indeed, one of the criticisms of the movement was that it created too many organizations—perhaps as many as 800—with diverse goals and diverse means to goals. Organizations developed in response to particular circumstances of time and place. Some were narrow in the membership they served and in the goals they sought. Many were only for educators; some for engineers, businessmen, or lawyers. Some were for Chicanas only.

During the 1960s and 1970s Chicanas in increasing numbers participated actively in various movimiento groups, particularly in student organizations. This involvement of Chicanas, like other aspects of the movement, was not completely new. As far back as the late nineteenth century Mexican American women took part in auxiliaries of male organizations and in a handful of militant groups that would accept them as equals. A few were able to achieve leadership roles. At the beginning of the 1880s Lucía González Parsons was already deeply involved in midwestern radical labor movements and in 1905 became one of the founders of the Industrial Workers of the World (IWW). Two decades later María L. Hernández and her husband, Pedro, established the Knights of America. This San Antonio split-off from the Sons of America had an influential role in establishing LULAC at the end of the decade. During the 1930s María urged greater ethnic militancy and worked to end school segregation in Texas. After World War II she continued the struggle for Mexican American civil rights and later took part in the Chicano movement despite her advanced age.

One of María's younger contemporaries, Emma Tenayuca, in 1934 founded the radical San Antonio Workers Alliance, which soon claimed over 3,000 members, mostly among pecan shellers. Also prominent in the Alliance was Luisa Moreno, who went on to play an active role in organizing UCAPAWA in southern California during the 1940s. She was deported during the McCarthyite anti-Communist hue and cry of the fifties. Another contemporary and friend of Emma Tenayuca was fellow tejana Manuela Solís, who helped organize border garment industry workers, nearly all Chicanas, as well as farm laborers. In 1938 Manuela and Emma led San Antonio pecan shellers in their strike. After World War II both continued to be active in Mexican American causes, especially the Chicana movement. Some Chicanas were able to create limited local power bases in organizations like MAPA. During the late 1960s many helped form cadres of movimiento organizations.

In the 1960s women's liberation formed a vital part of the American civil rights movement. Although most Chicanas tended to be wary of Anglo feminist groups, they were influenced by the women's movement and greatly expanded their own activities. Most saw themselves as triply victimized—because of class, race, and gender. During the seventies, rape, abortion, and sterilization became issues widely and often vociferously discussed in Chicana meetings. Generally the community gave considerable support to strong feminist positions on these issues by Chicanas. Sexist machismo aroused strong, sometimes emotional feelings among Chicanas; a small minority viewed male sexism as an integral part of Mexican culture.

Chicanas' participation in the movimiento made them increasingly aware of the chauvinism of its male leadership. They found that they often were as much victims of sexist discrimination within the movement as they were victims of racist and ethnic discrimination outside it. Rejection of a Chicana rights resolution by Corky Gonzales's first Chicano Youth Liberation Conference at Denver in 1969 made clear their inferior position in the movement and pushed them to drive for equality. Their new awareness led at times to acrimonious debates with male leaders of movimiento groups and ultimately led to the founding of a number of Chicana organizations.

Throughout the 1970s activity by Chicanas expanded rapidly, especially in colleges and universities, where they organized numerous conferences and discussions. To free themselves from gender-based restrictions of their culture Mexican American women developed over forty regional and national groups by the early eighties. The first strictly Chicana organization was the Comisión Femenil Mexicana Nacional (CFMN), founded in California in October 1970. Less than a year later, in May, the first national conference for Chicanas, held in Houston, attracted some 600 Chicanas and served to rally tejanas to the feminist cause. At the National Chicano Political Conference in San Jose, California, during the 1972 elections, the Chicana Caucus was able to push through a position paper on its concerns, despite some male opposition.

During the second half of the 1970s a handful of national Chicana organizations were founded. Although they had only limited success, they did serve to bring Chicanas together and to make more of them aware of possible remedies for their problems. Through conferences and workshops, as well as by social and political pressure, Chicana groups strove to raise members' consciousness, to provide counseling and mutual support, to increase educational and professional opportunities, and to win equal rights.

Another important expression of Chicana liberation was the publication of journals dealing with Chicana interests. In its June 1971 issue *El Grito del Norte* in New Mexico devoted a special section to Chicana issues. Two years later the first feminist journal, *Encuentro Femenil*, edited by Anna Nieto-Gómez, appeared and was soon followed by half a dozen periodicals emphasizing Chicana concerns, including *Hijas de Cuauhtémoc*, *La Comadre*, *Intercambios Femeniles*, and *Hembra*. Within the academic community research on the history of Chicana activism also began. In 1976 Martha Cotera published *Profile on the Mexican American Woman*, a collection of essays on the accomplishments of Chicanas. This was followed in the next year by *Essays on La Mujer*, edited by Rosaura Sánchez and Rosa Martínez Cruz. In 1984 the National Association for Chicano Studies came under criticism from Chicana feminists who formed a Chicana caucus within the NACS and set the theme of the next conference: "Voces de La Mujer." The proceedings of this conference were published two years later as *Chicana Voices: Intersections of Class, Race, and Gender*, essays on topics of special interest to Chicanas. Since then Chicanas have published studies on various Chicana subjects as well as numerous articles in professional journals.

By the mid-1970s there were noticeable improvements in the position of Mexican Americans in American life, but the movimiento's deterioration was also clearly evident. Militancy was languishing among Chicano organizations as they moved from the activism of the 1960s toward the more restrained mood of the 1980s. Reies Tijerina, subdued because of his prison term, five years' parole, and rejection by other leaders, had left the national scene. Corky Gonzales largely stayed at home in Denver, and José Angel Gutiérrez had split the LRUP and left the Southwest. César Chávez had lost hard-fought gains in union contracts and faced insurgency within UFW ranks. Bitter controversy among second-level leaders and tensions between activists of middle-class and working-class backgrounds further weakened the movement.

At the same time American society appeared less concerned about the problems of Mexican Americans and other minorities. The civil rights crusade in the Southwest had been blunted by a combination of victories, accommodation, external pressures from authorities, and internal friction. Affirmative action seemed less urgent. Many Chicanos appeared more concerned about their individual economic improvement than the broader issue of quality of life for the underdog. To complete the picture, by the late 1980s the much heralded "Decade of the Hispanic" had clearly failed to live up to its promises.

However, the movimiento had been influential in organizing the enlarged Mexican American community and in alerting its members to their potential civic clout. In Texas particularly, it had undermined political structures that favored rural conservative domination in politics. By engendering pride in Mexican culture the movimiento created in American society a broader respect for Mexican Americans. It was also important in developing Chicana concerns, in increasing the number of active professionals and politicians, and, most important, in improving educational opportunities. As a result of the movimiento, more than fifty universities and colleges initiated Chicano/Mexican American studies departments and programs, and many high schools in the Southwest introduced classes in Chicano studies. However, that the battle for better education is far from over is indicated by recent high school blowouts by Mexican American students in Houston, Texas (1989), and Dinuba, California (1992).

16

THE CHICANO CULTURAL
RENAISSANCE

The massive immigration of Mexicans in the two decades from 1910 to 1930 brought with it no formal institutions to preserve and sustain their culture—no universities, few schools, no (Mexican) church. Nor did the immigrants develop important institutions to train intellectuals, writers, and other artists in a Mexican tradition. Because many folk practices of a Catholic-based Mexican culture persisted Mexicans were generally seen by the American Catholic Church as less than fully Catholic or at best as Mexican Catholics who needed to be reeducated to Northern European Catholicism. Their church, therefore, provided them with little cultural guidance or support in their new country.

Culture is, of course, constantly evolving. Until the 1930s Mexican American culture was largely set by the upper classes, who established the tone of the society. They tended to focus on Mexico and the past. In 1929 the League of United Latin American Citizens (LULAC) put forward the more democratic American ideals of the middle class. LULAC tempered upper-class cultural views and provided a more egalitarian viewpoint preferred by most Mexican Americans. Some have described this change as a move from a Mexican to a Mexican American mentality; it caused the 1930s to be seen as a decade of Americanization. The culture that evolved in the Southwest, derived from common customs, language, and especially shared religious beliefs and practices, more than strictly ethnic concerns, supplied cohesion to the movimiento.

In many ways the movimiento was the dividing line in the long history of the Mexican American search for cultural identity. The movimiento and the cultural renaissance of the late 1960s and 1970s clearly were mutually reinforcing. Artists drew inspiration from the movement as well as from their Mexican Indian background; some created a unique synthesis of the two. Most authors drew upon their life experiences for topics and themes, but some combined these with cultural elements from their Indian past. Notable Chicano artists—in the theater, painting (especially murals), music, literature, poetry, and the plastic arts— achieved wide public recognition.

The Mexican American community is one of great heterogeneity. Differences arise from occupations or professions, from levels of formal education and use of Spanish and English, from the degree of acculturation or assimilation into American society, from racial combinations, from regional Mexican cultural differences, and from the cultural climate in both Mexico and the United States at the time of migration. Mexicans are a diverse, multicultural people with many linguistic roots, physical types, and social levels. The immigrants who came in the 1980s clearly did not bring with them a Mexican culture identical to that brought by those who arrived during the 1910 revolution or in the late 1800s. Generations of Mexican immigrants from different parts of Mexico have interacted with each other and with the local cultures they encountered in rural and urban American environments. This process of mixing and blending over a period of more than a century, always deeply indebted to the past on both an individual and a community level, has resulted in identifiable regional and subregional cultures.

Despite this diversity, there are unifying factors: broad genetic makeup, language, country of origin, historical experiences in both Mexico and the United States, general cultural and social customs, and, above all, broadly common religious beliefs and practices. Racism, segregation, and discrimination arising from their minority position have also served to unite them. Mexican Americans have retained traditional aspects of their culture so long because of relative isolation in the United States, closeness to Mexico, ease of travel, and the Spanish-language media. These factors were all used by the movement to unify its supporters and promote its objectives.

The political, economic, and social objectives of the movimiento were in the long run, and perhaps primarily, cultural. The 1960s radicalization led to greater awareness of and pride in Mexican American cultural uniqueness. Most Chicanos, like their leaders, viewed themselves as deprived of, or at least separated from, their cultural roots. Chicano intellectuals suffered from a deep sense of alienation and experienced a need to explore and continue elaborating their culture, to construct their history, and to redefine their identity. This concern for self-definition is perhaps best illustrated by Corky Gonzales's poem "I Am Joaquín" (1967). From the beginning Chicano leaders in the movimiento saw the arts as an important tool to achieve their objectives. The arts became a powerful agency in redefining identity and expressing pride in ethnicity.

The Mexican American pursuit of self-definition sought to strengthen pride in Chicano cultural roots as it protested against domination by Anglo society and its denial of worth to mexicano culture. In its early stages the movement attacked the many offensive stereotypes—for example, the bandido and the lazy Mexican—and particularly their widespread use in advertising and films. Chicano leaders moved away from the melting-pot concept of Americanization to a salad-bowl analogy and emphasized their Amerindian roots. They identified with their Indian ancestors and with the Mexicas' mythological homeland, Aztlán. Out of this quest for a more positive identity, a new self-confidence was born. As self-esteem grew and Chicanos developed a greater sense of cultural continuity, the need for self-identification became less dominant.

An important current in the movimiento was an emphasis on literature, drama, and poetry. As the movement evolved, there was a flowering of novels, short stories, essays, poetry, and plays by Chicanos who pridefully emphasized their Mexican Indian heritage. Many wrote about Indian themes, and they gave their journals names like *El Azteca* and *Aztlán* and frequently used Aztec and Mayan figures and symbols to illustrate and decorate their books, poems, and articles. This literary renaissance both nourished the movement and was nurtured by it. Within its complexity it had many currents and directions. In literature, mural art, and *corridos* (popular ballads) immigration and the mexicano labor experience became major themes. Writers explored themes of prejudice, discrimination, and exploitation, as well as the pain of cultural adaptation. Some authors wrote in English, some turned to Spanish, some combined the two languages. To a considerable extent the writings were autobiographical.

Pocho by José Antonio Villarreal, the first significant Chicano novel, was published in 1959 by a major U.S. publisher, Doubleday. It was the semi-autobiographical story of a Chicano youth growing up in California's Santa Clara Valley. Unfortunately for Villarreal, it was ahead of its time and received scant attention. Not until the movimiento gathered impetus in the next decade did it achieve widespread fame. Villarreal described the immigrants' culture shock, the Mexican American experience in California, and societal pressures. In the mid-sixties Raymond Barrio, a Californian by adoption, wrote *The Plum Plum Pickers*, a more expository picture of socioeconomic injustices in American agriculture. The book detailed the experiences of a contemporary migrant couple trapped by an exploitive agricultural system. By the late sixties and early seventies greater interest in publishing Chicano works had developed, and a number of anthologies of Chicano short stories and excerpts appeared. In 1970 Richard Vásquez came out with his *Chicano*, a historical novel of the immigrant experience in the United States delineated in three generations of a family. *Peregrinos de Aztlán* (1974) by Miguel Méndez added the unhappy experience of undocumented immigrants to that of Chicanos living in the Southwest.

In 1970 Tomás Rivera's . . . *y no se tragó la tierra* won the first Premio Quinto Sol. Its publication the next year set high standards for a new generation of Chicano novels. Made up of twelve narratives thematically linked, the novel focused on the plight of migrant farm workers as seen through the eyes of a child. In that same year *Bless Me, Ultima*, a novel reflecting older, rural nuevomexicano life, by Rudolfo Anaya of New Mexico won the second Premio Quinto Sol award and was published a year later. The next Quinto Sol prize went to Rolando Hinojosa-Smith's picaresque *Estampas del valle y otras obras*, published in 1973; three years later his *Klail City y sus alrededores* won the highly respected international Casa de las Américas award.

Among other notable Mexican American novelists are Nash Candelaria, best known for his *Memories of the Alhambra* (1977), the first of a series of four novels about the Rafa family's search for identity; Ron Arias with his social commentary, *The Road to Tamasunchale* (1975); John Rechy, author of *City of Night* (1963) and six subsequent novels dealing with homosexual life in large urban centers; Oscar Zeta Acosta, *Autobiography of a Brown Buffalo* (1972), which tells of a search for machismo through drugs and sex, and *Revolt of the Cockroach People* (1973); Arturo Islas with his semi-autobiographical novels *The Rain God* (1984) and *Migrant Souls* (1990); and Victor Villaseñor's highly successful nonfictional *Rain of Gold* (1990), the story of his family's move from Mexico to California, depicting both the economic opportunity and the discrimination encountered. These and other Chicano works detail the experience of Mexican Americans and offer insight into their culture and the authors' artistic creativity. The best of Chicano writing, like other literature, has universal application.

Perhaps the most widely known Mexican American writer is the late Ernesto Galarza, one of the first Mexican Americans to receive a Ph.D. His autobiographical *Barrio Boy* (1971) provides personal details of the family move from Mexico as he remembered it; out of his adult experience came a large number of important works dealing principally with mexicano labor. The most controversial modern Mexican American author, Richard Rodríguez, is a second-generation writer who was born in San Francisco and, like Ernesto Galarza, grew up in Sacramento. In 1982 he published the autobiographical *Hunger of Memory: The Education of Richard Rodríguez*; its message upset many Mexican Americans. In it he argues that most immigrants want to be accepted in American society, but without feeling that they are betraying their Mexican culture. He also sees them dominated by nostalgia for the past because of American antipathy to things Mexican. His criticism of affirmative action and bilingual education have made his book especially controversial, while its clear prose has won him several awards. Success has enabled him to expound his views on acculturation and assimilation in prestigious journals and the popular media.

The short story, as well as longer fiction, has been a favorite Chicano literary genre, with numerous outstanding practitioners: Francisco Jiménez, Sabine Ulibarrí, Ron Arias, Estela Portillo Trambly, Miguel Méndez, Rosaura Sánchez, and Sergio Elizondo among others. The most recent short story star on the Mexican American literary horizon is Sandra Cisneros, whose work *Woman Hollering Creek and Other Stories*, published in 1991, has received rave reviews, even more than her earlier *The House on Mango Street*. Most Chicano short stories come out of the authors' experience; as a result, they tend to be regional, dealing mainly with the Southwest. Typically the stories portray a young Chicano's coming to grips with the realities of the American world. The Chicano short story, like the novel, is alive and flourishing. Mexican American writing is increasingly recognized by mainstream publishers, readers, students, and critics as a vital part of American literature.

Chicano dramatic works also give testimony to the creative talent in the movement. The plays of Carlos Morton (*The Many Deaths of Danny Rosales*, 1983), Estela Portillo Trambly (*Day of the Swallows*, 1971), and Luis Valdez have aroused widespread interest. Valdez's name has become virtually synonymous with Chicano drama. A student leader early in the movement, during "la huelga" he improvised numerous *actos*, one-act plays, for his Teatro Campesino. The biting satire of his early work shows a keen perception of the Chicano experience and a deep understanding of the farm workers' plight. His actos have been widely acclaimed, especially as he moved from harvest workers to barrio life for his themes. Over the years Valdez has become a model for Chicano dramatists.

Luis Valdez has been outstanding also as a theatrical and film producer. His Teatro Campesino, derived from a variety of sources, was begun in 1965 to support the United Farm Workers movement. It has inspired the formation of numerous other teatro companies in colleges, universities, and barrios all over the United States. Among the better known are the Teatro de Esperanza in Santa Barbara, Teatro Nuevo Siglo of the University of California at San Diego, Teatro Libertad in Tucson, and La Compañía del Teatro of Albuquerque. La Compañía has been especially important as a training ground for actors, and Nuevo Siglo has toured Europe. Under Valdez's leadership the various groups joined in 1970 to form a loose affiliation called TENAZ (Teatros Nacionales de Aztlán), which has held annual Chicano theater festivals.

The recent trend has been away from people's theater to diverse styles of drama. This move is illustrated by Luis Valdez's 1978 play, and later film, *Zoot Suit*, and his 1986 *I Don't Have to Show You No Stinking Badges*. Lately Teatro Campesino productions have turned to the problems of Chicanas; *Simply Maria* and *How Else Am I Supposed to Know I'm Still Alive?* are recent examples. Another example of the trend is Carmen Zapata's bilingual theater group, founded in the 1970s in southern California.

In films, outstanding independent Chicano producers are Moctezuma Esparza, Jesús Treviño, and Richard "Cheech" Marín. Excellent television films like *The Ballad of Gregorio Cortez* by Esparza and *Sequín* by Treviño, as well as the biculturally sensitive *Born in East L.A.*, written and directed by Marín, have helped make their names well known to the American public along with that of Valdez. Valdez is widely known for his highly successful film *La Bamba*. In addition to *Sequín* Treviño has also produced and directed a number of other documentaries. Paul Espinosa is noted as the producer of *Ballad of an Unsung Hero*, the story of Pedro González, a pioneering Los Angeles radio and recording star who was railroaded to prison. Gregory Nava's 1983 film, *El Norte*, about two Guatemalans enjoyed wide acceptance; it showed dramatically the problems faced by immigrants crossing the border from Mexico to the United States without documents. A very different sort of film was *The Milagro Beanfield War*, co-produced by Moctezuma Esparza. It painted an engaging picture of nuevomexicano small-town life and the struggle to preserve the old ways in the face of Anglo intrusion.

In addition to these filmmakers and directors there has been an appreciable increase in the number of younger actors, some made popular by television shows. Among them are Edward James Olmos, Andrés García, Lynda Córdoba Carter, Paul Rodríguez, "Cheech" Marín, and Guillermo Gómez-Peña. They join the company of veterans like Katy Jurado, Ricardo Montalbán, and Anthony Quinn. Not to mention mexicano film pioneers like Dolores Del Río, Lupe Velez, Ramón Novarro, Gilbert Roland, and Leo Carrillo.

From the beginning of the movement, and long before, poetry has been a literary form of great attraction for Chicanos; it has been highly experimental both in form and in language. Most Chicano poets draw their inspiration as well as their metaphors from the social conditions in which they find themselves. The 1960s saw an outpouring of verse, much of it political in nature and some at times strident and confrontational. The best-known poem and the most widely acclaimed piece of Chicano literature is Corky Gonzales's epic "I Am Joaquín," mentioned earlier. It weaves ancient Aztec myth, more recent Mexican history, and contemporary Chicano anguish into a moving epic. In 1969 "I Am Joaquín" was filmed by the Teatro Campesino, creating the poem in a new dimension.

Among those poets who follow closely behind Gonzales in poetic stature are Alurista (Alberto Urista Heredia), Abelardo Delgado, Lorna Dee Cervantes, Rafael Jesús González, José Montoya, Gary Soto, Omar Salinas, and Bernice Zamora—all of whom have earned national and international reputations. These and other Mexican American poets frequently combine hard realism from their daily life with mysticism and great lyricism. Some of their poetry combines Spanish and English powerfully in a single work. Their poetry reflects the frustration, suffering, and existential problems of survival that challenge Chicanos daily. Their principal message is an urgent call for change and greater tolerance in American society.

Rapid expansion of literature brought an explosion of Chicano journals and periodicals, popular and academic, transitory and enduring. The most important academic journals were *El Grito, Aztlán,* and *La Red/The Net. El Grito: A Journal of Contemporary Mexican American Thought* was first published in late 1967 in Berkeley by Quinto Sol Publications, headed by Professor Octavio Romano-V of the University of California and Nick Vaca. Octavio Romano-V played a fundamental role in the Chicano literary renaissance. He saw Mexican Americans deep in the process of self-identification and in need of a platform from which to express their views and articulate their concerns. *El Grito* provided that forum.

Aztlán: International Journal of Chicano Studies and Research, now subtitled more simply *A Journal of Chicano Studies,* began in 1970 as a quarterly published by the Chicano Studies Center at the University of California at Los Angeles under the guidance of Juan Gómez Quiñones. *La Red/The Net: The Hispanic Journal of Education, Commentary, and Reviews* is a quarterly which focuses on educational issues of importance to Chicanos. It developed out of an earlier monthly newsletter of the National Chicano Research Network. These journals and others of more irregular issue, such as *Atisbos, Campo Libre, Caracol, Chismearte, La Cucaracha, Con Safos, De Colores,* and *Tejidos,* carried poetry, short stories, and scholarly as well as popular articles on topics in the social sciences and arts. They made it possible for many young Chicanos to break into print.

There were other more regional and local publications, many published by Chicano studies centers; most of them appeared irregularly and disappeared by the mid-eighties. In addition there were a handful of more specialized journals, such as *Chicano Law Review,* concerned with issues affecting Mexican Americans; *Bilingual Review/Revista Bilingüe,* primarily a bibliographic and research journal; and *Revista Chicano-Riqueña,* now called *The Americas Review,* specializing in creative literature and literary criticism.

Popular periodicals have aimed at a broad middle-class Latino readership. The best-known are *Caminos, La Luz, Nuestro, Hispanic,* and *Réplica*—all national journals featuring articles on cultural events, current news, Latino personalities, and other topics of special interest to the nation's Hispanics. By 1980 *Hispanic Business,* published by Chicano Jesús Chavarría, had become the bible of the growing Mexican American business class.

Because most Chicano writers found it extremely difficult to get published by mainstream presses, the late sixties and early seventies saw an explosion of Chicano publishers and publishing houses. Inevitably many of these were ephemeral; some, like Raymond Barrio's Ventura Press, were essentially one-man operations. Among the most important companies were Quinto Sol Publications and its successors Tonatiuh International and Justa Publications in Berkeley; La Causa Publications, Inc., of Oakland, California, which published *El Plan de Santa Bárbara*; Trucha Publications in Lubbock, Texas; Mictla at El Paso; and Pajarito Publications at Albuquerque. Among the outstanding Chicano publishing organizations connected with academic institutions are the Chicano Studies Center at the University of California at Los Angeles; the Center for Mexican American Studies at the University of Texas in Austin; the Mexican American Studies and Research Center of the University of Arizona in Tucson; the Bilingual Press/Editorial Bilingüe at Arizona State University in Tempe; and Arte Público Press at the University of Houston. To a degree these publishing centers have provided for Chicanos the kind of intellectual and creative support that they might derive from having their own university bases.

The movimiento also challenged Chicanos to express themselves creatively in music. Rejecting society's view that Mexican American music had no place in the mainstream, Chicanos set off a musical renaissance, refurbishing and redirecting earlier musical forms. In the 1920s and 1930s, as the number of Mexican immigrants expanded rapidly, border radio stations began broadcasting a wide variety of contemporary popular Mexican music, as well as older folk music. In southern California, Pedro González and his Los Madrugadores became popular figures during the late 1920s with their daily radio program. Among other early popularizers of Mexican music were Lydia Mendoza, "The Lark of the Border," "Lalo" Guerrero, Santana, and Pete Escobedo. Little Joe and la Familia began a vamping to new musical styles, a trend best illustrated by Richie Valens's (Ricardo Valenzuela) adapting the song "La Bamba" to rock.

Beginning in the mid-sixties there was a surge of Mexican American songs, sometimes criticizing Anglo society's treatment of mexicanos and supporting "la huelga." From the Delano grape strike came an album titled *Viva la Causa—Songs and Sounds from the Delano Strike*. Corridos, frequently a form of oral history, were composed and sung about labor, mistreatment of Chicanos and Mexicans, the deaths of John F. Kennedy and his brother Robert, and the Vietnam War. In the entire border region so-called Tex-Mex music from southern Texas and northern Mexico developed wide popularity among Anglos as well as Mexican Americans. Los Tigres del Norte have been playing this revamped *norteño* (northern Mexican) music since the mid-sixties; their songs detail the immigrant's struggle, the pitfalls of alcohol and drugs, and the stresses of life in the United States.

Outstanding Mexican American singers like Linda Ronstadt, Joan Báez, Vikki Carr, Trini López, Andy Russell (Andrés Rabago), Freddy Fender (Báldemar Huerta), and, over a dozen years, Los Lobos with their melding of rock with traditional Mexican musical forms have helped make Spanish-language music more widely known and popular among both Anglos and Chicanos. The most recent album of Los Lobos, *Kiko* (1992), switches from earlier realistic looks at the barrio to an introspective look at the family, love, and spiritual forces. The success of Luis Valdez's film *La Bamba* (for which Los Lobos did the sound track) on the life of 1950s Chicano vocalist and teen idol Richie Valens and of Linda Ronstadt's exciting and triumphant stage presentation, *Canciones de Mi Padre*, illustrates the expanded appeal and popularity of Mexican music. The successful concert tour in 1990 of Raices Musicales (Musical Roots), a group sponsored by the National Council for the Traditional Arts, is another indication of a rising interest in and appreciation of mexicano music.

A considerable expansion of Chicano art and especially the developments in mural painting have been a prominent aspect of the movimiento from its beginnings. Based on traditions of Mexican muralists Diego Rivera and José Clemente Orozco, mural artists Judy Baca from Los Angeles, Manuel Martínez of Denver, and others painted barrio walls in virtually every city and town of any size in the Southwest, especially in California. By the late 1980s there were an estimated 1,000 or more murals in the Golden State alone. The paintings combine the Virgin of Guadalupe, the Mexican revolution, and the Chicano experience with pre-Columbian Toltec, Aztec, and Maya symbols. The muralists painted important scenes and figures from their history; on walls, buildings, and overpasses their passionate beliefs and feelings were displayed. Their styles range from harsh social realism to abstract expressionism. In addition to general statements of social protest, some mural art reflected specific concerns, indicated, for example, by the incorporation of the "huelga" black eagle in their works. These murals are a form of popular art aimed at the masses and have served both to engender self-pride and to help Mexican Americans recover their cultural heritage.

Artists of the movimiento were influenced by both Mexican and American models. Some explored themes only indirectly related to la raza. For example, Alfredo Arreguín, the outstanding Seattle artist whose poster won the competition to advertise the Washington State centennial in 1989, paints colorful scenes that are complex, finely detailed drawings, often with lush backgrounds reminiscent of tropical Mexico. Porfirio Salinas, a favorite of Lyndon Johnson, is widely acclaimed for his traditional "bluebonnet" (a wildflower) Texas landscapes, some of which the president hung in the White House. Consuelo González Amezcua of Texas is unique in her intricate multicolored ballpoint pen drawings in a primitive style. Melesio Casas, one of the founders of the militant Con Safos Painters, is well known for his Humanscapes and his social concerns for Chicanos. Rupert García and Malaquías Montoya have created international niches for themselves in graphic and poster art somewhat reminiscent of mural painting.

The artist Luis Jiménez, while also a muralist of note, is perhaps best known for his glossy fiberglass-and-epoxy "machine man" sculptures. Although Mexican American artists have been active in all fields of fine arts, including sculpture and wood carving, unquestionably the mural is the most significant, often combining historic ethnic roots and contemporary political objectives. The Chicano Park murals of Barrio Logan in San Diego provide an outstanding example of this combination.

The first publicized exhibition of works by Chicano painters did not take place until 1970. In that year three exhibitions were mounted in Texas and California. In them Chicano artists showed their popular, socially conscious paintings, a majority based on their Mexican heritage and their experience in the United States. In addition, community cultural centers where Chicano artwork could be exhibited were established by artists José Montoya of Sacramento, Melesio Casas of San Antonio, Salvador Torres of San Diego, Ernesto Palomino of Fresno, California, and others.

While not all agree, some Chicano art historians consider graffiti to be an acceptable form of popular art; indeed, at times there has been a melding of Chicano graffiti, often carefully organized complex sets of symbols, with murals. In addition to graffiti, low-rider automobiles, usually carefully remodeled and meticulously redecorated with great pride, are considered to be popular art among Chicano youths. The interiors may include crushed velvet, crystal chandeliers, and swivel seats. Some have seen a relationship to the highly decorated carts of peasant cultures in Costa Rica and Sicily. Particularly in California, low-riding is a widespread urban activity which brings a sense of pride to barrio youths. Low-rider clubs hold regular meets so members can admire each other's cars and compete for prizes; they are viewed by some as desirable alternatives to gang participation. There is even a northern California magazine named *Low Rider*, with a circulation of over 100,000, mostly among young Chicanos.

In the 1960s and 1970s there occurred a considerable expansion in the number of Spanish-language newspapers as well as radio and television stations. Historically the Spanish-language press in the Southwest antedates the United States' war with Mexico; after 1848 it was important in keeping Spanish alive. The number of Spanish-language newspapers grew from a mere handful in the 1840s to a nineteenth-century peak of 60 in 1895. In the first six decades of the twentieth century some 250 Spanish-language papers were established, but most proved to be ephemeral. By the beginning of the 1980s, despite heavy attrition, over 100 weekly and daily newspapers were still being published. They not only provided coverage of news of special interest to Mexican Americans but also frequently offered a showcase for poetry, short stories, and artwork. Some publishers attempted, with limited success, to develop a bilingual press, which stressed the value of learning English while it sustained loyalty to language and culture.

In addition to the printed medium, over 500 radio stations and a proliferation of 130 television stations broadcast in Spanish either partially or solely, full-time or part-time. Broadcasting in Spanish is most common in the large cities of the Southwest, and in New York, Miami, and Chicago. There was even a Mexican-owned network of Spanish-language television stations and cable companies—the Spanish International Network (SIN). More recently two U.S. Spanish-language networks, the New York-based Telemundo Group and the larger Miami-based Univisión Holdings, the latter owned by Hallmark Cards, have battled for preeminence. There is also a Spanish-language cable service, Galavisión, owned by the Mexican Grupo Televisa. While there has been a great upsurge in Spanish-language television, it remains largely under Anglo management and control.

A cause and result of this media growth has been an expansion of advertising directed specifically at the Mexican American market through both language and ethnic preferences. The number of Chicanos in skilled and semiskilled occupations became larger, and their incomes increased. Seeing the potential of the raza market, manufacturers and retailers responded with larger Spanish advertising budgets. The expanded use of Spanish in the media, especially in television, is seen by some as slowing down and even reversing acculturation to English. One result has been the development of greater cultural cohesiveness as raza consciousness grows. The expansion of Spanish advertising has aroused Anglo interest in the language as well as antagonism to both the people and their language.

However, use of Spanish among American-born Mexican Americans has decreased appreciably. A 1976 study by the Census Bureau indicated that third-generation Mexican Americans speak only a limited amount of Spanish. As one moves away from the bilingual border and away from recent immigrants, use of Spanish declines. Another factor has been a longtime negative American attitude toward the use of Spanish. By 1970 twenty-one states required that English be the exclusive language of instruction in public schools, and until fairly recently in many schools of the Southwest speaking Spanish was severely discouraged or even expressly prohibited, sometimes under penalty of physical punishment. A recent survey showed only 5.3 percent of Mexican Americans reporting that they spoke Spanish at home, although about 90 percent claimed they were able to speak or understood the language. Only 1.3 percent admitted that they spoke English poorly or not at all.

On the other hand, isolation, continued segregation, high levels of immigration from Mexico, and the relative ease of crossing the border for family visits, business, and tourism have constantly reinforced the use of Spanish. In the barrio Spanish remains, to a large extent, the language of a communication network that informally provides, particularly to the recently arrived, information about jobs, housing, social services, and unwelcome authorities. The movimiento's emphasis on bilingual literature contributed to greater interest in Spanish. In addition, to some extent there was a "Spanish is beautiful" sentiment in the movement; the language communicated and helped maintain the Mexican cultural heritage. Spanish is, after all, one of the world's great languages.

In 1974 bilingualism became a household word when the U.S. Supreme Court, in the case of *Lau* v. *Nichols*, unanimously held that failure of schools to provide programs tailored to meet the special language needs of minority children violated the 1964 Civil Rights Act and the Fourteenth Amendment as well. As a result of the Bilingual Education Act, special programs for Spanish-speaking (and other) children had already begun in 1968, but the Lau decision rapidly expanded bilingual classes as federal funding rose from $7.5 million in 1969 to $107 million by 1980 and as states passed bilingual education laws. The Lau case and state legislation also led to a strong reaction by conservative Anglos who felt that bilingual programs challenged basic American assumptions regarding cultural assimilation and might eventually lead to a separatist movement. Letters to the editor and press interviews with opponents of bilingual education spoke of the "menace" of Spanish and even referred to it as "subversive."

Mexican Americans reacted to these emotional nativistic views with bewilderment and some anger. An overwhelming majority recognized the paramount need to speak English proficiently. They did not and do not view speaking Spanish as negative and strongly resent any implication that Spanish is inferior. Spanish is the language of family, home, friendship, and la raza. Bilingual adult education programs also provided older Mexican Americans with greater economic mobility through an improved command of English. Further, bilingual programs help their children learn English more quickly and focus attention on the educational plight of those who enter school speaking little or no English. Some view bilingual programs as a way of fighting discrimination and increasing respect for their language and culture.

Funding for bilingual education has never comprised more than a tiny fraction of the federal education budget, but with a rising tide of xenophobia it has become a highly emotional issue. Under the Reagan administration, from 1981 to 1989, funding for bilingual education was regularly reduced. On the positive side, the issue stimulated many

Mexican American parents to take more active roles in school affairs. An important negative result was the rise of chauvinist groups like U.S. English, which added to the nativist backlash.

The English Only movement was initiated in 1978 by Emmy Shafer, angry when she was unable to find an English-speaking clerk in a Dade County, Florida, government office. Spurred by growing prejudice against people of color, the movement quickly acted to counter the "undermining of American society." U.S. English, a national organization based in Washington, D.C., got English Only legislation introduced into the U.S. Congress by its honorary chairman, S. I. Hayakawa. It has since conducted well-financed campaigns to introduce similar legislation at the state level. By 1989, prodded by U.S. English and English Only, seventeen states had approved legislation making English the official language, as had over forty towns, including tiny Los Altos, California, despite its charming Spanish name.

U.S. English funds supported attacks on bilingual programs as part of its campaign against Mexican immigration. The group also urges a written English-proficiency test for naturalization. Shrill and hostile in tone, U.S. English seems aimed primarily at Spanish speakers and talks about "defending" English, as though it were under attack. The fact is that Mexican immigrants and their offspring learn English at the same rate as European immigrants did a century ago.

Illustrating the group's intolerance were racist remarks in October 1988 by co-founder John Tanton that caused the resignation of U.S. English's president, educator and Republican politician Linda Chávez, and other officers. Although able to arouse considerable thoughtless support, the group appears to create a certain amount of amused toleration among thinking persons. Virtually all Mexican Americans agree that America should have only one public language.

Mexican American children, regardless of the environment and language at home, are constantly exposed to American mass culture— national products and tastes, Anglo heroes and social values. They grow up speaking English and accepting the Puritan ethic of work-as-virtue. They believe in commonly held goals: individual achievement, success, and status. Through exposure to movie and television stars, singers, musicians, and prominent athletes they have been made aware of national norms in dress and conduct. They accept national socioreligious holidays like Thanksgiving. The Northern European Christmas tree and Santa Claus have been widely adopted, while, in exchange, Cinco de Mayo has become virtually an American holiday in the Southwest, not unlike St. Patrick's Day and Chinese New Year elsewhere.

Mexican American culture, although under attack, is alive and flourishing. It is constantly changing, influenced by the dominant society and heavy immigration from Mexico as well as the diverse Latino cultures of Puerto Rico, Central and South America, and the Caribbean, especially Cuba. As a result, Mexican Americans have a clearer vision of a future shared with other Hispanics in the United States. Greater inter-ethnic cooperation and affiliation have already helped them win elections and influence government and will undoubtedly have even more impact in the future. With increased political sophistication Mexican Americans will be able to use their larger numbers in American society and support from fellow Latinos to greater social and political advantage.

17

JOBS, BUSINESS,
AND POLITICS

Although the migration to the cities of the Southwest began with the great exodus from Mexico brought on by the 1910 revolution, until the 1920s the mexicano population remained largely rural and relatively stable. Before World War I the Southwest experienced limited economic transformation and continued to be dominated by subsistence agriculture, sheep and cattle raising, mining, lumbering, and, in Texas, cotton culture. During the 1920s approximately half a million Mexicans immigrated legally to the United States; thousands more entered without benefit of documentation. This heavy immigration had a tremendous impact on patterns of residence. Thousands of the new immigrants found shelter in existing urban barrios, while other thousands settled in cheap-housing colonias nearby. At the same time Mexican Americans began moving from rural areas to towns and cities.

As a result of this urban movement, Mexican American society underwent a powerful upheaval. Not only was the demographic pattern greatly changed but the rural subculture itself now became modified by urban influences. As more Mexican Americans found urban employment, the authority of the family patriarch was diminished and the family became less cohesive. With its members no longer working together as a unit and further separated by urban living, the family's social fabric weakened. In the barrio children no longer felt close familial and societal supervision, and many turned to their peers for acceptance, seeking status and identity in the urban gangs that quickly developed.

As rural Mexican Americans joined the new immigrants in seeking year-round jobs in the towns and industrial work in the cities, San Antonio quickly became the "mexicano capital" of the Southwest. By the 1920s it was "shipping out" nearly a quarter of a million workers annually. Many of these were in transit from Mexico, using the city as an employment base. Mexicano labor was essential to the rapid economic transformation of the Southwest. As a result of the move to the cities and increased industrialization, many Chicanas entered the industrial labor market for the first time. In turn, female employment as well as stable employment for males provided the financial basis for expansion of small family businesses and pushed some mexicano families into the middle class and upper middle class. Most of these businesses serviced the mexicano community.

The steady flow of rural people to the city in recent decades has been a worldwide phenomenon. For Mexican Americans especially, World War II was a major factor in the movement to urban centers, as they found employment in west coast and inland industrial centers. In the postwar years continuing heavy migration of agricultural workers north from Mexico added to the pressure on Mexican Americans to move to cities as jobs in agriculture became less available and financially less attractive. The changing economy in the Southwest—a shift from agriculture, ranching, lumbering, and mining to manufacturing, government installations, and service industries in which long-term and usually better-paying employment existed—pulled more into big-city barrios. In 1930 nearly half of all employed Mexican Americans worked in agriculture; by 1982 less than 7 percent were so employed. Already in 1950 two-thirds of Mexican Americans lived in towns and cities, and by 1990 an estimated 94 percent of them were urban dwellers. However, a few rural areas remained predominantly Chicano—for example, southeastern Texas and northwestern New Mexico. The two areas tended to continue to be characterized by rural poverty as well as physical and social isolation. In New Mexico welfare became a way of life for many of those who remained as, decade after decade, nuevomexicano youths left for Albuquerque and urban California.

During the first half of the twentieth century most Mexican Americans remained heavily concentrated in low-skill, low-pay rural and urban employment. In the cities they were kept separate as a labor source by a variety of restraints: low levels of skills, discrimination in employment and wages, labor union policies, segregated housing, school segregation and limited educational opportunities. Typically encouraged to enter the United States as agricultural labor, by the 1920s they had already begun to move into unskilled industrial work as they became more and more urbanized. By the decade's end a majority in Los Angeles worked in the building trades and in a wide variety of other jobs: canneries, inter-urban railways, street paving, meat packing, restaurants, laundries, and foundries. Only about one-third in California still depended solely on agriculture for their livelihood. Even a majority of these lived in urban areas and commuted to the fields.

Urban housing segregation was largely by class rather than by ethnicity, although the two often coincided. In the larger cities mexicanos tended to live close to the workplace. However, as transportation improved, some moved to new, sometimes suburban, neighborhoods. In Los Angeles only after the mid-1920s did large numbers of Mexican Americans move eastward out of the older central city area.

World War II had a major impact on Americans of Mexican descent. In the course of the war discriminatory practices diminished somewhat. The massive war effort created previously undreamed-of opportunities for economic advancement for both men and women. Many workers, especially young men from New Mexico, moved to west coast cities like Los Angeles, San Pedro, and Richmond to work in shipyards and other industries. From Texas others went north to Chicago, Detroit, Denver, and Kansas City. On the west coast and in the urban Midwest they encountered conditions that were often less restrictive, allowing them to expand their horizons and to harbor hopes for a better future.

The war greatly reduced Mexican Americans' isolation and opened new employment possibilities. As wartime demands for labor rapidly expanded the urban movement, more workers were able to obtain semiskilled and skilled work. In southern California postwar manufacturing and industrial expansion were encouraged by a large labor reservoir and in turn attracted heavy immigration, both legal and undocumented. After the war the number of Chicanos moving from agriculture to light manufacturing and service industries grew rapidly. Although their upward mobility increased, they continued to be greatly underrepresented in professional, managerial, and technical ranks despite better education and training with the help of the GI Bill. They also remained largely excluded from policy-making positions.

At the end of the fighting some of the gains made during the war years were lost. Wartime jobs disappeared, some social advances were not retained, and many Chicano veterans returned to find little, if any, increase in acceptance. On the other hand, with an intensified ethnic awareness, many refused to submit to indignities and discriminatory practices of the past. There was a postwar reaffirmation of their cultural *mexicanidad*, a greater reluctance to conform to Anglo norms, and a seeking for a model of cultural pluralism. Determined to have the rights and opportunities for which they had fought and for which many had shed blood, some used the GI Bill to obtain college educations or on-the-job training, to start businesses, and to buy homes. Clearly the GI Bill was a significant agent of upward mobility in the two decades after the war. These years from 1945 to 1965 have been seen by some historians as a time when Mexican Americans devoted their energies largely to personal economic and social betterment. However, it was also a time when the groundwork for the politics of protest was being laid.

In the post-World War II years Mexican Americans' improvements in income and employment were dwarfed by greater Anglo advances. Chicanos' occupational patterns changed primarily as a result of internal migration, urbanization, and new technology. Agriculture became more mechanized with the introduction of cotton-picking machines, mechanical tomato pickers, and other inventions and techniques. As more canneries and other food-processing plants automated, thousands of jobs that once were the first rung on the ladder to better-paying urban employment were eliminated. Employment opportunities for urban Chicanos developed or increased in construction, building maintenance, trucking, refineries, smelters, the garment industry, assembly-line work, hotels and restaurants, retail clerking, gardening, and domestic service. By the 1980s about two-thirds of Mexican Americans had skilled, semiskilled, or white-collar employment. The demands of rapidly expanding new industries like electronics led to a notable increase in jobs for Chicanas.

By 1970 a small Mexican American merchant and entrepreneurial sector began to emerge. Typically barrio businessmen might be contractors, restaurant operators, grocers, bakers, garage owners, metal-workers, or small publisher-printers. In some towns and cities of the Southwest they formed Mexican American Chambers of Commerce and other service organizations. During the 1970s Latino businesses grew by 200 percent. In the five years between 1982 and 1987 Latino-owned businesses jumped 70 percent from 248,000 with $15 billion in sales to 422,000 with sales of over $50 billion. By 1990 there were more than half a million Latino businesses in the United States, a majority of them in California; they generated nearly $100 billion in annual revenue. California alone claimed 250,000 Latino business owners, a majority mom-and-pop entrepreneurs in service industries. Some see this development as proof of increasing upward mobility, and it certainly marks an increase in the size of the raza middle class.

The urban movement was not free of difficulties and trauma. As Mexican Americans relocated, they encountered a serious new problem, a housing shortage that in some cities was acute because little construction had taken place since the beginning of the Great Depression at the end of the 1920s. Much of the housing available to them was slum, substandard, or old and in need of extensive repairs. Gradually they found shelter as well as jobs, became aware of community organizations and social services, and began timidly to seek political influence. The urban communities developed networks which in turn led to political organization and potential political power. The enlarged urban Mexican American population often was led by members of the business and professional classes who formed the basis for more aggressive community groups. Politically conscious veterans organizations found fertile fields for proselytizing.

The organizing vitality among Chicanos in the Southwest after World War II was supplied primarily by veterans. These second-generation Americans, children of migrants who had come to the United States during the 1920s, had learned how the American system functioned on a day-to-day basis, how society could be influenced for change. Many had practical experience in leadership. They returned to barrios and colonias aware that, by organizing, they could use their newfound skills to obtain their rightful place in a democratic society. Certainly, roots of the movimiento were nourished by the civic and political awareness of returning veterans.

In the 1950s and 1960s the number of Mexican Americans elected to public office slowly increased. In 1961 Henry B. González of Texas won a seat in the U.S. House of Representatives. He was followed by

Edward Roybal from California, and in 1964 "Kika" de la Garza of Texas joined them. A decade later these three were influential in founding the National Association of Latino Elected and Appointed Officials (NALEO), for which Roybal became the chief spokesman. In Colorado the New Hispanic Party, organized because of discontent with the Democratic and Republican parties, flared up briefly and then disappeared after a lack of success in the 1966 election. The Congressional Hispanic Caucus (CHC) was established in 1976, with Roybal and Garza taking prominent roles in its founding. It concerns itself with issues like immigration, bilingual education, police brutality, and other concerns of Latinos. During the 1970s there was a 200 percent increase in the number of Mexican Americans elected to public office. Electoral success resulted from voter registration, activist leadership of World War II veterans, and organizational and union participation. Continuing success depends on the availability of experienced, able leaders, effective organizational support, and getting out the vote.

Although Mexican Americans have been minimally rewarded with government employment by both Republican and Democratic parties, since World War II job opportunities, mostly in state and local government, have been greater than in the private sector because of equal opportunity hiring of minorities. Within the public sector they have created organizations such as Incorporated Mexican American Government Employees (IMAGE) to encourage Chicano interest in government employment. IMAGE, founded in Denver in 1973, has nearly 100 chapters, which also strive to increase government employment opportunities for Hispanics. At higher governmental levels the National Association of Latino Elected and Appointed Officials, established in 1975, has pushed for hiring more Mexican Americans and other Latinos in government with some success.

In order to achieve economic and social progress some leaders saw an imperative need for Mexican Americans to enter the political process on a broad scale, from local to national levels. The politicization of leaders and communities by the Chicano movement after the mid-sixties gave rise to significantly increased political activism. Greater concentration of people in cities helped make possible what some observers called the politics of protest. This development was also aided by federal programs of the Kennedy and Johnson administrations, particularly civil rights legislation and the War on Poverty, which provided political and civic experience, especially to low-income Mexican

Americans. As the Chicano movement grew less militant during the mid-1970s, more moderate leaders brought a resurgence of middle-of-the-road forces. This change paralleled the more conservative political mood of the country. While Mexican American Democrats (MAD) to a degree took over the liberal objectives of La Raza Unida Party, some older traditional groups turned more to time-tested political techniques. In Texas redistricting lawsuits and extensive voter registration paid off in major gains in political representation. By the late 1980s Texas was second only to New Mexico in the number of Mexican American state and national legislators.

Historically the degree of Mexican American political participation has varied considerably from one part of the Southwest to another. New Mexico, with a hispano majority down to the Great Depression, has had continuous nuevomexicano political participation since the Treaty of Guadalupe Hidalgo. The long and successful political careers of Miguel A. Otero, Sr. and Jr., during the territorial era were followed by Ezéquiel Cabeza de Baca's election to the governorship of the new state in 1916. Two years later his Mexican-born friend Octaviano Larrazolo was elected over the Democratic candidate, Félix García. A decade later, in 1928, Larrazolo was elected to the U.S. Senate. After serving two terms in the House of Representatives, Dennis (Dionisio) Chávez in 1934 became U.S. senator from New Mexico, a position he held with great distinction and respect until his death in 1962. After Chávez moved to the Senate his House seat was filled, term after term, by middle-of-the-roader Antonio Fernández until he died in the mid-fifties. In the late forties and early fifties nuevomexicanos ran in the governorship race but lost; however, several were elected lieutenant governor during these years. Also many nuevomexicanos won election to the state legislature.

Nuevomexicano Joseph Montoya, after two decades of political experience in both houses of the state legislature and four terms in the lieutenant governor's chair, was elected to the U.S. House of Representatives in 1957 and then to the Senate. He was reelected senator until his defeat in 1976. He died two years later. An important nuevomexicano on the Washington scene is Manuel Luján, who was elected to his tenth term in the House in 1986. He was appointed Secretary of the Interior by President George Bush during the latter's first year in office. Needless to say, New Mexico's record in Mexican American political representation is unique among the states.

Generally, in the post-World War II years Mexican Americans remained greatly underrepresented in local and state governments as well as in Washington, although improvement began to appear during the 1960s. In 1974 two politically moderate Mexican Americans were elected state governors: Raúl Castro in Arizona and Jerry Apodaca in New Mexico. Subsequently the leadership mantle fell upon the postwar generation, among them Toney Anaya, governor of New Mexico from 1982 to 1986, and mayors Ray Salazar of El Paso, Henry Cisneros of San Antonio, and Federico Peña of Denver, the last two in President Bill Clinton's cabinet. These three followed in the footsteps of Raymond Telles, the cautious reform mayor of El Paso from 1957 to 1961. Charismatic politicians of moderate views, all three were able to attract support from Anglos as well as Mexican Americans. Cisneros, who holds an MBA from Harvard University and a Ph.D. from George Washington University, has been described as a conservative liberal and has been mentioned as a possible presidential or vice presidential candidate. A milestone of sorts was marked in 1984 when Raúl González became the first tejano elected by popular vote to a statewide office, associate justice of the Texas Supreme Court. Since then Dan Morales has been elected Texas attorney general and has been touted as the "Henry Cisneros for the '90s." In August 1992 John Méndez of California became the only United States attorney from a minority background.

In 1986 the National Association of Latino Elected and Appointed Officials reported 304 county officials, 1,048 municipal officials, and 530 court and law enforcement officers of Mexican descent. There were also 183 Latino mayors. Four years later there were two Latino Cabinet members, eleven members of the House of Representatives, one state governor, two big-city mayors, and about 130 state legislators, but no U.S. senators. Although the total Mexican American population has increased from about 2 million in 1930 to nearly 6 million in 1970, and to 13 million in 1990, Mexican Americans have acquired relatively little decision-making power in politics.

The 1980s, widely touted as the "Decade of the Hispanic," were supposed to see the rise of Hispanics to their rightful place in the circles of political and economic power. This did not happen. Rather, a handful of prominent Mexican American political leaders lost their preeminent positions. In San Antonio, Mayor Cisneros resigned after his extramarital love affair became a public scandal. In California, state senator Joseph Montoya was indicted on twelve counts of selling his vote to lobbyists, and federal district judge Robert Aguilar was indicted on charges of trying to influence two judges in criminal cases.

In California the number of voting-age Latinos increased a dramatic 117 percent in the 1970s. By 1990 Latinos comprised 25 percent of the state's population; yet they wielded very limited political power. In the Southwest nearly 665,000 Chicano voters were registered between 1976 and 1980. Yet in the off-year election of 1982 only 52 percent of eligible southwestern Latinos were registered and only 37 percent voted. Nationally more than one million new Hispanic voters registered during the 1980s, raising hopes for greater representation. Despite this numerical increase, between 1986 and 1990 total voter registration of Latinos fell from 36 percent to 32 percent and in the 1990 election only 34 percent of those registered voted. Such levels of registration and voting militate against any increase in political clout. Clearly, Mexican Americans need greater motivation to vote.

Why do Mexican Americans have lower levels of participation in the political process than the general population? The answer lies in many factors. A few are cultural, but most derive from their low socioeconomic position and discrimination against them. By far the most important factors in their political disenfranchisement are: gerrymandering areas in which they form a majority, at-large rather than single-district elections, intimidating election practices such as economic threats, and, until fairly recently, poll taxes. Residency requirements have also reduced political participation by those who remain in the migrant stream. Moreover, Mexican Americans change residence at twice the rate Anglos do and thereby may lose their registration.

Poverty and low-paying jobs correlate with low levels of both naturalization and political participation. In 1940 Mexican American family income averaged only 60 percent of the federal minimum standard for a family of four. Although Mexican American income levels have improved, in 1981, 23.5 percent of families remained below the poverty level. For Mexican Americans the 1980s were a decade of stagnant income levels; during the eight years of the Reagan administration the percentage of persons at poverty levels actually increased slightly. The 1990 census showed that, while family incomes had improved, 25 percent of all Mexican-origin families were still below the poverty level. That economic inequity is paralleled by severe underrepresentation in terms of elected and appointed officials is scarcely coincidental.

In addition to poverty, there are a cluster of factors that further reduce

Mexican American political participation. It is a matter of statistical record that youth and low levels of education have a negative effect on voter registration and turnout. In all three categories—poverty, age level, and education—Chicanos are at, or near, the bottom in American society. In 1990 the median age of Mexican Americans was 24.3 years; for the non-Hispanic population it was 33.8 years. The fact that Mexican Americans have proportionately a far larger under-voting-age population than non-Hispanics, as well as low registration levels, helps explain why Mexican Americans, despite their numbers, failed to achieve greater political power. About 50 percent of Chicanos do not complete high school today and in the recent past the percentage was higher. An additional factor is the fact that convicted felons cannot vote. For a variety of reasons, especially poverty, Chicanos are in that category in higher percentages than the general population. A final factor is a widely held cynicism among Mexican Americans about politicians and the political process. This may come from historical experience both in Mexico and in the United States.

To participate in the electoral process one must be a citizen. Over 30 percent of Mexican Americans are not citizens, compared to 3 percent for the total population. The fact that they form a large part of the most recent immigrant wave partially explains this difference in citizenship rates. Additionally, first-generation Mexican Americans are often made to feel like foreigners even after they achieve citizenship, and tend to retain some sense of being sojourners. Positive factors affecting naturalization seem to be property ownership, marriage to an American citizen, and children, especially those born in the United States.

——————

At the national level government recognition of an intensified Chicano demand for greater political power has led to some improvement. In response to Mexican American demands, President Lyndon Johnson chose to deal with the moderate GI Forum and LULAC, ignoring more importunate voices. In June 1967 he announced the formation of the Inter-Agency Committee on Mexican American Affairs and appointed moderate Vicente Ximenes to head the new office. Two years later it became a Cabinet Committee on Opportunities for Spanish Speaking People. Johnson's successor, Richard Nixon, formulated a sixteen-point program to hire the Spanish-speaking in government and named more to federal jobs than any previous president. However, during his five and a half years in office he appointed fewer than a dozen Latinos to upper-level positions. Gerald Ford, who followed him, in two and a half years made over twenty high-level appointments, including that of Fernando DeBaca as Special Assistant for Hispanic Affairs.

Between 1977 and 1981 President Jimmy Carter appointed about 200 Latino officials, many to high-level positions. Among these were Professor Ralph Guzmán to the Department of State and three ambassadors: Raúl Castro to Argentina, Julián Nava to Mexico, and Marí-Luci Jaramillo to Honduras. Under his successor, Ronald Reagan, the total was down, but Reagan did appoint the first Mexican American to a Cabinet post. Lauro Cavazos, president of Texas Technological University in Lubbock, became Secretary of Education in September 1988 and in the following year he was reappointed to that position by the newly elected president, George Bush. With Bush's subsequent appointment of Congressman Manuel Luján of New Mexico as Interior Secretary there were two Mexican Americans in the Cabinet. In December 1990, Cavazos resigned under pressure from the arrogant White House chief of staff, John Sununu.

In 1991, of an estimated 4,000 elected Hispanic officials, approximately half were in Texas. This improvement in political representation in Texas is the result in large measure of voter-registration efforts by MALDEF and the Southwest Voter Registration Education Project (SVREP) during the 1970s and 1980s. California, which has 50 percent more Latinos than Texas, has the next-largest number of Hispanic officials. Latinos make up over 25 percent of the population, but they hold only 7 percent of elected offices. Clearly Mexican Americans are becoming an important force in the political process. While they often seem less than firmly committed to Latino unity, which might give them greater political power, they clearly have moved beyond brown-power rhetoric and sloganeering toward a strong political base for seeking solid social benefits. In the 1990s they are likely to tip the balance in many local elections from school boards and city councils to state offices and are certain to be wooed by both major parties at the national level.

Chicanas have done well in politics. They comprise some 40 percent of Hispanics elected and appointed to municipal offices in smaller towns of the Southwest. Among those elected to city councils were María Berriozabal in San Antonio, Gloria Molina in Los Angeles, and Debbie Ortega in Denver. At Crystal City, Virginia Musquiz, one of the founders of the LRUP, took an active role throughout the sixties in organizing the Mexican American community for political action. In the 1964 election she ran for the Texas House of Representatives, but lost. Also active during the sixties was María Hernández, a founder of the Knights of America. She appeared frequently as a spokesperson for young Chicanos at political rallies in Texas and stumped widely in support of La Raza Unida Party candidates.

In southern California many Chicanas became active in political and community affairs. Among them, Francisca Flores, a founder of the California League of Mexican American Women, played a major role in politics and other Chicana concerns. For a while at the end of the sixties she published at her own expense a four-page newsletter that addressed Chicana feminist and activist issues, titled *Carta Editorial*. Then, in 1970, it was absorbed into a journal which she also published, *Regeneración*, evocative of the earlier publication of Mexican revolutionary precursor Ricardo Flores Magón. In the field of welfare rights another active Los Angeles leader in the late sixties was Alicia Escalante, who was deeply involved with the Chicano National Welfare Rights Organization and the militant Católicos Por La Raza. She was also one of the founders of the Chicana Service Action Center, along with Francisca Flores, who became its first director.

Not only in the struggle for social justice and Chicana rights did Chicanas find new political opportunities. In 1971, Romana Acosta Bañuelos, an outstanding businesswoman and banker of Los Angeles, was appointed Treasurer of the United States by President Nixon; and a decade later nuevomexicana and later California banker Katherine Ortega succeeded to that same position. The most highly placed Chicana in the federal government was Marí-Luci Jaramillo, a second-generation Mexican American from New Mexico. After a distinguished career at the University of New Mexico she was appointed U.S. ambassador to Honduras in 1977. This handful of successful Chicanas are representative of the new spirit animating the entire group. Many other Chicanas have held influential positions in state and national government, have become important leaders in national and community organizations, and have had an impact far beyond the Mexican American community.

Chicanas also began to assert themselves as workers. Historically Mexican American culture relegated Chicanas to caring for home and children. They were seen as guarding cultural traditions, and women who worked (outside home and family) were typically resented by Mexican American males. In agriculture a large number of wives worked in the harvest fields alongside their men in family teams. In many cases children accompanied their parents in the fields, adding their bit to the family income. Outside agriculture, however, relatively few Chicanas found employment except as domestics or laundresses. The El Paso laundresses' strike at the end of World War I illustrates both the increase in Chicanas working outside the home and their rising militancy.

By the 1920s working women formed about one-third of the immigrant Mexican labor force. In Texas they were employed mostly as laundresses, domestics, and salesclerks, while in California they tended to work in packinghouses, canneries, and the garment industry as well as in laundries. During the 1930s about one-third of the new border garment industry's employees were Chicanas, and in the Texas pecan-shelling businesses they comprised over three-fourths of the workers.

Typically these women, mostly young and unmarried, worked for wages that often were below the code levels established in 1933–1934 by the New Deal's National Recovery Administration (NRA). During World War II years many Chicanas entered the industrial labor market in war production factories, in shipyards, and on the railroads at higher wages. Their increasing participation in the work force and higher levels of education weakened patriarchal authority among all urban Mexican Americans and contributed to a growing independence and consciousness of self among Chicanas. In 1950 about 20 percent of them were officially in the work force; by 1982 the percentage had risen to 49.1, compared to 52.3 percent for women not of Hispanic origin.

In California, Dolores Huerta is an outstanding example of the emancipated Chicana. After working for years in the Community Service Organization, she became deeply involved in the United Farm Workers union, in which she served as an organizer, contract negotiator, and lobbyist. Soon she had become a UFW vice president and was widely recognized as an articulate and effective labor leader. She has received numerous honors, including having a corrido written about her. In Colorado, Helen Gonzales, wife of Corky, played an energetic role in the Crusade for Justice, which from its beginnings emphasized family involvement.

In the business world a few Chicanas have been able to achieve leadership roles. One of them, Romana Acosta Bañuelos of Los Angeles, beginning in the 1950s developed a food-processing business and later moved into banking as well. In 1969 she was named Outstanding Businesswoman of the Year in Los Angeles. Nuevomexicana Katherine Ortega, who financed her college education by working in an Alamogordo bank, became the founder of a successful accounting firm and later became a well-known southwestern banker. Also in New Mexico, Nina Otero Warren, although primarily an educator most of her life, came to be a prominent leader in the real estate and insurance business in Santa Fe. Tejana Cathi Villalpando achieved distinction in the oil business and in communications, and in California actress Lynda Córdoba Carter has her own dramatic production company and is also an entrepreneur in the cosmetics industry. During the eighties Ofelia Montejano became recognized as an outstanding fashion designer. Nearly all of these Chicanas also took active roles on a variety of fronts through community groups, social agencies, unions, and networks in law, business, and higher education.

In 1991 the Census Bureau reported that 50.6 percent of Chicanas were active in the labor force, close to the national average for all U.S. women. However, they earned only about 82 percent of the income of non-Hispanic women. Since 1940 there has been small but consistent movement from low-pay unskilled jobs to higher-pay skilled or semiprofessional employment. Still, 65.8 percent of Chicanas, according to the 1990 census, are mostly in low-pay jobs in sales, service, clerical, and factory work. Less than 15 percent have broken new ground to become professionals, educational administrators, and business managers.

The 1990 census indicated that Chicana employment had brought about improvement in family incomes; however, Mexican American families had only about two-thirds of Anglo family income, just as they had ten years earlier. About 25 percent of all Mexican American families and nearly 46 percent of families headed by women had incomes below the poverty level. Chicanas from rural and small-town families, especially, still had totally inadequate incomes and opportunities. Whereas Chicanos may encounter discrimination on the basis of race and class, Chicanas as a group suffer from a triple handicap, the burden of their gender, race, and social class.

18

EPILOGUE

The history of Mexican Americans is so much a story of migration that American immigration policy has been a paramount concern of the community. For more than a hundred years Mexican workers have been encouraged to come to the United States when their labor was desired; when times turned bad they were harassed, even victimized and sent back. Sometimes attitudes of encouragement and harassment existed side by side. The evidence indicates that immigrant labor has always had, and continues to have, an overall long-term positive impact on the U.S. economy; nevertheless, periods of depression have invariably brought forward a "deport the Mexican" solution. On both sides of the border the immigration issue continues to be a vital concern.

The migratory flow from Mexico appears to have a life of its own. After a century and a half this movement to the United States has become so widespread and institutionalized as a means of economic survival that its control or eradication is difficult in the extreme. It has become deeply embedded in both the socioeconomic fabric of Mexico and the economic structure of a large part of the United States.

Of all concerns about mexicanos the economics of immigration is the least amenable to a rational approach. The immigration debate, typically conducted within a framework of economic slump and high levels of unemployment, has caused Mexican workers to be seen as both an economic and a cultural threat. Emotion, opinion, prejudice, and fear have long ago driven out logic, reason, and any sense of fairness. As a result, the immigration problem has no clear definition that is widely accepted, only a broad range of often conflicting interests, typically economic. It probably will never be completely resolved.

Immigration to the United States was unrestricted by law for the first century after 1776. During the next half-century U.S. immigration legislation was aimed at excluding immigrants who were diseased or considered to be racially or culturally inferior and less suitable for assimilation than Northern Europeans. It was firmly rooted in the xenophobia and widely held racism of the late nineteenth century. The term "race" often referred to what today we call a culture—for example, "Italian race." Despite its racism, nineteenth-century immigration policy seems to have been motivated as much by economics as by cultural differences.

Because annual immigration ran at nearly 900,000 per year during the first decade of the twentieth century, there developed widespread concern about the changing sources of immigration from Northern to Southern and Eastern Europe. In 1924 Congress enacted the Johnson-Reed National Origins Act. By setting country quotas and a ceiling for Eastern Hemisphere immigration and excluding Western Hemisphere countries from this system the law strongly encouraged the movement of workers north from Mexico; it helps explain the extraordinarily heavy Mexican immigration of the second half of the 1920s. Many of these immigrants entered without documents. A Border Patrol was first established in 1924, but its 75 members could not effectively patrol the 2,000-mile frontier. Besides, undocumented entrance was not prohibited until 1929, and even then it was only a misdemeanor with no legal penalty. Thousands of Mexicans, with and without visas, supplied labor for the boom of the 1920s. After the repatriation of the 1930s labor needs of the United States in World War II led to the bracero program and greatly augmented use of Mexican workers.

Only in the postwar era did American immigration policy cease to be molded almost solely by the economic concerns of agriculture, railroads, mining interests, and other employers. In the immediate postwar period the desperate plight of hundreds of thousands of refugees and other factors created a climate in which attitudes toward immigrants became less restrictive. There was some turning away from earlier racist judgments. Foreshadowing the concept of family reunification as the primary basis of immigration policy, in 1946 Congress passed the War Brides Act, under which more than 100,000 foreign-born wives, husbands, and children of members of the armed services entered the United States.

By the early 1960s it was widely agreed that U.S. immigration policy needed a complete overhaul. President John F. Kennedy urged a comprehensive revision with a view to ending the national quota system and its ethnic discrimination. After extensive hearings Congress in 1965 passed the Hart-Celler Immigration and Nationality Act by a large majority. It went into effect three years later. Although not without its shortcomings, the Hart-Celler Act ended the national origins basis of admission to the United States. For the Eastern Hemisphere the individual country quota principle was replaced by a system of preference categories which established family reunification as the basic principle of immigration policy. Western Hemisphere immigration continued to remain outside the system, but for the first time was included in the overall immigration ceiling.

Many saw inclusion of the Western Hemisphere in the total number of immigrants as the beginning of an effort to limit Mexican immigration. This interpretation was strengthened in the mid-1970s when Congress in the Western Hemisphere Act extended both the preference system and the 20,000-per-country limit to North and South America. The 20,000 ceiling on legal immigration led to a 173,000 backlog in Mexican visa requests by 1980 and to an equally massive increase in illegal entrance.

The composition of immigration to the United States was dramatically changed by the Hart-Celler Act's exclusion of first-preference immigrants from the 20,000 limitation. Before the act's implementation in 1968 approximately 60 percent of immigrants came from Europe, 36 percent from Latin America, and 3 percent from Asia; after Hart-Celler went into effect Asian and Latin American first-preference immigration rose sharply. By the second half of the 1980s Latin Americans and Asians accounted for nearly 90 percent of immigrants and Europeans for only about 5 percent. Most of the Mexicans and Asians qualified for visas as first-preference immigrants. Mexicans continued to form the largest single national group in the new immigration. During the 1970s documented Mexican immigration averaged 64,229 persons per year. In the 1980s legal Mexican immigrants averaged over 100,000 per year out of a total average annual immigration of more than 600,000.

The heavy undocumented immigration of the 1970s and 1980s co-incided with persistent high levels of unemployment in the United States. The result was an ongoing search during those two decades for a revised policy to deal with illegal entrance. In 1975 the INS commissioner officially estimated that there were between 4 and 12 million undocumenteds, mostly Mexicans, in the United States. A year later he modified that estimate to between 6 and 8 million; in 1978 the new commissioner, Leonel Castillo, lowered the INS estimate to 3 to 6 million. The numbers game and the immigration debate developed a widespread perception that illegal immigration had suddenly skyrocketed and aroused the specter of a Latinized United States. As a result, there was insistent demand that Congress solve the perceived problems.

Prompted by this pressure, in 1978 Congress created a sixteen-man Select Commission on Immigration and Refugee Policy, headed by the Reverend Theodore Hesburgh, longtime president of Notre Dame University. After considerable research and extensive hearings in a dozen cities, in March 1981 the commission released its final report. Among hundreds of recommendations it strongly favored sanctions for employers of undocumenteds and an amnesty or legalization program. Sanctions, amnesty, and an expanded Border Patrol were accepted by many as ways to control undocumented immigration.

Out of the commission's report came the 1982 Simpson-Mazzoli immigration reform bill. Its main features included: employer penalties, amnesty and the possibility of ultimate legalization for certain undocumenteds, expansion of the Border Patrol, and an absolute annual limit on immigration which would include first-preference immigrants. Various Hispanic groups strongly opposed aspects of the proposed legislation.

For the next three years Congress was unable to reach agreement on bills promising immigration reform. A proposed national identity card aroused angry objections from many Mexican Americans and civil libertarians; the idea was finally dropped. Other Mexican American concerns were that the proposed legislation might lead to increased exploitation of undocumented workers, exacerbate racial feelings, and possibly arouse a discriminatory backlash. The principal stumbling block was the inclusion of a guest-worker program for agriculture which, opponents argued, would tend to encourage illegal immigration. By

1985 it had become clear that the guest-worker provision was pivotal to any immigration reform legislation.

In 1985 no compromise was reached. During the first half of the following year House Judiciary Committee discussions, chaired by Congressman Peter Rodino, sought compromises that might end the impasse. Early in June, Congressman Charles Schumer introduced an amendment to the Simpson-Rodino bill, which was being considered in the House. His amendment replaced the guest-worker concept with a second amnesty category, Special Agricultural Worker (SAW), made up of undocumenteds who had worked twenty days in perishable agriculture between May 1, 1985, and May 1, 1986. To guarantee farm interests a continuing ready supply of workers it also provided that those who qualified under SAW and later left farm work might be replaced through a Replenishment Agricultural Worker program (RAW). The reduced eligibility requirements and the flexibility of the SAW-RAW amendment provided an alternative to the guest-worker concept acceptable to agricultural employers by assuring them a virtually inexhaustible pool of workers.

After a mixed initial reception, on October 9 the Schumer amendment passed in the House by a vote of 230 to 166. Five days later a House-Senate committee hammered out a compromise bill. The next day the House voted to accept the new version, 238 to 173, and two days later the Senate followed suit, 63 to 24. During the final debate there was strong feeling that the Simpson-Rodino Immigration Reform and Control Act (IRCA) was not a "good" law, but nobody could present a better alternative that could be passed. Representative Romano Mazzoli called it the "least imperfect bill." Latino leaders both in and out of Congress were deeply divided over the legislation. The sentiment that some action had to be taken won out, and the IRCA was passed. On November 6, 1986, President Ronald Reagan signed it into law.

The law has three principal provisions: a beefed-up Border Patrol, employer sanctions, and two categories of amnesty. Of these three, amnesty was, for Mexican Americans, the most important. The basic concept of amnesty was not a new idea. It was embodied in earlier legislation, the 1929 Registry Act and the McCarran-Walter Act of 1952. As finally passed, the IRCA listed two ways by which aliens might qualify for amnesty: (1) provable residence in the United States since January 1, 1982, and (2a) provable employment in farm work for 90

days between March 1985 and May 1, 1986, or (2b) 90 days' employment in any three years since 1983 plus 90 days' residence. This second
part, (2a) and (2b), created the SAW category.

The complete amnesty process consisted of three stages to be passed:
first application, resulting in temporary legal alien status; second application, leading to permanent legal status; and lastly citizenship. The
law also limited or excluded the amnesty recipients from receiving
government assistance for five years.

On Cinco de Mayo in 1987, the Immigration and Naturalization
Service began accepting applications for legalization. Meanwhile the
law and its interpretation by the INS created confusion, uncertainty,
and fear among undocumenteds. Initially a decline in border area arrests
occurred, but no flood of undocumenteds returning to Mexico developed, as some had predicted. There is no evidence that those who were
ineligible left the United States.

By the May 4, 1988, deadline for stage one 1.4 million applicants
had registered under the general provision (form I-687); about half listed
southern California as their area of residence. Some 480,000 had also
signed up under the Special Agricultural Worker program, whose deadline was extended to November 30. Ultimately SAW applications ex-
ceeded INS predictions by hundreds of thousands. The total number
of aliens who applied for amnesty by January 1989 was about 3.096
million: 1.789 million general (I-687) and 1.307 million SAW (I-700).
Approximately 100,000 Mexicans registered and were accepted for the
RAW pool.

Of the applicants for general admission, approximately 70 percent,
or 1.25 million, were Mexican, of whom 43 percent were female. Of
the SAW applicants, 81 percent, or 1.059 million, were Mexican, of
whom 18 percent were female. Of the 3 million amnesty applicants,
55 percent were in California. Overwhelmingly the general amnesty
applicants were U.S. residents. Most of the SAWs appeared to be sojourners with residence in Mexico; however, the IRCA encourages them
to become settlers.

Six years after the passage of the IRCA what can be said about its
impact, its effectiveness in controlling and reducing undocumented
immigration? Clearly it created opportunities for more than 3 million
undocumented workers to legitimize their presence and ultimately to
integrate into American society if they wish to. There is no evidence
that employers have felt it necessary to improve working conditions or

wages to attract workers. In fact, since IRCA the number of reported violations of minimum wage legislation has tripled. A recent survey indicated that only 15 percent of the applicants saw any appreciable benefit for themselves coming out of the IRCA. Moreover, its ostensible purpose of reducing undocumented Mexican immigration has not been accomplished.

The IRCA basically tries to achieve internally contradictory goals: to reduce immigration without restricting immigrant labor. Its implementation was initially followed by a decline in arrests for illegal entry. Various factors contributed to this trend. Fluctuations in apprehensions by the Border Patrol seem to be more closely related to policy and emphasis than to changes in the volume of undocumented immigration. In mid-1987 a noticeable upswing in undocumented entrance was recorded; it continued during the rest of the year. By May 1988 the numbers were back up to pre-IRCA levels. In 1991 the Border Patrol apprehended 1.13 million persons trying to enter the United States without documents and 1992 apprehensions approached 1.5 million. It appears unlikely that a socioeconomic process as complex as Mexican migration can be substantially altered by unilateral legislation like IRCA.

There is general agreement that the new law has not stopped undocumenteds as its supporters had promised and the INS first claimed. The February 1989 proposal to dig a deep four-mile ditch at Otay Mesa near San Diego and an earlier suggestion for a razor fence, the completion two years ago of a six-mile ten-foot-high steel barrier and fence, referred to in the press as a "recycling of the Berlin Wall," and the even more recent Army Corps of Engineers' thirteen miles of border floodlights seem tacit admissions that, so far, the Simpson-Rodino law has failed to establish control at the border. A more pedestrian illustration is the signs on Interstate 5 south of San Diego warning CAUTION and showing silhouettes of two running adults and a small child. Students of undocumented immigration declare that the United States is relatively limited in what it can do at the 2,000-mile border to prevent entrance.

Because of Simpson-Rodino the number of women and children in the flow has increased. More undocumented workers now bring their families and remain in the United States, thereby becoming settlers rather than sojourners. Ultimately this change will lead to increased use of educational, health care, and other social services, and may cause some communities to be burdened with a disproportionate share of the costs.

What has been the impact of employer sanctions? To begin with, they did not result in any appreciable return migration as IRCA backers had argued they would. Has the threat of employer sanctions caused employers to cease hiring undocumenteds? The answer seems to be: not really. There appears to be little reduction in employer demand for undocumented labor, despite sanctions. Some larger employers have stopped hiring undocumenteds. However, many agricultural employers have insulated themselves from sanctions by operating through labor contractors, who have proliferated since IRCA. Clearly the thousands who hire maids, gardeners, and other domestics as well as employers of two, three, or four workers have been little affected by the legislation. The IRCA has created an immense oversupply of legal labor which competes with Mexican American workers, undermines their opportunities especially in agricultural employment, and holds down farm wages.

The Simpson-Rodino IRCA has led to numerous problems, some anticipated, some not. Clearly there has been a massive increase in the use of fraudulent documents by illegals and in their acceptance by employers. The press has reported a flourishing industry in counterfeit green cards, social security cards, and other documents useful to immigrants at less than $50 per set. Much more fraud is anticipated.

There has been a rapid rise in reports of employer discrimination against minority citizens and green carders on the basis of their possible illegal status. Complaints have been numerous. In 1990 the California Fair Employment and Housing Commission, having held public hearings, reported that "widespread discrimination" was being practiced in the state as a result of IRCA. Generally, it appears that the IRCA has not changed the dynamics of Mexican migration to the United States, but has given rise to greater complexity in the movement. Its full impact can be measured only after longer experience.

There are questions still to be answered. What will be the impact of stage two with its hurdles? How many undocumenteds will be able to move from temporary to permanent legal status and ultimately to citizenship? What will happen to those who do not complete the qualification process? Will they become a permanent underclass? What will be the ultimate impact of IRCA on the border region of both countries? What will be the final costs, financial and economic, to the undocumenteds? To the United States? Will immigration continue to be the dominant force for Mexican Americans that it has been in the past? How will the North America Free Trade Area (NAFTA) pact, if approved, affect Mexican immigration to the United States? Is it a step toward a solution to the undocumented problem? Is the only realistic long-term solution to the problem greater economic development in Mexico, as some suggest? Will NAFTA lead to sufficient economic improvement in Mexico so that Mexicans will remain in their own country to seek a better economic future? The answers to all these questions are of great importance to the Mexican American community. They will affect how Mexican Americans view themselves and are perceived by others.

Today a broad consensus exists among Mexican Americans that it is high time that they shared in the benefits that other Americans enjoy. One can hope that the twenty-first century will provide them with greater opportunities than they have yet had. Perhaps most important, they all should have certain access to a first-rate education. Most Mexican American parents recognize that education is the most likely road to personal achievement and upward mobility. However, many simply do not know how to use the American educational system effectively to help their children. The system often fails adequately to meet the psychological and social needs of raza students. To do a poor job of educating children is a criminal waste of talent and does an immense disservice to both them and the nation.

Despite some progress, Chicanos' high school graduation rates remain lower than those of blacks and Asians as well as Anglos. Many high school students feel that education is irrelevant to the future assigned them by society and the effort required is therefore futile. A high school dropout rate of 50 percent and a college graduation rate of between 5 and 10 percent mock our proclamations of equal opportunity. At both levels poverty is one of the principal problems. In education much remains to be achieved.

Increased opportunities in politics during the 1970s and 1980s were largely the result of the civil rights movement, the Chicano movimiento, and especially voter registration and other civic activities of various organizations. There were important gains at local, state, and national levels. On the national scene there were two Cabinet members, nearly a dozen ambassadors by the end of the eighties, and a growing number of important federal departmental figures. At the beginning of the 1990s there were more than 4,000 elected and appointed Hispanic officials. Of special note was the greatly increased role of bright young Chicanas in politics and officeholding.

In addition to supplying their labor, Mexican Americans, as we have seen, have also enriched American culture with their architecture, literature, art, music, theater, and cuisine. Perhaps the most satisfying and promising field has been in the arts and letters, where Mexican Americans have achieved distinction as writers, poets, musicians, painters, singers, actors, dramatists, and cinematographers. Their poetry, dramas, novels, and short stories both interpret and explicate la raza and at the same time often have universal appeal. Their murals decorate hundreds of walls in dozens of our cities, and their music gladdens the hearts of thousands.

The Mexican American work force showed no measurable gains during the 1980s in obtaining its share of white-collar jobs, although Chicanas reduced their underrepresentation. Despite some improvement during the 1980s, at the beginning of the 1990s the Mexican American median family income, $23,200, is 36 percent lower than the $36,300 of Anglo families. Although 80 percent of Mexican American males participate in the work force, compared to 74 percent for Anglos, their unemployment rate is 30 to 40 percent higher than for Anglos (10.6 percent compared to 7.4 percent in March 1991). Similarly, the unemployment rate for Chicanas is over 50 percent higher than for Anglo women. As a result, one out of three Mexican American children lives in poverty. As the gap separating the poor from the rich widens, more Mexican Americans live below the poverty level than did at the beginning of the 1980s, the "Decade of the Hispanic."

In health care also, Mexican Americans remain near the bottom of the ladder. Consigned all their lives to jobs that offer low pay and no pension plans or health benefits, many live in poverty with limited and inferior health care. About a third lack health insurance because their employment does not provide it and they cannot afford it on their incomes. Elderly Mexican Americans are particularly affected. The two-thirds of a million over the age of sixty-five have more health problems than other Americans of comparable age, but are less likely to receive help from Medicare, social security, or private insurance. A 1989 study found that half of them said they were in poor or only fair health, largely the result of a lifetime of hard physical labor.

While some progress has been achieved, Mexican Americans continue to face economic, social, and political handicaps. The pace of improvement during the 1960s and 1970s obviously slowed down during the 1980s. Today the nation appears to have little concern for equal opportunity for all, and discrimination and racism seem to be on the rise, at least at the moment. Continuing serious efforts need to be made to eliminate stereotyping and racial stigma and to open the American system wider to Mexican Americans and other minorities.

In spite of the many imperfections of life in the United States for people of Mexican descent, most remain hopeful. Thrust out of their homeland by desperate poverty and lack of opportunity, Mexicans continue to cross the border, legally or without documents, to seek the promise held out by the United States. In 1900 there were slightly more than 100,000 people of Mexican birth living in the United States. Between 1900 and 1990 the total number of Mexicans legally migrating to the United States was about 3.5 million. Additionally, perhaps half that many who came as undocumented sojourners remained as settlers. Clearly the overwhelming majority of the 13.3 million persons of Mexican descent counted in the 1990 census are willing immigrants and their descendants. This ongoing elective immigration has shaped and continues to reshape Mexican American culture and community.

ABBREVIATIONS AND ACRONYMS

ACCPE: American Coordinating Council of Political Education
AFL: American Federation of Labor
AFL-CIO: American Federation of Labor and Congress of Industrial
Organizations
AGIF: American GI Forum
ALRB: Agricultural Labor Relations Board (California)
AMAE: Association of Mexican American Educators
ANMA: Asociación Nacional México-Americana
AWOC: Agricultural Workers Organizing Committee (an AFL-CIO
union of the 1960s)

BIP: Border Industrializing Program (Mexican)

CAP: Community Action Patrol
CASA: Centro de Acción Social Autónoma
CASO: Chicano Associated Students Organization
CAWIU: Cannery and Agricultural Workers Industrial Union
(Communist-affiliated)
CHC: Congressional Hispanic Caucus
CIO: Congress of Industrial Organizations
CMAU: Congress of Mexican American Unity
COPS: Communities Organized for Public Service
CPLR: Católicos Por La Raza
CRLA: California Rural Legal Assistance
CROM: Confederación Regional Obrera Mexicana (a leading Mexican
labor union)
CSO: Community Service Organization (founded in latter 1940s)
CUCOM: Confederación de Uniones de Campesinos y Obreros
Mexicanos
CUOM: Confederación de Uniones Obreras Mexicanas

CYA: Chicano Youth Association
CYO: Catholic Youth Organization

DQU: Deganiwidah-Quetzalcoatl University

FAIR: Federation for American Immigration Reform
FEPC: Fair Employment Practices Commission
FERA: Federal Emergency Relief Administration
FSA: Farm Security Administration

IMAGE: Incorporated Mexican American Government Employees
INS: Immigration and Naturalization Service
IRCA: Immigration Reform and Control Act (Simpson-Rodino)
IWW: Industrial Workers of the World (a revolutionary syndicalist labor organization founded in 1905)

LRUP: La Raza Unida Party
LULAC: League of United Latin American Citizens (founded in Texas in 1929)

MACC: Mexican American Cultural Center
MAD: Mexican American Democrats
MALCS: Mujeres Activas en Letras y Cambio Social
MALDEF: Mexican American Legal Defense and Education Fund
MANA: Mexican American Women's National Association
MAPA: Mexican American Political Association (California)
    Mexican Americans for Political Action (Texas)
MASA: Mexican American Student Association,
MASC: Mexican American Student Confederation
MAUC: Mexican American Unity Council
MAYO: Mexican American Youth Organization
MEChA: Movimiento Estudiantil Chicano de Aztlán
MMAS: Mexican Mutual Aid Society

NACS: National Association for Chicano Studies
NALEO: National Association of Latino Elected and Appointed Officials
NCCHE: National Chicano Council on Higher Education
NCLR: National Council of La Raza

NFLU: National Farm Labor Union
NFWA: National Farm Workers Association (founded by César Chávez in the 1960s)
NLRB: National Labor Relations Board
NMU: National Miners Union
NOMAS: National Organization of Mexican American Services
NRA: National Recovery Act

PADRES: Padres Asociados Para Derechos Religiosos, Educativos, y Sociales
PASSO/PASO: Political Association of Spanish-Speaking Organizations
PLM: Partido Liberal Mexicano

SIN: Spanish International Network
SVREP: Southwest Voter Registration Education Project

TELACU: The East Los Angeles Community Union
TENAZ: Teatros Nacionales de Aztlán
TUUL: Trade Union Unity League (Communist-affiliated labor organization)

UCAPAWA: United Cannery, Agricultural, Packing, and Allied Workers of America
UFW: United Farm Workers
UFWOC: United Farm Workers Organizing Committee (formed by merging NFWA and AWOC in 1966)
UMAS: United Mexican American Students
UNO: United Neighborhood Organization
USES: United States Employment Service

WFM: Western Federation of Miners (a left-wing labor organization in the U.S. Southwest)
WPA: Works Progress Administration

GLOSSARY

ALAMBRISTA   A person who crosses the border illegally by (presumably) climbing a fence; from *alambre*, "wire"

ALELUYA   A Protestant, especially an evangelical

ALIANCISTA   A member of any alianza, especially the Alianza Federal de Pueblos Libres, Reies López Tijerina's organization

ANASAZI   An early Indian culture in the American southwest; flourished from the sixth to the fourteenth century A.D.

ANGLO   Short for Anglo American; in the Southwest sometimes designating all non-Hispanic-descent Americans

AZTEC   Middle American Indian group of Nahua stock who dominated south-central Mexico in the fifteenth century; also called Mexica

AZTLÁN   Mythical homeland of the Aztec or Mexica Indians

BARRIO   District; in the United States, Mexican American/Latino quarter of town

¡BASTA YA!   Enough!

BLOWOUT   School walkout by students

BOLILLO   Tejano term for an Anglo; literally a French roll or a stiff lace cuff

BRACERO   A worker, a (hired) hand; particularly a Mexican brought to the United States under a labor contract; from *brazo*, "arm"

CABALLERO   Knight, horseman, gentleman, Sir (in direct address)

CALIFAS   Caló dialect term for California

CALIFORNIO/CALIFORNIANO   Original Hispanic-Mexican inhabitant of California, or his/her descendant; loosely any Californian of Spanish-Mexican descent

CALÓ   Spanish dialect, used mostly by urban youths

CAMPESINO   Farmer, farm worker

CARNAL   "Brother," friend, buddy

LA CAUSA   Descriptive name for the farm workers' movement under César Chávez

CHICANO   Mexican American; form of "mexicano" truncated by dropping the first syllable and pronouncing the initial X as in Nahuatl; used since the turn of the century and popularized by the movement in the 1960s, today often with overtones of ethnic nationalism and activism; offensive to some older conservative Mexican Americans because originally it was applied to lower-class Mexicans

LA CHINGADA   Literally, "the raped one," particularly Malinche, Cortés's Indian mistress; an unfortunate woman; the phrase has many shades of meaning

CHOLO   Pejorative term in California for Mexican immigrant

LOS CIENTÍFICOS   Mexican followers of the Positivist philosophy of the Frenchman Auguste Comte; they supported President Porfirio Díaz

CINCO DE MAYO   Commemoration celebrating the Mexican defeat of the invading French army at Puebla, Mexico, on May 5, 1862

COFRADÍA   A brotherhood; a society with a religious basis, usually the devotion to a particular saint

COLONIA   Small settlement, sometimes part of a town, inhabited by mexicanos

COMPADRE   Godfather (in relation to biological father); loosely, friend, buddy (colloquial)

COMPAÑERO   Companion, friend

CONTRATISTA   Labor contractor, usually for agricultural work

COYOTE   Person who organizes illegal border crossing; sometimes a labor contractor who "sells" strikebreakers

CRIOLLO   Colonial term referring to American-born person of Spanish/European parentage

CURANDERO/A   A curer; folk medicine practitioner

CURSILLO   A mexicano religious and social movement in the U.S. Southwest

DORADO   Literally, "gilded"; refers to a member of Pancho Villa's elite cavalry, because of their highly decorated uniforms

EJIDO   A communal landholding, usually belonging to a village

EMPRESARIO   Land grantee who was required to recruit a specified number of settlers in order to validate his grant

ENGANCHISTA   Literally an entrapper, a hooker; one who recruits farm labor; a contratista

GABACHO/GAVACHO   Strongly pejorative term for Anglo; originally referred to French (therefore foreign)

GACHUPÍN(ES)   Colonial term of derogation referring to peninsular Spaniards. Also cachupín

GENTE DE RAZÓN   Literally, "people of reason"; colonial term referring to members of the upper classes, usually Spaniards or criollos

GRINGO   Mildly pejorative term for a foreigner, in Mexico especially an Anglo-Saxon; originally from *griego*, "Greek," therefore foreign

GRITO DE DOLORES   Famous rallying cry of Father Miguel Hidalgo which initiated the 1810 Mexican revolution for independence

GÜERO   Blond, fair (referring to a person); therefore sometimes an Anglo

HERMANDAD   Brotherhood; usually a religious mutual-aid organization; see also cofradía

HIDALGO   A nobleman

HISPANIC   Term used (especially by government and other agencies) to include all persons of Spanish cultural background; used also by nuevomexicanos since the early 1900s to assert Spanish descent in order to distance themselves from poor immigrant Mexicans with limited formal education

HISPANO   New Mexican of Hispanic-Mexican origins; a nuevomexicano; also Hispanic as above

HOHOKAM   Ancient Indian culture in the Salt River valley of Arizona; flourished from about 300 B.C. to the thirteenth century A.D.

ILLEGAL   Foreigner in the United States without legal papers; an undocumented alien

JEFE/JEFA   Literally, "chief"; at times a term for parent

LATIN AMERICAN   A person from a Portuguese-, French-, or Spanish-speaking country of the Western Hemisphere; in Texas often a euphemism for Mexican

LATINO   A Latin American; this umbrella term includes all persons of Latin-derived cultural background, preferred by many to Hispanic;

originally promoted by France in the late nineteenth century to expand her influence in the Western Hemisphere by including French speakers

MACHISMO   Term used to connote a virile maleness (which may emphasize bravery, honor, and integrity); from *macho*, "male"

MADERISTA   Follower or supporter of Francisco Madero during the 1910 Mexican revolution

MADRINA   Godmother

MALINCHISMO   The selling out of one's own people or (Mexican) culture; from Malinche, the Nahua woman who helped Cortés in his conquest of the Aztecs

MANDE VD., SEÑOR.   Literally: "Command [me], sir." "At your service." Often used by Mexicans as a polite response of recognition when spoken to.

MANITO   Truncated form of *hermanito*, "little brother"; buddy; mildly pejorative term for Spanish-speaking New Mexican

MAPISTA   A member or supporter of MAPA, usually Mexican American Political Association in California

MAYA   An advanced Middle American civilization occupying southern Mexico and much of Central America; it flourished between 1000 B.C. and the fifteenth century A.D.

MEDIERO   Sharecropper on northern Mexican frontier, especially in New Mexico, until the twentieth century

MESTIZAJE   Process of the physical blending of Indians and Europeans

MESTIZO   Literally "mixed"; a person of mixed European and Indian ancestry

MEXICA   See Aztec

MEXICAN   A citizen of Mexico; a Mexican national

MEXICANO   Usually a person from Mexico; also a person of Mexican descent in the U.S. Southwest; used in the text when both categories are or may be included; even today, when Spanish is the language spoken, mexicano is widely used, and the distinction between Mexican American and Mexican national may rely on the terms *mexicano de este lado* and *mexicano del otro lado*

MOJADO   Literally, "a wet (one)"; one who enters the United States illegally, (presumably) by swimming the Rio Grande, therefore strictly only in Texas

MULATO A person of mixed European and African ancestry
MUTUALISTA Mutual-aid organization or a supporter thereof

NAHUA/NAHUATL An Indian language group which included Aztecs, Toltecs, Tlaxcalans, and Chichimecs
LOS NIÑOS HÉROES Mexican cadets who resisted American troops at Chapultepec in 1847
NORTEÑO Person from the northern states of Mexico; a northerner
NUEVOMEXICANO/NUEVO MEXICANO Hispanic-Mexican inhabitant of the area of New Mexico, especially in the nineteenth century

OLMEC Ancient Mexican Indian culture along the Gulf coast; flourished from 500 B.C. to 1100 A.D.

PACHUQUISMO/PACHUCO Pejorative term for a "hip" lifestyle within the barrio, followed usually by the young; a practitioner of the same
PADRINO Godfather
PARTIDO "Share" system used in sheep culture on the northern Mexican frontier; to establish his flock, a herder borrowed a number of sheep and later repaid the lender with "interest"
PATO/A Undocumented border crosser via the Rio Grande; literally, "a duck"; a patero is a person who guides a pato across
PATRIA CHICA Local region of one's birth and upbringing; literally, "little fatherland"
PATRÓN Boss, protector, patron; in Mexico and U.S. Southwest usually a large landowner
PELADO Literally, "a peeled one"; a rascal or low-class person; a misfit; one who is flat broke
PENITENTE Member of the Confraternidad de Nuestro Padre Jesús Nazareno, a Catholic lay religious group in New Mexico, also called the Brotherhood
PEÓN Worker, usually agricultural and tied to the land
PINTO Barrio term for a prison inmate
POBLADOR Settler, usually in a town
POCHO Pejorative Mexican term for a person of Mexican descent born in the United States or a Mexican who has become Americanized; less pejorative when used by a Mexican American
POLLO/A Undocumented land border crosser; literally, "a chicken"; a pollero is a person who guides pollos across the border

PORFIRIATO   Regime of Mexican president Porfirio Díaz, 1877–1911
PRESIDIO   Military fort or garrison
PRIETO/A   Dark-skinned (person); prieta is sometimes used as a term of endearment
PUEBLO   Township, village

QUETZALCOATL   The Feathered Serpent, principal god and legendary ruler of the Toltecs; god of the sun, the wind, and the morning star; adopted by other Middle American cultures

RANCHERO   Owner of a ranch; related to ranching or stock raising
RANCHO   Rural property, usually one on which cattle are raised
LA RAZA   Ethnic term for Spanish-speaking people, connoting a spirit of belonging and a sense of common destiny; popularized by the movement in the 1960s
LA RAZA UNIDA   Political party founded in Texas in 1970 by José Angel Gutiérrez and others
REBOZO   A long shawl or muffler worn (usually) by women
REPATRIADO   A person sent back to Mexico from the United States
RICO   Literally a rich person; used in the Southwest to denote a member of the elite upper class
RINCHE   (Texas) Ranger

SANTERO   Carver of wooden statues of saints
SINARQUISMO   Radical right-wing political philosophy originating in Mexico with the Unión Nacional Sinarquista
SOJOURNER   Person who enters a country not intending to remain permanently; temporary worker, not an immigrant
SOLAR(ES)   Lot for town house; also town house
SURRUMATO   Pejorative term for a Mexican, especially used in New Mexico; foolish person; origin uncertain

TEATRO   Theater
TECATO   A drug user, especially of heroin; a junkie
TEJANO   Latino-Mexican inhabitant of Texas area, especially in the Spanish and Mexican periods
TENOCHTITLÁN   Capital of the Aztec confederation; modern Mexico City

TERTULIA   An evening social gathering for conversation or entertainment

TÍO TACO   Chicano version of "Uncle Tom"; pejorative

TOLTEC   Nahuatl-speaking Indian culture of the Mexican plateau; flourished from the seventh to the fourteenth century

UNDOCUMENTED   Foreigner in the United States without legal documentation; most neutral, least emotion-laden term

VAQUERO   (Mexicano) cowboy/cowhand

VATO/BATO   "Dude"; "guy"; a vato loco is a crazy mixed-up dude

VENDIDO/A   "Sellout," one who betrays la raza, often for his or her own benefit; see also Malinche

VIEJO/A   Literally, "old (one)"; endearing term for a parent

WETBACK   Pejorative term for an undocumented Mexican, presumably from crossing the Rio Grande into Texas; a mojado

ZAMBO   Person of mixed Indian and African descent

ZOOT SUIT   Term used to describe the exuberant clothing worn by some young urban males in the 1940s

FOR FURTHER READING

Any general history, by its very nature, is derived from sources far too numerous to list in a bibliography of works consulted. The following is a short list of recommended books generally available to the reader.

Acuña, Rodolfo. *Occupied America: A History of Chicanos.* 3rd ed. New York: Harper & Row, 1988.

Balderama, Francisco. *In Defense of La Raza: The Los Angeles Mexican Consulate and the Mexican Community, 1929–1936.* Tucson: Univ. of Arizona Press, 1982.
Bannon, John Francis. *The Spanish Borderlands Frontier, 1513–1821.* New York: Holt, Rinehart and Winston, 1970.
Barrera, Mario. *Race and Class in the Southwest: A Theory of Racial Inequality.* Notre Dame, Ind.: Univ. of Notre Dame Press, 1979.
Bean, Frank D., et al., eds. *Undocumented Migration to the United States: IRCA and the Experience of the 1980s.* Washington, D.C.: The Rand Corp., 1990.
Briggs, Vernon M., et al. *The Chicano Worker.* Austin: Univ. of Texas Press, 1977.

Camarillo, Albert. *Chicanos in a Changing Society: From Mexican Pueblos to American Barrios in Santa Barbara and Southern California, 1848–1930.* Cambridge, Mass.: Harvard Univ. Press, 1979.
Castañeda, Carlos E. *Our Catholic Heritage in Texas, 1519–1936.* 7 vols. Reprint, New York: Arno Press, 1976.
Chávez, John R. *The Lost Land: The Chicano Image of the Southwest.* Albuquerque: Univ. of New Mexico Press, 1984.
Cornelius, Wayne. *Building the Cactus Curtain: Mexican Migration and U.S. Responses, from Wilson to Carter.* Berkeley: Univ. of California Press, 1980.

Cortés, Carlos, ed. *Aspects of the Mexican-American Experience.* New York: Arno Press, 1976.

Corwin, Arthur F., ed. *Immigrants and Immigrants: Perspectives on Mexican Labor Migration to the United States.* Westport, Conn.: Greenwood Press, 1979.

Cotera, Martha P. *Profile on the Mexican American Woman.* Austin: National Educational Laboratory, 1976.

Day, Mark. *Forty Acres: César Chávez and the Farm Workers.* New York: Praeger, 1971.

De la Garza, Rudolph O., et al., eds. *The Mexican American Experience: An Interdisciplinary Anthology.* Austin: Univ. of Texas Press, 1985.

De León, Arnoldo. *The Tejano Community, 1836–1900.* Albuquerque: Univ. of New Mexico Press, 1982.

———. *They Called Them Greasers: Anglo Attitudes Toward Mexicans in Texas, 1821–1900.* Austin: Univ. of Texas Press, 1983.

Dinnerstein, Leonard, and David M. Reimers. *Ethnic Americans: A History of Immigration.* 3rd ed. New York: Harper & Row, 1988.

Dunne, John Gregory. *Delano.* New York: Farrar, Straus & Giroux, 1971.

Ehrlich, Paul, et al. *The Golden Door: International Migration, Mexico, and the United States.* New York: Ballantine Books, 1979.

Faulk, Odie B. *Land of Many Frontiers: A History of the American Southwest.* New York: Oxford Univ. Press, 1968.

Galarza, Ernesto. *Barrio Boy.* New York: Ballantine Books, 1971.

———. *Merchants of Labor: The Mexican Bracero Story.* Santa Barbara, Calif: McNally & Loftin, 1964.

Gamio, Manuel. *Mexican Immigration to the United States: A Study of Human Migration and Adaptation.* New York: Dover Press, 1971.

García, F. Chris, and Rudolph O. de la Garza. *The Chicano Political Experience: Three Perspectives.* North Scituate, Mass.: Duxbury Press, 1977.

García, Mario T. *Desert Immigrants: The Mexicans of El Paso, 1880–1920*. New Haven: Yale Univ. Press, 1981.

———. *Mexican Americans: Leadership, Ideology, and Identity, 1930–1960*. New Haven: Yale Univ. Press, 1989.

García, Richard A. *Rise of the Mexican American Middle Class: San Antonio, 1929–1941*. College Station: Texas A&M Univ. Press, 1991.

Gómez-Quiñones, Juan. *Chicano Politics: Reality and Promise, 1940–1990*. Albuquerque: Univ. of New Mexico Press, 1990.

González, Nancie G. *The Spanish-Americans of New Mexico*. Albuquerque: Univ. of New Mexico Press, 1967.

Grebler, Leo, Joan W. Moore, and Ralph Guzmán. *The Mexican-American People: The Nation's Second Largest Minority*. New York: Free Press, 1970.

Griswold del Castillo, Richard. *La Familia: Chicano Families in the Urban Southwest, 1848 to the Present*. Notre Dame, Ind.: Univ. of Notre Dame Press, 1984.

———. *The Los Angeles Barrio, 1850–1890: A Social History*. Berkeley: Univ. of California Press, 1979.

Hammerback, John C., et al. *A War of Words: Chicano Protest in the 1960s and 1970s*. Westport, Conn.: Greenwood Press, 1985.

Handlin, Oscar. *The Uprooted: The Epic Story of the Great Migrations That Made the American People*. New York: Little, Brown, 1951.

Higham, John, ed. *Ethnic Leadership in America*. Baltimore: Johns Hopkins Univ. Press, 1978.

Hoffman, Abraham. *Unwanted Mexican-Americans in the Great Depression: Repatriation Pressures, 1929–1939*. Tucson: Univ. of Arizona Press, 1974.

Horgan, Paul. *The Heroic Triad: Essays in the Social Energies of Three Southwestern Cultures*. New York: Holt, Rinehart and Winston, 1970.

Hundley, Norris, Jr., ed. *The Chicano*. Santa Barbara, Calif: Clio Press, 1975.

Jamieson, Stuart. *Labor Unionism in American Agriculture*. Washington, D.C.: U.S. Government Printing Office, 1945.

Kibbe, Pauline. *Latin Americans in Texas*. Albuquerque: Univ. of New Mexico Press, 1946.

Lamar, Howard Roberts. *The Far Southwest, 1846–1912: A Territorial History*. New Haven, Conn.: Yale Univ. Press, 1966.

Langley, Lester D. *MexAmerica: Two Countries, One Future*. New York: Crown, 1988.

Larralde, Carlos. *Mexican-American Movements and Leaders*. Los Alamitos, Calif: Hwong, 1976.

Larson, Robert W. *New Mexico's Quest for Statehood, 1846–1912*. Albuquerque: Univ. of New Mexico Press, 1968.

Martínez, Oscar. *Border Boom Town: Ciudad Juárez Since 1848*. Austin: Univ. of Texas Press, 1978.

Mayer, Vicente V., Jr., ed. *Utah: A Hispanic History*. Salt Lake City: American West Center, Univ. of Utah, 1975.

Mazón, Mauricio. *The Zoot-Suit Riots: The Psychology of Symbolic Annihilation*. Austin: Univ. of Texas Press, 1984.

McWilliams, Carey. *North from Mexico: The Spanish Speaking People of the United States*. New ed. Westport, Conn.: Greenwood Press/ Praeger, 1990.

Meier, Matt S., and Feliciano Rivera, eds. *Readings on La Raza: The Twentieth Century*. New York: Hill and Wang, 1974.

Meinig, Donald W. *Imperial Texas: An Interpretive Essay in Cultural Geography*. Austin: Univ. of Texas Press, 1969.

―――. *Southwest: Three Peoples in Geographical Change, 1600–1970*. New York: Oxford Univ. Press, 1971.

Mirandé, Alfredo, and Evangelina Enríquez. *La Chicana: The Mexican-American Woman*. Chicago: Univ. of Chicago Press, 1979.

Montejano, David. *Anglos and Mexicans in the Making of Texas, 1836–1986*. Austin: Univ. of Texas Press, 1987.

Moore, Joan W. *Homeboys: Gangs, Drugs, and Prison in the Barrios of Los Angeles*. Philadelphia: Temple Univ. Press, 1978.

―――― with Harry Pachon. *Mexican Americans*. 2nd ed. Englewood Cliffs, N.J.: Prentice-Hall, 1976.

Moquin, Wayne, and Charles Van Doren, eds. *A Documentary History of the Mexican-American*. New York: Praeger, 1971.

Muñoz, Carlos, Jr. *Youth, Identity, Power: The Chicano Movement*. New York: Verso, 1989.

National Association for Chicano Studies. *Chicana Voices: Intersections of Class, Race, and Gender.* Austin: Center for Mexican American Studies, Univ. of Texas, 1986.

———. *The Chicano Struggle: Analyses of Past and Present Efforts.* Binghamton, N.Y.: Bilingual Press/Editorial Bilingüe, SUNY, Binghamton, 1984.

North, David S. *The Border Crossers: People Who Live in Mexico and Work in the United States.* Washington, D.C.: TransCentury Corp., 1970.

———. *Through the Maze: An Interim Report on the Alien Legalization Program.* Washington, D.C.: TransCentury Corp., 1988.

Nostrand, Richard L. *Los chicanos: geografía histórica regional.* Mexico, D.F.: SepSetentas, 1976.

Perales, Alonso S. *Are We Good Neighbors?* San Antonio: Artes Gráficas, 1948.

Perrigo, Lynn I. *Hispanos: Historic Leaders in New Mexico.* Santa Fe, N.M.: Sunstone Press, 1985.

Pitt, Leonard. *The Decline of the Californios: A Social History of the Spanish-Speaking Californians, 1846–1890.* Berkeley: Univ. of California Press, 1966.

Reisler, Mark. *By the Sweat of Their Brow: Mexican Immigrant Labor in the United States, 1900–1940.* Westport, Conn.: Greenwood Press, 1976.

Robinson, W. W. *Land in California.* Berkeley: Univ. of California Press, 1948.

Romo, Ricardo. *East Los Angeles: History of a Barrio.* Austin: Univ. of Texas Press, 1983.

Rosaldo, Renato, et al., eds. *Chicano: The Evolution of a People.* Minneapolis: Winston Press, 1973.

Rosenbaum, Robert J. *Mexicano Resistance in the Southwest: "The Sacred Right of Self-Preservation."* Austin: Univ. of Texas Press, 1981.

Ross, Stanley R., ed. *Views Across the Border: The United States and Mexico.* Albuquerque: Univ. of New Mexico Press, 1978.

Samora, Julián. *Los Mojados: The Wetback Story.* Notre Dame, Ind.: Univ. of Notre Dame Press, 1971.

————, ed. *La Raza: Forgotten Americans*. Notre Dame, Ind.: Univ of Notre Dame Press, 1966.

Sánchez, George I. *Forgotten People*. Albuquerque: Univ. of New Mexico Press, 1940.

Sánchez, Rosaura, and Rosa Martínez Cruz. *Essays on La Mujer*. Los Angeles: Chicano Studies Research Center, Univ. of California, 1977.

San Miguel, Guadalupe, Jr. *"Let All of Them Take Heed": Mexican Americans and the Campaign for Educational Equality in Texas, 1910–1981*. Austin: Univ. of Texas Press, 1987.

Servín, Manuel P. *The Mexican-Americans: An Awakening Minority*. Beverly Hills: Glencoe Press, 1970.

Shockley, John Staples. *Chicano Revolt in a Texas Town*. Notre Dame, Ind.: Univ. of Notre Dame Press, 1974.

Simmen, Edward. *Pain and Promise: The Chicano Today*. New York: New American Library, 1972.

Spicer, Edward H., and Raymond Thompson, eds. *Plural Society in the Southwest*. New York: Interbank, 1972.

Steiner, Stan. *La Raza: The Mexican Americans*. New York: Harper & Row, 1970.

Stoddard, Ellwyn R. *Mexican Americans*. New York: Random House, 1973.

————, Richard L. Nostrand, and Jonathan P. West, eds. *Borderlands Sourcebook*. Norman: Univ. of Oklahoma Press, 1983.

Taylor, Paul S. *Mexican Labor in the United States: Chicago and the Calumet Region*. Berkeley: Univ. of California Press, 1932.

Trejo, Arnulfo D., ed. *The Chicanos: As We See Ourselves*. Tucson: Univ. of Arizona Press, 1979.

Valdés, Dennis Nodín. *Al Norte: Agricultural Workers in the Great Lakes Region, 1917–1970*. Austin: Univ. of Texas Press, 1991.

Van Ness, John R., and Christine M., eds. *Spanish and Mexican Land Grants in New Mexico and Colorado*. Santa Fe, N.M.: Center for Land Grant Studies, 1980.

Vigil, Maurilio E. *Los Patrones: Profiles of Hispanic Political Leaders in New Mexico History*. Washington, D.C.: Univ. Press of America, 1980.

Weber, David J. *Foreigners in Their Native Land: Historical Roots of the Mexican American*. Albuquerque: Univ. of New Mexico Press, 1973.

————. *The Mexican Frontier, 1821–1846: The American Southwest Under Mexico*. Albuquerque: Univ. of New Mexico Press, 1982.

Westphall, Victor. *The Public Domain in New Mexico, 1854–1891*. Albuquerque: Univ. of New Mexico Press, 1965.

INDEX